FROM *POLYPRAGMON* TO *CURIOSUS*

From *Polypragmon* to *Curiosus*

Ancient Concepts of Curious and Meddlesome Behaviour

MATTHEW LEIGH

OXFORD
UNIVERSITY PRESS

OXFORD

UNIVERSITY PRESS

Great Clarendon Street, Oxford, OX2 6DP,
United Kingdom

Oxford University Press is a department of the University of Oxford.
It furthers the University's objective of excellence in research, scholarship,
and education by publishing worldwide. Oxford is a registered trade mark of
Oxford University Press in the UK and in certain other countries

British Library Cataloguing in Publication Data

Data available

ISBN 978-0-19-966861-8

Printed in Great Britain by the
MPG Printgroup, UK

For Victoria

Preface

This is a study of a group of words in Greek and Latin that are used to describe curious and meddlesome behaviour. It works outwards from the words themselves and traces the variety of meanings that each acquires across time. It also seeks to work between Greek and Latin and to trace the degree to which patterns in Latin usage reflect the expanding semantic range of their Greek equivalents. Some readers will wish to study the book as a whole; others will prefer to seek clarification of what a specific passage means by *polypragmon*, *periergos*, or *curiosus*. Throughout I have aimed to produce a work that is not just meticulous and useful but also entertaining and creative. It is for others to say whether I have attained any of these goals.

I began to research this topic in the final months of the Philip Leverhulme Prize Fellowship that I held for the academic years 2001–3. Further progress was made in the course of periods of study leave granted to me by St Anne's College and the Faculty of Classics in Oxford University for the first six months of 2008 and the last three months of 2011. I also gained great benefit from the five weeks that I spent as a Tytus Visiting Fellow at the University of Cincinnati in the summer of 2008 and for the hospitality offered by Mrs Margaret Kwee and the Fondation Barrymore in the summers of 2010 and 2011. The time available for research has otherwise been severely restricted by my responsibilities in teaching, administration, and fundraising, but I do not underestimate my good fortune in having easy access to the wonderful resources of the Bodleian Library.

I am very grateful to Hilary O'Shea at Oxford University Press for her support for this project. The two anonymous readers offered very helpful advice, which I have attempted to take on board. Rowena Anketell was meticulous in her copy-editing and Taryn del Neves persistent and energetic in all matters regarding production and marketing. To all I offer my sincere thanks.

Various friends have discussed this project with me or have read sections of my work. I must offer particular thanks to Roger Crisp, Rhiannon Ash, John Marincola, and Stephen Harrison, as well as to the two anonymous OUP referees, who read the completed typescript and offered much sage advice. I have also had the opportunity to present my ideas to audiences in Cambridge, Durham, Exeter, Ljubjana, London, Oxford, Padua, Sydney, and Turin. The Brasenose–St Anne's Classics Research Symposium, the JACT Latin Summer School at Wells, and the Godolphin and Latymer Classics Breakfast Club provided particularly stimulating and supportive conversation.

Throughout this time I have been proud to be part of the Classics School at St Anne's College. My colleagues are among my dearest friends. The intellectual energy and good cheer that our students bring to their work is a constant inspiration. I am also mindful of what it means to be the successor, however inadequate, to as great a scholar as Margaret Hubbard. Her death in the spring of 2011 brought great sadness; but her enormous generosity to St Anne's means that the Classics School will continue its work for decades to come.

My greatest debts are personal. Victoria Kwee kept faith with me through difficult times and remained convinced, even when I was not, that the project could be completed. My parents stayed close to me and never turned the telephone off. I do not know how to repay their love.

Contents

Abbreviations

All abbreviations of the names or works of ancient authors are based on those of the *Oxford Classical Dictionary*, 3rd edn., eds. Simon Hornblower and Antony Spawforth. The following works are cited in abbreviated form:

AJAH *American Journal of Ancient History*
AJPh *American Journal of Philology*
ANRW *Aufstieg und Niedergang der Römischen Welt*
BICS *Bulletin of the Institute of Classical Studies*
CGL *Corpus Glossariorum Latinorum*, ed. G. Goetz and G. Gundermann (Leipzig, 1888–1923)
CIL *Corpus Insciptionum Latinarum*
CJ *Classical Journal*
C&M *Classica et Medievalia*
CPG *Corpus Paroemiographorum Graecorum*, ed. E. von Leutsch and F. W. Schneidewin (Göttingen, 1839–51)
CPh *Classical Philology*
CQ *Classical Quarterly*
CW *Classical World*
FGrH *Die Fragmente der Griechischen Historiker*, ed. F. Jacoby (Berlin and Leiden, 1923–58)
GCN *Groningen Colloquium on the Novel*
HSCP *Harvard Studies in Classical Philology*
ILS *Inscriptiones Latinae Selectae*, ed. H. Dessau (Berlin, 1892–1916)
JHS *Journal of Hellenic Studies*
JRS *Journal of Roman Studies*
K-A *Poetae Comici Graeci*, ed. R. Kassel and C. Austin (Berlin and New York, 1983–)
MD *Materiali e discussioni per l'analisi dei testi classici*
MH *Museum Helveticum*
OED *Oxford English Dictionary*, 1st edn. (1909)
OGIS *Orientis Graeci Inscriptiones Selectae*, ed. W. Dittenberger (Leipzig, 1903–5)
OLD *Oxford Latin Dictionary*, ed. P. G. W. Glare (Oxford, 1982)
Peter H. Peter (ed.), *Historicorum Romanorum Reliquiae*, 2nd edn. (Leipzig, 1914)
RhM *Rheinisches Museum für Philologie*

RSI   *Rivista storica italiana*
SIFC   *Studi italiani di filologia classica*
SO   *Symbolae Osloenses*
SVF   *Stoicorum Veterum Fragmenta*, ed. H. von Arnim
           (Leipzig, 1903–24)
Syll.   *Sylloge Inscriptionum Graecarum*, ed. W. Dittenberger
           (Leipzig, 1915–24)
TLL   *Thesaurus Linguae Latinae* (Leipzig, 1900–)
WJA   *Würzburger Jahrbücher für Altertumswissenschaft*
WS   *Wiener Studien*

Introduction

(1) THEME AND METHOD

The immediate origins of this project lie in my experience almost a decade ago of reading the *Histories* of Polybius and in the surprise I experienced at the employment in this work of the Greek adjective and substantive *polypragmon*, the abstract noun *polypragmosyne*, and the verb *polypragmonein*. These were words that had mattered to me as an undergaduate student of the Greek history of the fifth and fourth centuries, and I knew that in this I was far from alone. To many the concept of *polypragmosyne* encapsulated the restless meddling and intervention of individual Athenian citizens in the lives of their peers as well as that of the Athenian state as a whole in the affairs of its neighbours and beyond.[1] Yet now I was confronted with a writer whose usage went well beyond that with which I was familiar. Accusations of *polypragmosyne* were still heard as one state decried the intervention of another in affairs outside what was held to be its proper domain. At the same time, however, the sheer nosiness that seemed to drive the individual citizen's interest in the affairs of others and led to accusations of malicious prosecution or sykophancy, appeared to have undergone a form of rehabilitation. For *polypragmosyne* had become a key concept in Polybius' description of scholarly research and of the energy driving such endeavours. Three questions quickly formed in my mind. First, what were the origins of this version of *polypragmosyne* and how far did it reach in the Greek writers of Polybius' period and after? Second, how important was it that this less familiar usage should be found alongside

---

[1] The classic statement of this position is Ehrenberg (1947). That my then teacher was thinking through these issues will be clear from Brock (1998).

references to that state *polypragmosyne* that I already knew from the
fifth-century texts, and how could this help me think about the role
of Polybius as a scholar conducting investigations under the aegis
of an ever-expanding Roman empire? Third, what might be the
relationship between how Greeks spoke of *polypragmosyne* and
how Latin writers employed their own terms *curiosus* and latterly
curiositas?

This book is the product of a project that began in those three
questions but swiftly ramified and took in other usages, other discourses as well. For it was soon apparent that it would be impossible
to study *polypragmosyne* without also engaging with its recurrent
synonyms *philopragmosyne* and *periergia*, each of which came
equipped with its own adjective-cum-substantive (*philopragmon*,
periergos) and verb (*philopragmonein*, *periergazdesthai*).[2] In contrast
to this richness of terms deployed by Greek writers, the more parsi-
monious Romans engaged with the same ideas by reference to one
adjective-cum-substantive (*curiosus*) and only latterly to its related
abstract noun (*curiositas*). The principal issue was therefore to identify those instances in which *curiosus* was being used in a manner
equivalent to that associated by the Greeks with *polypragmon* and its
synonyms as opposed to those in which it meant nothing more
challenging than 'careful'.

In order to answer the questions that I set myself it has been
necessary to adopt the methods of the lexicographer. I have made
no little use of the various electronic resources that have so acceler-
ated the first stages of any word search, but am also in debt to the
work of those less technologically privileged inquirers who issued the
first concordances to individual authors or composed the meticulous
entries to be found in Stephanus' *Thesaurus Linguae Graecae* and the
Thesaurus Linguae Latinae. More often than not, however, I have
found that to leap in and out of a text only where a particular word is
to be found can lead to but a superficial understanding, and have
therefore taken the time to read whole works through where it
seemed important to do so. The decision to devote two summers to
reading in their entirety the *Geography* of Strabo and the *Natural
History* of Pliny certainly did not hasten the completion of this
project, but I cannot regret the effort this involved.

---

[2] Ehrenberg (1947), 62 engages only cursorily with *periergia*.

(2) PRINCIPLES OF INQUIRY

This study works outwards from the ancient terms themselves and then identifies the categories to which they are applied, rather than working backwards from modern categories of thought and then finding the ancient terms that most closely approximate to them. When in recent years colleagues from other disciplines asked me what I was working on, I often found it easier to occlude this approach and to state that I was studying ancient ideas about curiosity. This response had some advantages. Most knew something of the early Christian critique of vain curiosity or were familiar with emblematic figures of mortal curiosity such as the Ulisse of canto 26 of the *Inferno* or Goethe's Faust. There was also a burgeoning body of scholarship on attitudes to and expressions of curiosity from the church fathers through to the eighteenth century, and this continues to grow.[3] Some of these studies were indeed content to apply their own conception of curiosity and then to seek comparable phenomena in different cultures and ages;[4] but those from which I learned most began with the words themselves and constructed a world of thought from them.[5]

What was it in the description of my project as a history of ancient ideas of curiosity that made me wince or cross my fingers behind my back? The crucial point here was that the very words that could denote curiosity could also describe a variety of other phenomena as well. The essence of this project was therefore to trace that plurality of meanings and to identify the connecting thread or threads that drew them together. *Polypragmon* and its synonyms were fascinating precisely because they could mean not only curious but also meddlesome, driven, undisciplined as well. It is this nexus of meanings that the following chapters are designed to identify and to interpret.

The decision to focus on specific words and their meaning offers the chance to say something more precise but perhaps also more narrow than some contributions to the history of curiosity in the ancient world.[6] Having read and enjoyed these less lexically grounded

---

[3] I owe a lot to Kenny (2004). For other relevant studies, see Blumenberg (1983); Bös (1995); Shattuck (1996); Daston and Park (1998); Benedict (2001); Huff (2011).

[4] Shattuck (1996) falls into this category.

[5] Daston and Park (1998), 397 n. 57 is an important statement of method. Kenny (1998) is an essential preliminary to Kenny (2004).

[6] See e.g. C. Barton (1992), 85–167; André and Baslez (1993), 132–66, 317–72.

studies, I have no illusions that my own approach is the only, let alone the most attractive, way to conduct work in the history of thought. If I have stuck to it, it is because the most radically revealing results must emerge from the bottom up, that is to say from the nexus of associations implicit in the words we use to structure our thoughts.

Words, however, are problematic entities and I am only too aware of the ways in which the individual word can let one down. In Greek, for instance, *polypragmon* and *periergos* are strangers to the higher genres of epic and tragedy though the tragic poets do find a variety of circumlocutions by which to express the same ideas that others express through these terms.[7] In Latin, meanwhile, the very fact that the first three syllables of *curiosus* scan long–short–long means that it can never feature in any work composed in the dactylic hexameter or pentameter. A history of ancient curiosity that excluded any reference to Lucretius, Vergil, Ovid, Manilius, or Lucan would surely look very strange, but such a work could only illustrate the contribution of these authors by reference to words other than *curiosus*.

A further and fundamental feature common to both the Greek and Latin usage of the terms under investigation dictates that they can only speak to one part of what modern English usage understands by curiosity: they are all applied to the inquirer and not the object of inquiry.[8] Where those of more recent ages may collect curios, open cabinets of curiosities, or pay a visit to the old curiosity shop, ancient writers would call such objects *thaumata* or *mirabilia*. The final chapter of this work looks in some detail at the paradoxographers, that is to say those ancient writers who collected strange and wonderful stories from a variety of largely historical and scientific sources, but where the words at the centre of this study appear is in relation to those whose curiosity led them to accumulate the data that these works then set out.[9]

---

[7] See Ch. 1 Sect. 4.

[8] Kenny (2004) deploys the useful distinction between subject-oriented and object-oriented curiosity. See Ch. 2 Sect. 10 for my reasons to discount what the *TLL* takes to be an anomalous example of object-oriented curiosity at Petron. *Sat.* 92. 4. The next such instance suggested by the *TLL* is from Tertullian.

[9] Note also Plut. *Mor.* 520C: those who visit the monster market at Rome and stare at those with three eyes or heads like ostriches may be *polypragmones* but those they stare at are prodigies (*terata*) and not curiosities.

(3) SIGNIFICANCE AND SYNONYMITY

What underpins the close relationship between *polypragmon, philopragmon*, and *periergos* in Greek and *curiosus* in Latin, and connects the various fields to which they are applied, is the combination of a basic term for an occupation or preoccupation (*pragma* and *ergon* in Greek, *cura* in Latin) with an intensifying prefix (*poly-, philo-, peri-*) or suffix (*-osus*). In the case of *polypragmon*, the prefix *poly-* can imply both 'much' or 'many' and the term can therefore describe a human subject who either focuses intensely on one particular object or whose engagement is with many different objects at once. The *polypragmon* can thus be a meddler who is invited to look only to his own concerns and not to those of others or a creature of unrestrained curiosity who cannot help but hop from one topic of inquiry to another. The *periergos* is often indistinguishable from the *polypragmon*, but the prefix *peri-* can also suggest preoccupation with that which is peripheral as opposed to what is essential, and the concept of *periergia* is often associated with the purely ornamental and perhaps needlessly elaborate. The *philopragmon* in turn displays many of the traits of both the *polypragmon* and the *periergos*, but the prefix *philo-* suggests an essential disposition, a positive relish for different forms of engagement. In Latin *curiosus* is applied to all these traits. The key feature here is the suffix *-osus*, which is often associated with an excessive proclivity.[10] Varro himself makes just this claim with regard to *curiosus* itself.[11]

The essential synonymity of the three Greek terms is explicitly acknowledged by a number of ancient sources and is evident from various recurrent ways in which the words are used. The earliest explicit statement of this relationship is to be found at *Topica* 111a9–10, where Aristotle claims that *philopragmosyne* is a synonym for *polypragmosyne*. The philosopher does not expand on this statement, but it is perhaps significant that the less common term is said to be a synonym for the more common and not vice versa; for not only is *philopragmosyne* rarer than *polypragmosyne* but also there is little evidence to suggest that it covers an independent semantic field

[10] Ernout (1949).   [11] Varro, *Ling.* 6. 46.

where the latter might not as easily be employed.[12] The meddling and intrigue to which *philopragmosyne* refers is a social ill, and the *philopragmon* is most characteristically at home in the assembly, the courts, and all the other gathering places of the city.[13] He hunts down gossip,[14] instigates vexatious litigation,[15] and is an enthusiastic participant in political plotting and agitation.[16] All this is in turn familiar from the semantic field of the claimed synonym *polypragmon*.[17] So too, though less commonly noted, is Strabo's approving use of *philopragmon* to describe one who puts energy into his scholarly work.[18]

That *periergos* is also a synonym for *polypragmon* is explicitly stated by Photius.[19] This, however, is evident from Plato onwards. Consider that passage of the *Apology*, where Socrates quotes the charge against him, that he acts unjustly, is meddlesome in his investigation of the things of the world below and the heavens above, makes the weaker argument the stronger, and teaches others to do the same.[20] This phrasing may now be compared with the later dialogue, the *Laws*. Here the Athenian summarizes the view of those who disavow not only investigation of the greatest god and of the whole cosmos but also the meddlesome investigation of causes, for this is not pious.[21] In the first passage the concept of unwelcome or

---

[12] For synonymity, see also Poll. *Onom.* 4. 36 and 38; Hsch. π. 2914, cf. β. 146, γ. 652. For a somewhat different view, see Alex. in Arist. *Top.* pp. 156 l. 20 – 157 l. 17, cf. Suda s.v. πολυπραγμοσύνη καὶ πολυπράγμων, where to call someone φιλοπράγμων implies a basic disposition to meddle whereas it is possible to call a person πολυπράγμων without implying any underlying fault. For a modern view, see Dover (1974), 188–9.

[13] Philo *Ebr.* 79; *Abr.* 20; *Spec. Leg.* 2. 44.

[14] Philo *Agr.* 34.

[15] Pl. *Resp.* 549c; Dem. 39. 1; Isoc. 4. 30; Lyc. *Leocr.* 3, 5–6; Dion. Hal. *Lys.* 24; Din. 13; Philo *Som.* 2. 148.

[16] Philo *In Flacc.* 20, 41.

[17] The same point may be made with regard to the statement at Philo *Som.* 2. 225 that the beloved of God escape the storm of trouble/business (τὸν φιλοπραγμοσύνης χειμῶνα ἀποδιδράσκοντες) to come to the calm port of virtue. There is little difference between this and Philo *Spec. Leg.* 1. 69, where people come to the temple from all over the world as a secure refuge from a stressful life (οἷά τινα κοινὸν ὑπόδρομον καὶ καταγωγὴν ἀσφαλῆ πολυπράγμονος καὶ ταραχωδεστάτου βίου).

[18] Str. 1. 1. 7; 17. 1. 5.

[19] Phot. *Lexicon* ii. 416. 23 Porson: περιεργάζεσθαι· ἀντὶ τοῦ πολυπραγμονεῖν.

[20] Pl. *Ap.* 19b: Σωκράτης ἀδικεῖ καὶ περιεργάζεται ζητῶν τά τε ὑπὸ γῆς καὶ οὐράνια καὶ τὸν ἥττω λόγον κρείττω ποιῶν καὶ ἄλλους ταῦτα ταῦτα διδάσκων.

[21] Pl. *Leg.* 821a: τὸν μέγιστον θεὸν καὶ ὅλον τὸν κόσμον φαμὲν οὔτε ζητεῖν δεῖν οὔτε πολυπραγμονεῖν τὰς αἰτίας ἐρευνῶντας· οὐ γὰρ οὐδ' ὅσιον εἶναι.

meddlesome speculation is expressed through the conjunction of the verb *periergazdesthai* and the present participle of a verb for searching; in the second it is *polypragmonein* that is conjoined to the participle. All else is essentially the same. What is apparent from Plato is also clear from a variety of ancient sources. The *Peri Polypragmosynes* of Plutarch, for instance, on five occasions substitutes *periergia* for *polypragmosyne* and on another two speaks of *philopragmosyne*; the term changes but the subject does not.[22] This interchangeability of terms is also apparent elsewhere in the same writer's work. Of particular interest in this respect are the three different occasions on which he retails the same anecdote, in which Aemilius Paullus deprecates any attempt to interfere with his duties as general; in two cases he describes such interference as *polypragmosyne*, in the other as *periergia*.[23]

A further and widespread indication of synonymity is the tendency of writers to couple two or more of the key terms together without any suggestion that they represent clearly distinct facets of the same phenomenon: Philo includes all three terms in the same paragraph as he deplores the social ill of meddling,[24] and does so again as he considers Moses and the burning bush;[25] elsewhere the same writer yokes *philopragmosyne* and *periergia* together as he describes the thirst for gossip;[26] Epictetus twice conjoins *periergos* and *polypragmon* in descriptions of different forms of meddling;[27] Dio does the same with regard to the meddlesome character of the emperor Hadrian;[28] Aelian speaks of *polypragmosyne* and *periergia* as he describes the vice of fussy and excessive ornamentation

---

[22] For *periergia*, see Plut. *Mor.* 516A, 517E, 519C, 521A, 522B. For *philopragmosyne*, see Plut. *Mor.* 515F, 523A.

[23] Plut. *Aem.* 13. 6; *Mor.* 198A; cf. *Galb.* 1. 2.

[24] Philo *Abr.* 20.

[25] Philo *Fug.* 161–3. Moses is led on by his desire for knowledge (161 προαχθεὶς ὑπὸ τοῦ φιλομαθοῦς), and, when asking why the bush burns but is not destroyed (Exod. 3: 2–3), he treads on untrodden land proper to the gods alone (162 ἄβατον [οὐ] πολυπραγμονεῖ χῶρον, θείων ἐνδιαίτημα φύσεων). God tells Moses not to draw near (Exod. 3: 5), and this is a warning against meddlesome pursuit of knowledge (163... ἴσον τῶι μὴ πρόσιθι τοιαύτηι διασκέψει· περιεργίας γὰρ καὶ φιλοπραγμοσύνης μείζονος ἢ κατὰ ἀνθρωπίνην δύναμιν τὸ ἔργον· ἀλλὰ τὰ μὲν γεγονότα θαύμαζε, τὰς δ' αἰτίας, δι' ἃς ἢ γέγονεν ἢ φθείρεται, μὴ πολυπραγμόνει).

[26] Philo *Agr.* 34.

[27] Epict. *Diss.* 3. 1. 21; 3. 22. 9.

[28] Cass. Dio 69. 5. 1.

in women;[29] and Galen bemoans those associates of the patient who get in the way and insist on knowing more of his condition.[30] The same pattern holds for the relationship between the Greek terms and Latin *curiosus*. The second chapter of this study engages with a number of passages illustrative of this process, but it may be noted in advance that the late-antique bilingual glossaries render both *periergos* and *polypragmon* as *curiosus* and *periergazdomai* as *curiose ago*.[31] This usage in turn corresponds to that of the first Latin translations of the New Testament. In the Acts of the Apostles, the devotees of magic confronted by Paul at Ephesus are described in the Greek text as performing *perierga*;[32] in the Vulgate they are said to pursue *curiosa*,[33] and in the alternative early Latin translation from around the fifth century AD as performing *curiositates*.[34] This, however, is nothing new. From Plautus and Terence onwards, that is to say the first extant examples of the word, *curiosus* is the Latin equivalent of *periergos* and its synonyms, and it will retain this status throughout the centuries that follow.[35]

(4) STRUCTURE AND PARAMETERS
OF INVESTIGATION

The five chapters of this study begin with two preliminary surveys of important patterns of usage in the Greek writers of the fifth and fourth centuries BC, then in classical Latin literature up to the end of the first century AD. The first of these considers Greek in and of itself; the second interprets the various senses applied to *curiosus* by the Latin writers in the light of the changing semantic range of its Greek synonyms in the Hellenistic period and beyond. The Latin term is

[29] Ael. *VH* 12. 1.
[30] Gal. XVIIIb. 687–8 Kühn: περιεργαζόμενοι και πολυπραγμονοῦντες ἐπίστασθαι τὰ τοῦ κάμνοντος.
[31] *CGL* ii. 19, 402; iii. 179, 251, 335, 373; Kramer (2001), 61, 64.
[32] Acts 4. 19. 19: τῶν τὰ περίεργα πραξάντων.
[33] Vulg. act. 4. 19. 19: 'qui fuerant curiosa sectati'.
[34] Vet. Lat. act. 4. 19. 19: 'qui curiositates gesserunt'. For the dating of the Vulgate translation of Acts and of that marked as Vetus Latina cod. e, see the *TLL* index.
[35] Note, however, *CGL* ii. 412–13: 'πολυπραγμονω sciscito' and 'πολυπραγμων scrutor sciscitator'. The Latin verb and nouns cited are indicative of determined inquiry.

always already coloured by the awareness of Greek categories of thought. The three chapters that follow then work between Greek and Latin as each addresses a specific theme around which the key terms tend to cluster: the role played by imperial expansion in the growth of geographical knowledge; the connection between curiosity and impious investigation of the divine; and the association of the key terms with a highly ornamental literary style or with a mode of investigation that prizes the decorative but useless over the useful and profound. In the first of these I engage most closely with the questions with which the study of Polybius first confronted me. The key issue here is the ability of *polypragmosyne* to stand within the same work both for the unwarranted intervention of one state in the affairs of another and for the geographical and ethnographic investigations that just such intervention allows. The pattern of usage best exemplified by Polybius will also be found in Diodorus and in Arrian. Where it is not to be found—as in the *Geography* of Strabo—it will prove valuable to consider the writer's general attitude to empire. The same issue also arises when we contemplate the failure of Roman writers to deploy *curiosus* even in those critiques of their power that they put into the mouths of subject peoples. Where this language will come to the fore is rather in Tacitus' account of the unconcern of Tiberius to expand the borders of the empire and its constraining impact on the subject matter available to the historian.[36] In the final two chapters, by contrast, *curiosus* is no less constant a presence than its Greek equivalents. In each case what is fascinating is the degree to which a predominantly pejorative phrase can take on more positive associations or can even be adopted as a badge of pride by those against whom it is turned. The curious investigator of the heavens can as readily be celebrated for following the will of nature as he can be condemned for his impious meddling in provinces beyond the proper concern of man. Fascination with apparently marginal, even trivial, topics can be deplored or praised with exactly the same words; the defining factor is the artistic commitment of the individual critic.

---

[36] Tac. *Ann.* 4. 33–4 was very much in my mind as I first wrestled with the implications of Polybius' usage. The indifference Tiberius here displays to the expansion of the frontiers of the empire may be compared with Suet. *Tib.* 70. 3 and his ardent concern with the sort of philological trivia associated with *periergoi* and *curiosi*, to which I turn in Ch. 5. The figures he cuts in these two chapters are two sides of the same coin.

This study does not engage with equal intensity with each and every ancient usage of the Greek and Latin terms at issue. Some are of no real interest and to discuss them at any length would be an imposition on my reader. I have, for instance, passed over those instances where Isocrates and Aristotle employ *periergon* as they dismiss a particular topic as irrelevant to the matter in hand.[37] Nor have I concerned myself with all those instances where Galen or the doctors he describes decline to concern themselves (*polypragmonein*) with a given procedure or investigation.[38] As regards *curiosus*, I have found it important to note those instances where the sense is closer to 'careful' than to 'curious', but have only gone into this matter in detail in those instances where the two senses appear to bleed into each other.

Those studying the concept of *polypragmosyne*, particularly in the political and judicial discourse of the fifth and fourth centuries BC, will inevitably also encounter the antithetical notion of *apragmosyne*. The quietism that this latter term implies can be attributed to a state that declines to intervene overseas; to a countryman who avoids the city and all its machinations; to a defendant fallen victim to what is represented as vexatious litigation; and to a philosopher and his followers who choose to steer clear of politics. Much has been written on the topic and I engage repeatedly with these studies, especially in the next chapter.[39] Inasmuch as *apragmosyne* figures as a reaction to the ardent activism of so many individual citizens as well as of Athens as a whole, it is a concept that speaks most eloquently to the earliest period of this study. In later centuries its principal point of reference is to the quietism of the philosopher and, by extension, to the gods of Epicurus.[40] The only other antonym of any significance

---

[37] Isoc. 4. 7, 33; 6. 25; 8. 8; Arist. *An. pr.* 47a18–19; *Eth. Eud.* 1214b28–9, 1216b35–9, 1221b3–5; *Metaph.* 1036b23, 1038a21; *Part. an.* 642b7–9, 644a1; *Pol.* 1315a40–b4; *Rh.* 1369a10, 1414a19–21; *Top.* 139b17, 140a36, 140b1, 140b9, 141a12, 151b20–3.

[38] Gal. I. 85, 86, 88, 463–4; II. 126, 284–5, 345–6; III. 155–6, 468; VII. 763, 888; VIII. 496–7, 783–4; X. 9, 117; XI. 793; XIII. 436; XVIIa. 766 Kühn. For such phrasing, see also Diogenes of Oenoanda F. 4. 2. 1–9 Smith.

[39] Nestle (1926); Grossmann (1950); Dienelt (1953); Kleve (1964); Lateiner (1982–3); L. B. Carter (1986); Demont (1990), 28, 89–113; Bearzot (2007).

[40] For the philosopher as quietist in later Greek literature, see Philo *Quaest. Gen.* 4. 47a; Plut. *Num.* 5. 7; *Pelop.* 5. 3; *Mor.* 945A, 1043A–C. Contrast Ael. *VH* 3. 17 for a long list of philosophers who have engaged in politics, which closes with the comment: εἴ τις οὖν ἀπράκτους λέγει τοὺς φιλοσόφους, ἀλλὰ εὐήθη γε αὐτοῦ καὶ ἀνόητα ταῦτα· ἐγὼ μὲν γὰρ τὴν σὺν αὐτοῖς ἀπραγμοσύνην καὶ τὸν τῆς ἡσυχίας ἔρωτα κἂν ἁρπάσαιμι ἐπιδραμών. For the gods of Epicurus as a reflection of his own quietism, see Ch. 2 Sect. 3.

for this study is *aperiergos*. This figures often in discussions of the plain style in dress and rhetoric and is discussed in the final chapter of this study. It is otherwise central to a story from the *Life of Aesop*, in which Aesop is challenged to find a man who can dine with his master Xanthos without displaying the meddlesome character of the *periergos*.[41] Aesop first seeks for an *aperiergos* in the marketplace, but is let down when at dinner the man intervenes three times to question the decisions of Xanthos.[42] It is therefore only when he looks to the countryside that he finds a figure sufficiently indifferent to provocation to prove himself truly *aperiergos*.[43] That it is a rustic and not a man of the city who fits the bill will surprise no reader of Aristophanic comedy.[44] Yet the same perspective can also be found in eminently more serious authors such as Philo of Alexandria, for whom the city and its institutions are ever the home of meddlesome injustice and the country the home of the virtuous *apragmon*.[45]

The biblical exegesis of Philo is prominent in this chapter and elsewhere in this study. That, however, is about as far as I have strayed into Judaeo-Christian texts. This is thus a contribution to the understanding of pagan antiquity and not of the early church. The range of texts addressed in the ensuing chapters has already taken me into areas in which I have no claim to any sort of expertise. Yet my relative innocence when faced with the ancient philosophers is as nothing compared to my utter helplessness as a theologian. I have learned what I could of St Augustine from scholars such as Marrou, O'Donnell, and Bös, and very occasional references to his works may be found here and there.[46] If the material that I have collected proves to be of use to future students of patristics, I will be delighted, but I cannot pretend that this study is preliminary to any such investigation of my own.

It should finally be stated that the close attention given to the changing meanings of individual words is likely to lend this work a somewhat forbidding aspect for those studying the ancient texts in translation. Yet those same students may well profit from consultation of individual sections of this work and I have attempted to set out my material in such a way as to make this possible for them.

---

[41] *Vita Aesopi* 55–64; Hunter (2009).   [42] *Vita Aesopi* 57–8.
[43] *Vita Aesopi* 59–64.   [44] See Ch. 1 Sect. 6.
[45] Philo *Spec. Leg.* 2. 44–5, 47; *Abr.* 19–23; cf. Plut. *Mor.* 518E–519B, 521E.
[46] Marrou (1938); O'Donnell (1992), ii. 150–1, iii. 223–4; Bös (1995).

Wherever appropriate in the main text I have transliterated the key Greek terms under discussion. Where a specific passage is essential to understanding, I have either printed my own translation alongside the Greek or Latin text or have paraphrased the words in question and then printed the original in a footnote or very occasionally in brackets.

(5) SOME KEY TEXTS

This study ranges widely over the extant remains of ancient literature. Yet some texts are more explicitly engaged with the concepts at its heart than are others. One such is the portrait of the *Periergos* in Theophrastus, *Characters* 13, and a brief discussion of this passage will be found in the first chapter of this study. A second is the *Metamorphoses* of Apuleius, where the most important trait of the central character and narrator, Lucius, is his *curiositas*, just as it is his *periergia* in the much shorter *Onos* attributed to Lucian. These works are examined in depth in the fourth chapter. One other text, however, stands out and inevitably takes a prominent position in discussions of this topic—the *Peri Polypragmosynes* of Plutarch—and it may therefore be appropriate to say something in advance about a work to which I have already referred more than once and that is destined to feature repeatedly in the pages that follow.

The *Peri Polypragmosynes* is a short essay on the psychological ills of curiosity and is to be found in the *Moralia* just after the closely related essay on garrulousness.[47] It defines *polypragmosyne* as a love of learning about the ills of others and concerns itself entirely with the individual *polypragmon*.[48] Nothing is said about *polypragmosyne* and the interventionist state. In this sense it is most closely related to those texts of the Hellenistic and Roman periods with which all but the first chapter of this study is most closely engaged. Yet earlier periods of Greek culture are far from absent and with them come some of the preoccupations more typical of the fifth and fourth centuries: verses are quoted from tragic and comic texts, some

---

[47] For the *Peri Adoleschias*, see Plut. *Mor.* 502B–515A. For the *Peri Polypragmosynes*, see Plut. *Mor.* 515B–523B.

[48] Plut. *Mor.* 515D: ἡ πολυπραγμοσύνη φιλομάθειά τίς ἐστιν ἀλλοτρίων κακῶν.

more closely in context than others;[49] Cleon and Oedipus both emerge as figures of *polypragmosyne*;[50] sykophants are decried;[51] and reference is made to the 443 BC foundation of Thurii in the Magna Graecia.[52]

To Plutarch, *polypragmosyne* is one of the passions, sick and harmful and a source of storm and darkness for the mind.[53] These we must either extirpate or turn to a better end.[54] The *polypragmon* is blind to all that is wrong with himself and his own home, but constantly alert to any scandal lurking in the homes of others.[55] He roams from house to house peering inside in search of new horrors.[56] He has no respect for secrets and lives to pass on what he has learned to others.[57] His natural environment is the city, in particular the marketplace and the port.[58] Much of this we will see in later chapters, be it in the Terentian Chremes fascinated by the sorrows of his neighbour Menedemus, Cicero the *curiosus* famished for news of political life at Rome, or the historian Theopompus, who brings suffering on himself by seeking to uncover and to broadcast the secrets of the divine.

A further feature of this essay that merits particular attention is the response that it prescribes. Plutarch is not sanguine about the

---

[49] For verses quoted in context, note esp. Plut. *Mor.* 515D = com. adesp. fr. 725 K-A: τί τἀλλότριον, ἄνθρωπε βασκανώτατε, | κακὸν ὀξυδορκεῖς τὸ δ' ἴδιον παραβλέπεις; The same lines are quoted at Plut. *Mor.* 469B as being addressed to a *polypragmon*.

[50] Plut. *Mor.* 517A, 522B-C.

[51] Plut. *Mor.* 517A, 523A bis, 523B bis.

[52] Plut. *Mor.* 519B.

[53] Plut. *Mor.* 515C: πάθη νοσώδη καὶ βλαβερὰ καὶ χειμῶνα παρέχοντα τῇ ψυχῇ καὶ σκότος. The language of the passions suggests Stoicism. Hense (1890) argues convincingly for the direct or indirect influence of the Stoic Ariston of Chios, whom Plutarch cites at *Mor.* 516F.

[54] Plut. *Mor.* 515C-D.

[55] Plut. *Mor.* 515E-516B, cf. 521A.

[56] Plut. *Mor.* 516E-F.

[57] Plut. *Mor.* 518C-E; cf. 508C for the connection between *adoleschia* and *periergia*. On the same point, see also Porphyrio at Hor. *Epist.* 1. 16. 4: 'loquaciter] bene loquaciter quasi curiose audituro et scire cupienti'.

[58] Plut. *Mor.* 519A, cf. 521D-E. Note here Hsch. β. 146: βαλανεύς· πολυπράγμων, περίεργος and CPG ii. 64: β α λ α ν ε ύ ς: ἐπὶ τοῦ πολυπράγμονος. οὗτοι γὰρ σχολὴν ἄγοντες πολυπράγμονες εἰσίν. One of the functions of the bathkeeper is to cut hair and beards. He may therefore be connected to the hopelessly garrulous barber of Plut. *Mor.* 505B, 508F, 509A. The last passage emphasizes that it is at barbers' shops that gossips love to gather. This leads into the tale told at 509A-C, cf. Plut. *Nic.* 30 of how the news of the disaster in Sicily was first told to a barber in the Piraeus, who then rushed up to the city to pass on the news.

14 *Introduction*

polypragmon's ability to root out his malady though he does suggest various therapeutic procedures designed to take the edge off our hunger for new knowledge: the advice to set aside newly received letters and read them only at a later date brings to mind the Seneca of *Epistle 77*, whose unconcern for what is morally indifferent sets him apart from the people of Puteoli rushing to the port to pick up their letters from the Alexandrian mailboats.⁵⁹ Otherwise all that one prey to an overwhelming hunger for knowledge can do is to turn it to less damaging ends. Hence Plutarch's suggestion that the *polypragmon* embrace natural science and reminder that nature will never take offence at anyone investigating her secrets.⁶⁰ Yet should this all prove just too pure, it will at least be possible to turn to history, replete as it is with every type of scandal. The *polypragmon* can sate his evil appetite with such stories and yet cause no hurt to any of those around him.⁶¹ This association of *polypragmosyne* with different fields of scholarly inquiry will become prominent in the Hellenistic period and will be examined repeatedly from the second chapter of this study onwards.

One last aspect that must be noted is the concept of *polypragmosyne* as a passion (*pathos*). The concept is Stoic and it is evident that *polypragmosyne* is to be regarded as a subset of the generic passion of *epithymia* or desire. The appetitive character of *polypragmosyne* has already been seen in Plutarch's exhortation to turn to history and sate oneself on the scandals that it offers.⁶² It is also apparent in his description of how the soul of the *polypragmon* feeds and fattens all that is wrong with it by seeking out the sorrows of others,⁶³ or of how some bite through the seal on a letter as if eating the news that it contains.⁶⁴ *Polypragmosyne* is a form of want of self-control (*akrasia*) and the best way to express this is to describe it as an appetite beyond control.⁶⁵ Elsewhere in this study we will find Cicero ravenous with

---

⁵⁹ Plut. *Mor.* 521E–522E. For not opening letters at once, see Plut. *Mor.* 522D; cf. Sen. *Ep.* 77. 3. Hense (1890), 549–50 compares Ariston's prescription of self-training (*askesis*) against all four generic passions at Clem. Al. *Strom.* II p. 486 P.
⁶⁰ Plut. *Mor.* 517C–E, esp. D: καὶ ταῦτ᾽ ἀπόρρητ᾽ ἐστὶ φύσεως, ἀλλ᾽ οὐκ ἄχθεται τοῖς ἐλέγχουσιν.
⁶¹ Plut. *Mor.* 517E–F.
⁶² Plut. *Mor.* 517F: ἐμπίμπλασο.
⁶³ Plut. *Mor.* 516D: βόσκουσα καὶ πιαίνουσα τὸ κακόηθες.
⁶⁴ Plut. *Mor.* 522D: τοῖς ὀδοῦσι τοὺς δεσμοὺς διαβιβρώσκοντες.
⁶⁵ For *akrasia*, see Plut. *Mor.* 519E.

curiosity,[66] and hear Lucius introduce himself as a thirster after novelty.[67] In Aelian the greed and thirst of the eye will induce a *polypragmon* to violate the mysteries of Demeter and meet an unhappy end.[68] The connection drawn between two very different levels of appetite—that of the belly and that of the soul—is thus an indispensable metaphor in ancient evocations of man's sometimes overwhelming need to know.

I close this Introduction with the ancient view of curiosity as a passion because it is all too easy to recognize that feature in myself and in the energy that has sustained this project. Colleagues have had little difficulty in recognizing this book as a form of confession, as a way of thinking about my own inability to sit still and focus on one author, one text. Archilochus tells us that the fox knows many things but the hedgehog one big thing, and on that definition I must admit to being a fox.[69] Yet the pages that follow should offer something for those who identify with both species: the detailed investigation of one specific concept but with a range of reference and a diversity of sources sufficient to stave off boredom in the constitutionally restless. I can only hope that the reader will now approach the rest of this study in the same spirit of ravenous curiosity with which it was composed.

---

[66] Cic. *Att.* 2. 12. 2: 'sum in curiositate ὀξύπεινος'.

[67] Apul. *Met.* 1. 2: 'sititor alioquin nouitatis'.

[68] Ael. fr. 46 D–F. For the phrasing adopted here, cf. Eur. *Hipp.* 912–13 with Barrett (1964) ad loc.; *CPG* ii. 170: ἡδὺ τἀπόρρητα λιχνεύειν· ἐπὶ τῶν πολυπραγμόνων.

[69] Archil. fr. 201 West: πόλλ' οἶδ' ἀλώπηξ, ἀλλ' ἐχῖνος ἓν μέγα.

1

Polypragmosyne and *Periergia* from Thucydides to Theophrastus

(1) INTRODUCTION

The first place in which almost all of us encounter discourses of *polypragmosyne*, and latterly of *periergia*, is in the literature of fifth- and fourth-century BC Athens. In famous scenes from the historians, the tragedians, and the orators, these terms are applied to the conduct of individual citizens and communities alike. Those to whom such features are ascribed contest the ethical underpinnings of the claim, seek positive terms in which to describe themselves, and construct myths that encode favourable assessments of their conduct. These are always profoundly subjective terms: nobody ever saw a *polypragmon* or a *periergos* on the streets of Athens, only someone he or others held to be such. The aim of this chapter is therefore to trace the most significant discourses and patterns of thought in this period in which talk of *polypragmosyne* and *periergia* is to be found. Yet I will also draw attention to some more unusual ways of using these terms, ways which perhaps point forward to the usage and the preoccupations of later periods. In this way I aim to set the ground for the more thematically focused chapters to follow.

(2) *POLYPRAGMOSYNE* AND THE BOUNDARIES OF PROPRIETY

Of signal importance for ancient thinking on *polypragmosyne*, and recurrent in later texts, is the definition of justice quoted by Socrates at *Republic* 433a–b and described as one which both he and others have previously endorsed: to do that which is proper to oneself and not to meddle.[1] It is therefore important to consider both the antecedents of this claim and the sense applied to it by Plato himself.[2] In the first book of the *Histories* of Herodotus, when Gyges is invited to gaze on the naked form of Candaules' wife, he instinctively refuses, stating that it is the wisdom of the ancients that every man should look at that which is proper to him.[3] Asheri's note on this passage of Herodotus traces this ancient wisdom back to Pittacus of Mytilene, one of the Seven Sages, though the passage that he quotes more specifically insists that every man should accept his own station in life.[4] No less relevant in this context must also be the dictum attributed to Chilon by Demetrius of Phalerum urging us to hate the man who meddles with the affairs of another.[5]

A similar pattern of thought is also visible in the early dialogue of Plato, the *Charmides*, where Charmides himself quotes what is soon revealed to be the dictum of Critias, that the wisdom of self-restraint or temperance (*sophrosyne*) is to do that which is proper to oneself.[6] Socrates in turn introduces the further idea that *sophrosyne* is the

---

[1] Pl. Resp. 433a–b: καὶ μὴν ὅτι γε τὸ τὰ αὑτοῦ πράττειν καὶ μὴ πολυπραγμονεῖν δικαιοσύνη ἐστι, καὶ τοῦτο ἄλλων τε πολλῶν ἀκηκόαμεν καὶ αὐτοὶ πολλάκις εἰρήκαμεν. The translation that I have offered of τὰ αὑτοῦ as 'that which is proper to oneself' is designed to encapsulate the two perspectives that can here come into conflict. On the one hand the individual minding his own business can claim that he is concerned with 'my proper affairs'. On the other the outsider telling another to mind his own business is defining what it is and is not 'proper' for him to do. See *OED*, VII. ii. 1469–70 s.v. 'proper'. I.1 and III.9.

[2] Mewaldt (1929), 89 describes 'justice is doing that which is proper to oneself' as 'der alles Umschliessende Leitsatz von Platons Πολιτεία'. This being so, it is absolutely important to identify exactly what Plato means by this claim.

[3] Hdt. 1. 8. 4: πάλαι δὲ τὰ καλὰ ἀνθρώποισι ἐξεύρηται, ἐκ τῶν μανθάνειν δεῖ· ἐν τοῖσι ἓν τόδε ἐστί, σκοπέειν τινὰ τὰ ἑωυτοῦ. See the discussion of Raubitschek (1958) and of Tosi (1991), 571–2, who aptly compares Men. *Monost.* 629 Jäkel: πράττων τὰ σαυτοῦ, μὴ τὰ τῶν ἄλλων φρόνει.

[4] Asheri (2007) ad loc. citing, inter alia, the wisdom of Pittacus as recorded at Callim. *Epigr.* 1 Pf. = Diog. Laert. 1. 79–80 = *Anth. Pal.* 7. 89. See also Raubitschek (1958), who connects this to Aesch. *PV* 887–93 and esp. the scholion to v. 887 identifying the wise man alluded to as Pittacus.

[5] Chilon ap. Stob. *Flor.* 3. 1. 172: τὸν τὰ ἀλλότρια περιεργαζόμενον μίσει.

[6] Pl. *Chrm.* 161b = Critias D–K 88B 41a: σωφροσύνη ἂν εἴη τὸ τὰ ἑαυτοῦ πράττειν. For Critias' responsibility for this formulation, see Pl. *Chrm.* 161b–c, 162b–c; Rademaker (2005), 330–2. For a helpful survey of 5th-century views of *sophrosyne*, see Tuckey (1951), 5–9; North (1966); Rademaker (2005).

opposite of *polypragmosyne*.[7] He therefore implies that which the *Republic* will go on to make explicit: that *polypragmosyne* is the opposite of doing that which is proper to oneself. The problem, as Socrates himself insists, lies in identifying that which is, or is not, proper to oneself.[8] To an Athenian of the period, the phrase 'to do that which is proper to oneself' is indeed part of the common currency and could more loosely be translated as 'to mind one's own business'.[9] It is the voluntary circumscription of one's own activities and is the opposite of unwelcome or uninvited intervention in that which is proper to others.[10] Yet it also admits of a more prescriptive application if we do not ourselves decide what is our proper business but have that decision made for us.[11] It is therefore important that the originator of the claim should here be unmasked. For Charmides himself belongs to the category of the beautiful but dim and is as unable at this point to resist Socrates' objections as he is at any other in the dialogue.[12] Critias, by contrast, is a distinctly more self-confident and developed thinker, and would appear to have no doubt of his own ability to remind each and every one of his proper place.[13] It is by no means insignificant that between the dramatic date of the dialogue and its actual composition lies Critias' involvement in the second oligarchic coup of 404 BC.[14]

Both Herodotus and the *Charmides* can offer some insight into the rhetorical and philosophical strategies of the *Republic*. It will be noted that in the passage quoted above from *Republic* 433a–b

---

[7] Pl. *Chrm.* 161e: ἦ οὖν ἐπολυπραγμονεῖτε καὶ οὐκ ἐσωφρονεῖτε τοῦτο δρῶντες.

[8] Pl. *Chrm.* 161c, 162b complains that the phrase is an enigma. G. Schmidt (1985), 15 observes that the phrase τὸ τὰ ἑαυτοῦ πράττειν is 'mehrdeutig' and demonstrates various possible senses. Hazebroucq (1997), 201–30 is strikingly verbose on the idea of the 'enigma'. For Socrates' objections and Critias' response, see also Tuckey (1951), 20–3.

[9] Hyp. 3. 21; Lys. 19. 18; 26. 3; Dem. 10. 72.

[10] τὰ ἑαυτοῦ are thus the opposite of τὰ ἀλλοτρία. See e.g. Ar. *Plut.* 931 for the sykophant τἀλλοτρία πράττων; Isoc. 15. 24, 230.

[11] See e.g. Soph. *El.* 678.

[12] For the beauty of Charmides, see Pl. *Chrm.* 157d. His intellectual helplessness is evident at every stage of his participation.

[13] This would be particularly true could the account of the social benefits of *sophrosyne* at Pl. *Chrm.* 171d–e be taken as a proper reflection of the historical Critias' thought. See also Mewaldt (1929), 85–9; Rademaker (2005), 331.

[14] Pl. *Chrm.* 153a and c date the dialogue to the moment of Socrates' return from the Potidaea campaign of 435–430 BC. The dialogue is thought to have been composed in the 390s BC. For Critias in the *Charmides* and in history, see Tuckey (1951), 15–17; North (1966), 154; Rademaker (2005), 5–6.

Socrates states that many others before him have often claimed, as has he, that justice is to do that which is proper to oneself and not to meddle. This is important for two reasons: first, it implies that this is a form of traditional wisdom of the sort to which the Herodotean Gyges refers; second, the very fact that many have been able to make the same claim may suggest that it is as loose and in need of further definition as Socrates himself found the definition of *sophrosyne* in the *Charmides*. Both these suspicions are confirmed by closer examination of the text.

What is crucial here is that Socrates introduces this avowedly commonplace definition of justice into some decidedly uncommon reflections on the proper ordering of the state.[15] Essential here is the principle posited at the outset of the description of the ideal state and repeatedly echoed thereafter, that each man should do only one thing: a cobbler should mend shoes, a carpenter work wood, a soldier defend the state by force of arms, a guardian rule and give out orders.[16] The one thing each man does will be that which is fitting for him.[17] Each generation starts afresh and it is quite possible for a son to be suited to a task, hence a class, quite different from that of his father;[18] but the nature and capacities with which we are born do not allow for further transformation, and any attempt to exchange one's proper task for any other, or even to take on more than one task at once, will be dangerous to the state and therefore unjust.[19] There may be relatively little communal danger to be feared from cobblers and carpenters swapping tasks, because they both belong to the same basic class of producers, but it will be eminently hazardous should the same cobbler seek to be a soldier or a guardian.[20]

It is only if we trace the development of this very particular model of society that we can see how different are the ends to which Socrates puts the traditional definition of justice from what may be assumed to be its more conventional application. An ordinary

---

[15] For the rhetorical cunning displayed, see Andersson (1971), 102 n. 2; Blössner (1997), 258 n. 726. Blössner makes the important point that the grounds on which the premise that one man should do one thing is introduced are apparently innocuous ('aus unverfänglich scheinenden Gründen'). This is far from the truth by the time that Socrates has finished expounding his model for the state and this has huge implications for the traditional model of justice only latterly brought in at 433a–b.

[16] Pl. *Resp.* 370b, 374a, 394e, 397e, 400e, 406d–e, 421b, 433a, 433d, 441d, 442b, 443b.

[17] Pl. *Resp.* 433a.   [18] Pl. *Resp.* 423c–d.

[19] Pl. *Resp.* 434a–c.   [20] Pl. *Resp.* 434a–b.

Athenian, I suggest, who caught sight of a farmer tilling his own field and disinclined to tell others how to live, might nod admiringly and opine that 'the just man minds his own business'.[21] Were he to discover that the same farmer also made his own shoes or did his own carpentry, this would be little cause for shock. He might even regard this as coherent with ideals of self-sufficiency or *autarkeia*.[22] Were he then to peer into the farmer's cottage and discover a hoplite panoply hanging on the wall should it ever be necessary to take action in defence of the state, this too would surely be admired; for there is nothing so incompatible with minding one's own business as to have an enemy invasion force minding it for one, and the Athenian way to see off invasion is through the readiness of the ordinary citizen to take up arms as and when required rather than through the maintenance of a standing army subjected to the ceaseless drilling of the Spartans.[23] Yet according to the model Socrates offers for his city, this would constitute the intervention of the producer class in the proper work of the military and would constitute *polypragmosyne*. In this state, to do any more than that one thing to which one is suited is to do too many (*polypragmosyne*) and its complement is to do just one thing but that which is still appropriate to another and not oneself (*allotriopragmosyne*).[24] If the state can sustain itself through the assent of the ruled to the powers of the ruler, all the better. This can even be called *sophrosyne*.[25] If not there will be plenty of ways to

---

[21] Consider Pl. *Grg.* 526c where the soul of the ἀνδρὸς ἰδιώτου ἢ ἄλλου τινός, μάλιστα μέν ... φιλοσόφου τὰ αὑτοῦ πράξαντος καὶ οὐ πολυπραγμονήσαντος ἐν τῷ βίῳ passes straight to the isles of the blest. This dialogue is certainly concerned with the definition of justice, but the concept of *polypragmosyne* is introduced only in passing at a very late stage. Socrates has already conceded that it is possible to engage with the affairs of the city in a just manner (521d, 526a). What therefore matters about the private man or philosopher here described is that he has shunned political positions which make it all too easy to do wrong (525d).

[22] Pl. *Resp.* 565a speaks admiringly of *autourgoi* and Arist. *Rh.* 1381a23 confirms that this is a widely held view. See also Eur. *Or.* 920.

[23] Thuc. 2. 39. 1 is Pericles' classic statement of the difference between Spartan and Athenian methods. Hornblower (1991) ad loc. should be consulted for evidence undermining any impression of total amateurism. For the panoply, see Ar. *Plut.* 951, where the Just Man possesses one, and compare Pl. *Menex.* 249a–b, which describes how, when the child of a citizen slain in war reaches manhood, the state furnishes him with a panoply with which to return to his hearth.

[24] Pl. *Resp.* 444a–b.

[25] Pl. *Resp.* 431d–e; Rademaker (2005), 344.

compel such cooperation.[26] From start to finish the city is built from the top down and is profoundly anti-democratic in its spirit.[27] It is important to recall that Socrates' discussion of the just state is first introduced as an analogy for the just soul.[28] Though the focus through much of books 2–4 appears to be solely on the city qua city, this original perspective is resumed at 443c as Socrates reminds Glaucon that all his talk of cobblers and carpenters and their doings has been but an image of the inner man and of the competing elements within his own soul.[29] Yet if the state is a way of thinking about the individual, the opposite is also true and Socrates' description of the soul can seem but a reflection of the anti-democratic elitism of his political thought: the appetitive part of the soul is far larger than the rational and the spirited,[30] but a just and temperate soul will be one in which the appetite concedes to reason its right to rule over it.[31] The version of *polypragmosyne* that Socrates here fears is not that in which reason seeks to usurp the proper province of appetite but rather the opposite; for all then will be confusion and error, injustice and licentiousness, cowardice and stupidity.[32]

---

[26] For persuasion and coercion as means to the same end, see Pl. *Resp.* 421b: ἀναγκαστέον ... καὶ πειστέον, 519e πειθοῖ τε καὶ ἀνάγκηι.

[27] Adkins (1976) answers back to good effect.

[28] Pl. *Resp.* 368c–369a.

[29] This is strongly implied at Pl. *Resp.* 443c. By 444a, however, Socrates again talks of the just man and the just city. For how this analogy can play out in the later books of the *Republic*, consider Pl. *Resp.* 549c–550c on the origins of the timocratic man and the timocratic polity. Socrates imagines the situation of a son living in an ill-established city whose virtuous father flees honour, power, court cases, and all *philopragmosyne* (φεύγοντος τάς τε τιμὰς καὶ ἀρχὰς καὶ δίκας καὶ τὴν τοιαύτην πᾶσαν φιλοπραγμοσύνην) and accepts low status if it will keep him out of trouble (ἐθέλοντος ἐλαττοῦσθαι ὥστε πράγματα μὴ ἔχειν). Yet when the son sees those who do what is proper to themselves called fools and dishonoured (τούς ... τὰ αὑτῶν πράττοντας ἐν τῇ πόλει ἠλιθίους τε καλουμένους καὶ ἐν σμικρῷ λόγῳ ὄντας) and hears both his mother and the house-slaves criticize the father for being so passive as not even to prosecute those who owe him money, he turns against his influence. For all that the father seeks to nurture the rational over the appetitive and spirited portions of the son's soul (τοῦ μὲν πατρὸς αὐτοῦ τὸ λογιστικὸν ἐν τῇ ψυχῇ ἄρδοντός τε καὶ αὔξοντος, τῶν δὲ ἄλλων τό τε ἐπιθυμητικὸν καὶ τὸ θυμοειδές), the son eventually adopts an attitude halfway between that of his parent and that of the society around him and becomes high-spirited and ambitious (ὑψηλόφρων τε καὶ φιλότιμος). This is also how the timocratic polity comes into being.

[30] Cf. Pl. *Resp.* 431b–c for how few people in the state are led by reason.

[31] Pl. *Resp.* 443d–e, cf. 431c–432b.

[32] Pl. *Resp.* 444a–b.

In the *Charmides* Socrates bridles at the want of definition in the claim that 'temperance is to do that which is proper to oneself'. In the *Republic*, by contrast, he subjects the very similar claim that 'justice is to do that which is proper to oneself and not to meddle' to a definition that detaches it radically from any plausible reconstruction of conventional social attitudes. It is this transformation of commonplace but hazy categories of popular ethics into a system both clear and uncompromising that underpins the singularly alarming character of his ideas.

(3) ARISTOTLE AND POLITICAL
POLYPRAGMOSYNE

Aristotle puts considerably less weight than does Plato on the concept of *polypragmosyne*, but what he has to say is still of considerable interest. In particular what he illustrates is the gulf in response between the orator successfully accommodating his language to the ingrained prejudices of his audience and the ethical philosopher whose task it is to challenge just those views.

In the *Rhetoric* Aristotle advises the aspiring orator to know in advance what are the beliefs of his audience and to adapt his speech to take due account of this. Aristotle therefore asserts that the Athenian jury will revere those who are gentlemanly, courageous, and just, and states that they regard as just those who do not live off others but profit from their own labours. They also revere the prudent because they are not unjust and the quietist for the same reason.[33] An evident and not unfamiliar ideal is being sketched out— the Attic landsman whose efforts permit him to stand alone and to minimize his interaction with society—and this is an ideal which Aristotle himself is not embarrassed at times to endorse.[34]

If the quietist is commonly admired because just, is the man who engages in the collective decision-making of the community seen as a meddler and therefore unjust? Aristotle does not say as much in the

---

[33] Arist. *Rh.* 1381a20–6: καὶ τοὺς σώφρονας, ὅτι οὐκ ἄδικοι. καὶ τοὺς ἀπράγμονας διὰ τὸ αὐτό.
[34] Arist. *Pol.* 1292b22–33, 1318b6–16, 1319a30–8; cf. Pl. *Resp.* 565a; Eur. *Or.* 917-22; Grossmann (1950), 26–30; L. B. Carter (1986), 76–98.

Rhetoric, but something approaching this view is to be found in that work transmitted in the corpus of Aristotle's writings under the title *Rhetorica ad Alexandrum* but now more commonly identified as the *Ars Rhetorica* of Anaximenes.[35] This is a guide to various modes of oratory and the issue of *polypragmosyne* arises as the author considers how the past or current conduct of an orator can undermine his position. Those, therefore, who speak often are apt to be regarded as meddlers and are exposed to opprobrium for this.[36] It is just such a view that Aristotle himself contests in book 6 of the *Nicomachean Ethics*. Here he notes the popular belief that to be wise is to look to that which concerns oneself as an individual, but argues that there are various forms of wisdom, from household management to legislation to state affairs, be they matters of policy or judicial decision.[37] Wise though it is to look to what concerns oneself, the belief that politicians are busybodies[38] is erroneous because it can prove impossible to look to what concerns oneself without engaging in household management or politics.[39] Aristotle does not set out to create an ideal state but to consider how it is possible to live well in that which currently exists, and what appears as a first principle in Plato recurs here as a popular prejudice which reflects all too inadequately the realities of the human community: if all political activity is to be decried as *polypragmosyne*, how many of the manifest benefits of that community will be lost?

(4) THE INDIVIDUAL AS *POLYPRAGMON*

What emerges most clearly from Aristotle's account of *polypragmosyne* is that the active citizen constantly runs the risk of being

---

[35] For brief exposition of the evidence supporting this attribution, see Fuhrmann (2000), pp. xxxix–xl.

[36] Anaxim. *Ars rhet.* 29. 18: ἔπειτα ἐὰν συνεχῶς εἰώθῃ λέγειν· πολυπράγμων γὰρ εἶναι δοκεῖ οὗτος.

[37] Arist. *Eth. Nic.* 1141b29–33: δοκεῖ δὲ καὶ φρόνησις μάλιστ᾽ εἶναι ἡ περὶ αὐτὸν καὶ ἕνα· καὶ ἔχει αὕτη τὸ κοινὸν ὄνομα, φρόνησις· ἐκείνων δὲ ἡ μὲν οἰκονομία ἡ δὲ νομοθεσία ἡ δὲ πολιτική, καὶ ταύτης ἡ μὲν βουλευτικὴ ἡ δὲ δικαστική.

[38] Arist. *Eth. Nic.* 1142a1–2: καὶ δοκεῖ ὁ τὰ περὶ αὑτὸν εἰδὼς καὶ διατρίβων φρόνιμος εἶναι, οἱ δὲ πολιτικοὶ πολυπράγμονες.

[39] Arist. *Eth. Nic.* 1142a7–10: ζητοῦσι γὰρ τὸ αὑτοῖς ἀγαθόν, καὶ οἴονται τοῦτο δεῖν πράττειν. ἐκ ταύτης οὖν τῆς δόξης ἐλήλυθε τὸ τούτους φρονίμους εἶναι· καίτοι ἴσως οὐκ ἔστι τὸ αὑτοῦ εὖ ἄνευ οἰκονομίας οὐδ᾽ ἄνευ πολιτείας.

dismissed not as a patriot but as a busybody. The concern that the philosopher expresses is that any too restrictive definition of what it is to mind one's own business can so undermine any commitment to the collective that finally it puts what we regard as our personal affairs at risk. Further investigation will suggest that this is no new perception and that it is already deployed in fifth-century disputes about where good citizenship ends and meddling begins. The dramatists have much to contribute to our understanding of the topic.

It is not necessary to look very far for a first instance from the dramatists. For Aristotle himself turns to Euripides for an example of the common view that the wise mind their own business while politicians are busybodies.[40] The lines that he cites are from the speech of Odysseus in the prologue to the playwright's *Philoctetes*, in which the hero questions the merits of his own constant political activity when he could as easily lead a quiet life among the ranks of the army and gain no lesser reward.[41] Fuller versions of the same fragments are also given in Plutarch's work *On Self-Praise* while Odysseus' train of thought is indicated by Dio Chrysostom's versions at *Orations* 52. 11–12 and 59. 1–2.[42] Odysseus first questions whether he is indeed wise to act as he does.[43] What drives him on, the hero confesses, is the love of honour (*philotimia*),[44] for those who stand out are the ones to receive honour in the city and to be counted as men.[45] This is what constantly entangles Odysseus in affairs and induces him to lead a toilsome life.[46] For fear lest he lose the favour gained by his previous labours, he does not shun his present toil.[47] In its original context, therefore, what Odysseus has to say does not offer as perfect a match for the view that Aristotle describes as might be expected. He does question the wisdom of the active life and notes

---

[40] Arist. *Eth. Nic.* 1142a2–6.

[41] For useful discussion of the remains of this speech, see Müller (2000).

[42] Eur. fr. 787 Kannicht = Plut. *Mor.* 544C, fr. 788 Kannicht = Dio Chrys. *Or.* 52. 12 and Stob. *Flor.* 3. 29. 15; Eur. fr. 789 Kannicht = Plut. *Mor.* 544C.

[43] Eur. fr. 787 Kannicht: πῶς δ᾽ ἂν φρονοίην, ᾧ παρῆν ἀπραγμόνως | ἐν τοῖσι πολλοῖς ἠριθμημένῳ στρατοῦ | ἴσον μετασχεῖν τῷ σοφωτάτῳ τύχης;

[44] Dio Chrys. *Or.* 52. 12; 59. 2.

[45] Eur. fr. 788 Kannicht: οὐδὲν γὰρ οὕτω γαῦρον ὡς ἀνὴρ ἔφυ· | τοὺς γὰρ περισσοὺς καί τι πράσσοντας πλέον | τιμῶμεν ἄνδρας τ᾽ ἐν πόλει νομίζομεν.

[46] Dio Chrys. *Or.* 59. 2: ὑφ᾽ ἧς φιλοτιμίας κἀγὼ προάγομαι πλεῖστα πράγματα ἔχειν καὶ ζῆν ἐπιπόνως.

[47] Eur. fr. 789 Kannicht: ὀκνῶν δὲ μόχθων τῶν πρὶν ἐκχέαι χάριν | καὶ τοὺς παρόντας οὐκ ἀπωθοῦμαι πόνους.

that he could turn to quietism; this, however, is not because it is wiser
to mind one's own business, but rather because the activist receives
no greater material reward than the member of the common host. All
he can look to is honour and praise. At the same time, however, there
can be little doubt that Odysseus the political man par excellence is
apt to be regarded by his detractors as a meddler, as a *polypragmon*,
and his own phrasing employs terms suggestive of this view. As will
be seen in Section 8, the celebration of toil (*ponos*) is essential to the
positive construction of what others decry as the *polypragmosyne* of
the Athenian state, and in fr. 789 Odysseus explains why he does not
reject his current toil. In fr. 788. 2 he also refers to those who 'do
something more' (τι πράσσοντας πλέον) while in the version of the
speech at Dio Chrysostom, *Oration* 59. 2 he talks of himself undertaking 'many affairs' or 'facing great troubles' (πλεῖστα πράγματα
ἔχειν).[48] It is enlightening to compare Plato's myth of Er, where
Odysseus in the underworld has finally embraced the life of an
apragmon.[49]

The mockery of the politician as *polypragmon* is also attested by
Ps.-Xenophon, who claims that the only poor men to become victims
of comic mockery are busybodies or those on the make at the
people's expense.[50] Otherwise, the most common type of individual
polypragmon is the volunteer prosecutor or *sykophant*. The issue
goes to the heart of the Athenian legal system, where the task of
launching a prosecution is not given to any official director of public
prosecutions, but rather left to the individual citizen who perceives
wrongdoing in another and seeks redress. Certain modes of denunciation (*phasis*) and prosecution offer the prospect of financial
reward should the defendant be found guilty, but fines also exist to

---

[48] Eur. fr. 788. 2: τι πράσσοντας πλέον is a good example of the tragic poets'
penchant for more elegant alternatives to πολυπραγμοσύνη and πολυπραγμονεῖν.
See e.g. von Wilamowitz-Moellendorff (1895) at Eur. *HF* 266: 'πολυπραγμονεῖν ist
für die tragödie eine zu ἀγοραία λέξις, aber πολλὰ πράσσειν in dem Sinne hat Eur.
öfter'; Jebb (1906) at Soph. *Ant.* 67-8: περισσὰ πράσσειν and Jebb (1908) at *Trach.*
617: περισσὰ δρᾶν; Bond (1981) at Eur. *HF* 266-7 and 1163; Barrett (1964) at Eur.
Hipp. 785: τὸ πολλὰ πράσσειν. For comedy, see Dover (1993) at Ar. *Ran.* 228 and 749.
[49] Pl. *Resp.* 620c-d; Müller (2000), 164 even includes this passage among the
testimonia to the play.
[50] Xen. [*Ath. Pol.*] 2. 18: ὀλίγοι δέ τινες τῶν πενήτων καὶ τῶν δημοτικῶν
κωμῳδοῦνται, καὶ οὐδ' οὗτοι ἐὰν μὴ διὰ πολυπραγμοσύνην καὶ διὰ τὸ ζητεῖν πλέον
τι ἔχειν τοῦ δήμου. Cf. Plut. *Mor.* 519B for Charondas, lawmaker of Thurii, banning
comic mockery of anyone save adulterers and *polypragmones*; Christ (1998), 52-3.

punish those unable to convince at least one-fifth of the jury to convict.[51] This last provision should act as a bulwark against malicious and time-wasting legal action, but it scarcely safeguards the prosecutor against accusations of malice and self-interest. Anyone taking on the role of the good and active citizen and seeking to curb criminality therefore exposes himself to easy denigration. In institutional terms the prosecutor is 'the man who wishes to act' (ὁ βουλόμενος); in the powerfully pejorative terms of the speech for the defence, he is a sykophant.[52] Or even a sykophant and a *polypragmon*.[53] Sections 5 and 6 therefore consider how just such prejudices are exploited first in rhetoric, then in comedy. In all cases it will be important also to remain alert to traces of a more positive evaluation.

(5) SYKOPHANTS AND *POLYPRAGMONES* IN RHETORIC

The Athenian orators and logographers of the fifth and fourth centuries adopt a variety of positions as they deplore the meddling of their opponents; protest their own or their client's quietism; and assert the propriety of intervention in public life. We have already seen evidence for these approaches in the rhetorical treatises of Aristotle and Anaximenes, and this may now be compared with actual courtroom procedure. The instinctive sympathy of the jury for quietists and suspicion of those who speak too often surely underlies the opening to Lysias 7, *On the Stump*, where the defendant protests his previous quiet life and depicts himself as one fallen prey to wicked sykophants.[54] The ambition just to mind one's own business (τὰ ἑαυτοῦ πράττειν) is one attributed by the speaker of Lysias 19 to his father and reported in Lysias 26 as being made by Evander, compromised by involvement with the the the Thirty and now seeking to

[51] Andoc. 1. 33; Dem. 21. 47; 24. 7; 26. 9; 58. 6; A. R. W. Harrison (1968–71), ii. 83 n. 2.
[52] Osborne (1990).
[53] Isoc. 15. 225, 230; Aeschin. 3. 172 on ὁ περίεργος καὶ συκοφάντης Δημοσθένης; Christ (1998), 51 and n. 28.
[54] Lys. 7. 1; Lateiner (1982–3), 7; L. B. Carter (1986), 107–8.

pass scrutiny (*dokimasia*) as a citizen and potential magistrate.[55] Those, by contrast, who take pride in their own civic activities can, like Odysseus in Euripides' *Philoctetes*, refer to their desire for honour (*philotimia*), represent such conduct as in line with ancestral tradition, and remind the jury of their admiration for those who follow this course. Such is the Mantitheus of Lysias 16.[56] His opponents probably called him a *polypragmon*.

It is in this context that we may give detailed consideration to the *Antidosis* of Isocrates. The title of the speech relates to the process in Athenian law by which a man charged with the payment of liturgies could nominate another better placed to do so instead. The nominee could either agree to do so, thus admitting that he did indeed have greater resources on which to draw, or propose an exchange of his entire property with that of the man originally ordered to pay, or go to court and prove that he was indeed less well off.[57] The elderly Isocrates appears to have found himself nominated to pay the liturgies originally levied on another unnamed Athenian.[58] This affront in turn led him to invent a second and entirely fictional situation, in which, like Socrates before him, he would stand trial accused of corrupting the young.[59] Isocrates thus composes a speech complete with an invented prosecutor, Lysimachus;[60] addresses to an imaginary jury; and sundry references to the dripping of a non-existent water clock.[61] In it he defends his professional life as a teacher of rhetoric and the contribution of his art to the past, present, and future greatness of Athens. It is a copybook exercise but perhaps no less illustrative of actual practice for all that.

The case against Isocrates turns on the consequences of his thriving practice as a teacher of rhetoric to the young. If they have been corrupted by him, it must be because they have used the skills in argument and delivery acquired from him in the furtherance of

---

[55] Lys. 19. 18; 26. 3; Lateiner (1982–3), 6, 11; Bearzot (2007), 124, 129. For the regulations governing *dokimasia*, see A. R. W. Harrison (1968–71), ii. 200–7.

[56] Lys. 16. 20–1; Lateiner (1982–3), 9; Bearzot (2007), 126–8.

[57] A. R. W. Harrison (1968–71), ii. 236–8; Too (2008), 4–6.

[58] Isoc. 15. 4–5. Too (2008), 1 imports the name Megacleides from Ps.-Plut. *Vit.* 43.

[59] Isoc. 15. 7–8.

[60] Isoc. 15. 8, 14.

[61] For the water clock, see e.g. Isoc. 15. 54, 320.

political programmes inimical to the well-being of Athens. Lysimachus, of course, is an entirely invented foe, so he has little means of
defence when Isocrates accuses him of failing to give any firm proof
of how his pupils have been taught to enhance their property by
unjust means.[62] The teacher in turn can drive home this advantage
by citing all those who once associated with him and were later
crowned by Athens for their services to the state.[63] Yet now an
important objection is canvassed: those hostile to him may claim
that his contact with all the good men he names went no further than
being seen with them, while other pupils, whom he hides from the
jury, turned into *polypragmones*.[64] In order to answer this suspicion
he therefore turns to one former pupil, Timotheus, who did indeed
end his career as a commander convicted, fined, and forced into
voluntary exile rather than pay up. An extended encomium proves
that Isocrates has nothing to regret in his friendship with Timotheus;
that the punishment inflicted on him overlooked his many and signal
services to Athens; and that Timotheus' undoing was his failure to
lavish on his fellow citizens the charm that he exhibited towards
Athens' allies and defeated foes.[65]

The prejudice exploited by the prosecution is that which regards
skill in oratory as suspect and its possessors as men who use lies and
deception in order to gain that which they do not truly deserve.
Isocrates responds with a celebration of the rhetorical gifts of the
greatest Athenians from Solon to Cleisthenes and on to Themistocles
and Pericles. He also reminds the jury of the special prestige enjoyed
by Athens throughout the Greek world as the home of rhetoric: for
the city to punish one of its own for this practice would be as absurd
as for Sparta to punish its citizens for military training or the
Thessalians to turn against a Thessalian for training horses.[66] Most
of all, he insists on the distinction between the practice of rhetoric,
which is an essential skill in anyone seeking to contribute to public
life, and the moral qualities of the individual practitioners: if skill in
oratory *makes* us conspire to acquire the property of others, it follows

---

[62] Isoc. 15. 89–90.   [63] Isoc. 15. 93–6.
[64] Isoc. 15. 98: ἕτεροι δέ τινές μοι πολλοὶ καὶ πολυπράγμονες μαθηταὶ γεγόνασιν,
οὓς ἀποκρύπτομαι πρὸς ὑμᾶς.
[65] Isoc. 15. 101–39.
[66] Isoc. 15. 297–8.

that all men able to deliver a speech must also be sykophants and *polypragmones*.[67] One part of Isocrates' defence is thus to offer a rational defence of rhetorical training and a celebration of those who have benefited from it. Yet what makes the *Antidosis* so revealing is the manner in which it exploits to its own ends the very prejudices that elsewhere it contests. Essential to this is Isocrates' somewhat surprising self-presentation as an *apragmon* or quietist.[68] This may seem odd coming from a man so proud of his own contribution to collective counsel that he quotes large sections of his own speech to the people, *On the Peace*, as well as of his encomium to the city, the *Panegyricus*, and address to Nicocles, king of Cyprus.[69] Yet Isocrates can also note that he has never prosecuted anyone and that this is his first speech in any judicial context;[70] that he has been constant and uncomplaining in his payment of liturgies;[71] and that he has never sought any public office in return.[72] While he has mastered the higher forms of oratory and has done so through the study of philosophy, what gives men such as Lysimachus experience of judicial oratory is their inveterate meddlesomeness.[73] It is to deter such villains that the city publishes the names of sykophants and *polypragmones* alongside those of convicted criminals.[74]

---

[67] Isoc. 15. 230: εἴπερ ἡ περὶ τοὺς λόγους δεινότης ποιεῖ τοῖς ἀλλοτρίοις ἐπιβουλεύειν, προσῆκεν ἅπαντας τοὺς δυναμένους εἰπεῖν πολυπράγμονας καὶ συκοφάντας εἶναι.

[68] This is the only speech in which Isocrates explicitly claims to be an *apragmon*. He does, however, refer elsewhere (5. 81; 12. 9–10; *Ep*. 8. 7) to the weak voice and lack of courage that held him back from addressing the people.

[69] Isoc. 15. 59, 66, 73. Note also Isoc. 15. 260 describing himself as engaged περὶ τοὺς πολιτικοὺς λόγους. Too (2008), 124 argues that the only way to square Isocrates' claims to quietism with the statement at 15. 54 that he delivered these speeches is if he did so in front of a small, private group.

[70] Isoc. 16–21 are, in fact, judicial orations though the cases for which they were composed are most likely fictions.

[71] Isoc. 15. 145, 150. For this motif in the speeches of self-styled quietists, see also Lys. 19. 57–9; 21. 1, 5, 19; 26. 3; L. B. Carter (1986), 103–4; Bearzot (2007), 124–5.

[72] Isoc. 26–7, 144–5, 151: τὴν μὲν ἡσυχίαν καὶ τὴν ἀπραγμοσύνην ἀγαπῶν, 227-8: ἀπραγμονεστάτους μὲν ὄντας τῶν ἐν τῇ πόλει καὶ πλείστην ἡσυχίαν ἄγοντας, 238. For the quietist who loyally pays his liturgies while seeking no office in return, see Lys. 19. 2, 54–6; 21. 1–6, 19; Bearzot (2007), 124–5.

[73] Isoc. 15. 48: συνίσασι γὰρ τοὺς μὲν διὰ πολυπραγμοσύνην ἐμπείρους τῶν ἀγώνων γεγενημένους, τοὺς δ' ἐκ φιλοσοφίας ἐκείνων τῶν λόγων ὧν ἄρτι προεῖπον τὴν δύναμιν εἰληφότας.

[74] Isoc. 15. 237: ἔχω δὲ δεῖξαι καὶ τόπους, ἐν οἷς ἔξεστιν ἰδεῖν τοῖς βουλομένοις τοὺς πολυπράγμονας καὶ τοὺς ταῖς αἰτίαις ἐνόχους ὄντας, ἃς οὗτοι τοῖς σοφισταῖς

Lysimachus, as has been observed, does not exist. He is in no position either to celebrate his own *philotimia* or to explain why it is so clearly in the public interest that a pedagogue now well into his ninth decade should be brought to trial.[75] Instead, and almost ad nauseam, he is the embodiment of the sykophant and he lives to make trouble for others.[76] In other words, a speech that sets out to celebrate the contribution to society of rhetoric and rhetorical education depends for much of its effect on commonly held prejudices against the practitioners of just that art. It is one thing for a countryman in Lysias to portray himself as an innocent quietist fallen amongst sykophants and quite another for a rhetorician such as Isocrates to do just the same. That he turns to such a strategy even here where it seems so implausible may perhaps indicate quite how often it was adopted by speakers and logographers throughout this age.

(6) THE ARISTOPHANIC *POLYPRAGMON*

The works of Greek Old Comedy are rich in sykophants and *polypragmones*. So much is evident from play titles and stray fragments.[77] Yet far and away the best evidence is furnished by the works of Aristophanes and what makes these particularly interesting is the degree to which, even in this charmless stock character, traces can be found of a more positive evaluation.[78]

ἐπιφέρουσιν. ἐν γὰρ ταῖς σανίσιν ταῖς ὑπὸ τῶν ἀρχόντων ἐκτιθεμέναις ἀναγκαῖόν ἐστιν, ἐν μὲν ταῖς τῶν θεσμοθετῶν ἀμφοτέρους ἐνεῖναι, τούς τε τὴν πόλιν ἀδικοῦντας καὶ τοὺς συκοφαντοῦντας. The reference may be to the legal sanctions established for those not obtaining the votes of one-fifth of the jury after launching a prosecution.

[75] Isoc. 15. 9 states that Isocrates is now 82 years old.

[76] Isoc. 15. 8 is programmatic as Isocrates claims to have invented συκοφάντην ... ὄντα τὸν γεγραμμένον καὶ τὸν πράγματά μοι παρέχοντα. For further references to sykophancy see Isoc. 15. 21, 23, 66, 88, 96, 163, 164, 174, 175, 224, 225, 237, 241, 242, 288, 300, 308, 309, 312, 313 bis, 318, 320. For the sykophant and πράγματα παρέχειν, see Isoc. 15. 39, 148, 163, 241.

[77] For sykophants outside Aristophanes in Old Comedy, see Eupolis frr. 245. 2 and 259. 37 K-A. For references to *polypragmosyne*, see Eupolis fr. 238 K-A; Pherecrates fr. 163. 2 K-A. For *polypragmosyne* in Middle Comedy, see Heniochus fr. 3 K-A; cf. Timocles fr. 29 K-A.

[78] Ehrenberg (1947), 54–5 sees only hostility and a reflection of Aristophanes' fight against the demagogues.

In the parabasis to the *Acharnians*, the origins of the Peloponnesian War are traced to the sykophants' denunciation of illicit Megarian goods.[79] When, therefore, the hero Dikaiopolis creates his own private marketplace, it is one from which he bans all sykophants and denouncers.[80] They, however, do not pay heed and his attempt to complete a very favourable exchange with the starveling Megarian is interrupted by the arrival of a sykophant.[81] The language of denunciation is all around, but what the sykophant regards as the proper response to the discovery of enemy goods and citizens,[82] Dikaiopolis dismisses as meddling (*polypragmosyne*) and takes the risk upon himself.[83] Sykophants are now fair game to all: the chorus speculate on what will happen if Ktesias enters the marketplace or if Hyperbolos starts a trial;[84] the Theban declines to take a sykophant wrapped up in pottery in exchange for his eels; and Nikarchos the sykophant is given short shrift.[85]

In the *Acharnians*, therefore, the sykophant is both the cause of the war and the butt of the humble farmer's revenge. Yet it is worth noting that what Dikaiopolis can dismiss as meddling, the sykophant can represent as the performance of a patriotic duty. If the opposite of *polypragmosyne* is to mind your own business, it will be helpful first to define what is and is not one's business. This is what Aristotle will argue a century later in the *Nicomachean Ethics*, but it is clear that he is not the first to identify the problem.

The same issues are even more clearly debated in the sykophant scene of Aristophanes' late play the *Ploutos*.[86] Here the god of wealth is restored to sight and no longer bestows his gifts at random or on the undeserving. Various consequences ensue and not all of them as good as might at first be expected. One significant loser is the sykophant, who suddenly discovers that there are no more cases to be tried.[87] As he enters the stage, the sykophant is spotted by the Just Man, who can see from the start that he is a bad penny,[88] and prays that Ploutos should destroy all sykophants.[89] Yet in the exchange that ensues, the sykophant reveals a rather different understanding of his role. Indeed he professes to be a good man and one devoted to the

---

[79] Ar. *Ach.* 515–22. [80] Ar. *Ach.* 725–6. [81] Ar. *Ach.* 818–35.
[82] Ar. *Ach.* 819, 827. [83] Ar. *Ach.* 833.
[84] Ar. *Ach.* 839–41, 846–7. [85] Ar. *Ach.* 903–58.
[86] For intelligent discussion, see Christ (1998), 145–7.
[87] Ar. *Plut.* 859. [88] Ar. *Plut.* 862, cf. 957. [89] Ar. *Plut.* 877–9.

city.[90] True, he does not have the bile to be a farmer and is no trader unless he pretends to be one; rather he makes his living by concerning himself with the affairs of the city and of individual citizens alike.[91] To the Just Man it seems impossible that one meddling with that which is not his should be morally good,[92] but the sykophant merely asks why it should not be his business to benefit the city to the best of his ability.[93] Can meddling then be a benefit?[94] It certainly can be if it means supporting the established laws and suppressing wrongdoing.[95] Nor is this just a matter for jurors; for, as has been noted, the legal system requires individual citizens to be ready to launch a prosecution where they believe that a crime has been committed, and the sykophant is entirely ready to adopt that role. He can therefore argue that the affairs of the city really are his proper concern while the Just Man is left to complain that, if this is so, the city has a villain for its defender.[96]

In Aristophanes' *Clouds*, what makes the encounter of the Stronger and the Weaker Arguments so uncomfortable is the tension between the gut conviction that the Stronger Argument truly does represent the better position and the inability of that speaker to put his superiority into words.[97] Something very similar is going on here. For any ethical conflict between a Just Man and a Sykophant ought to have but one winner, but here it is actually the Sykophant who can answer every point and the Just Man who is finally driven to calling him names.[98] Aristophanic heroes creating new or better worlds often find themselves obliged to drive out sykophants, but even as they do so it can be difficult to dissimulate the indispensability to the

[90] Ar. *Plut.* 900.
[91] Ar. *Plut.* 907–8: τῶν τῆς πόλεώς εἰμ' ἐπιμελητὴς πραγμάτων | καὶ τῶν ἰδίων πάντων.
[92] Ar. *Plut.* 909–10: πῶς οὖν ἂν εἴης χρηστός, ὦ τοιχωρύχε, | εἴ σοι προσῆκον μηδὲν εἶτ' ἀπεχθάνει;
[93] Ar. *Plut.* 911–12: οὐ γὰρ προσήκει τὴν ἐμαυτοῦ μοι πόλιν | εὐεργετεῖν, ὦ κέπφε, καθ' ὅσον ἂν σθένω;
[94] Ar. *Plut.* 913: εὐεργετεῖν οὖν ἐστι τὸ πολυπραγμονεῖν;
[95] Ar. *Plut.* 914–15: τὸ μὲν οὖν βοηθεῖν τοῖς νόμοις τοῖς κειμένοις | καὶ μὴ 'πιτρέπειν ἐάν τις ἐξαμαρτάνῃ.
[96] Ar. *Plut.* 918–20: οὐκοῦν ἐκεῖνός εἰμ' ἐγώ. | ὥστ' εἰς ἔμ' ἥκει τῆς πόλεως τὰ πράγματα... νὴ Δία, πονηρόν γ' ἄρα προστάτην ἔχει.
[97] Ar. *Nub.* 1036–1104, esp. 1102–4 for the Stronger Argument's final surrender and defection to the opposite camp.
[98] L. B. Carter (1986), 86–7 discusses this passage but does not find anything to say for the sykophant.

proper functioning of the Athenian legal system of those men we might otherwise wish to dismiss as sykophants. This point is well made in Robin Osborne's study of the sykophant and it serves little to follow the example of David Harvey and note every other pejorative adjective characteristically used to describe what is already a deliberately pejorative term.[99] If it is funny for the sykophant of the *Birds* to identify himself as such, it is because those to whom he corresponds in contemporary society have many other more positive terms with which to describe their role.[100]

(7) THE PHILOSOPHER AS *POLYPRAGMON*

One last class of individual *polypragmon* may be considered: the philosopher. Socrates himself may decry *polypragmosyne*, but this does not rescue his own way of life from a very similar critique. The key passage here is one to which attention has already been drawn in the earlier discussion of the synonymity of *polypragmon* and *periergos*: Socrates' citation at *Apology* 19b of the claim that his investigations of the world below and the heavens above are unjust and meddling (ἀδικεῖ καὶ περιεργάζεται).[101] This indictment is of considerable importance for various facets of my argument; but for now it may suffice to juxtapose it with a further passage of the *Apology*, where Socrates acknowledges that he goes around counselling and interfering (πολυπραγμονῶ) with the affairs of individual fellow citizens while never daring to offer counsel to the city as a collective entity.[102] There is an obvious point of tension here and it is one to which later writers respond. For inasmuch as Socrates avoids any direct involvement in political decision-making, his lifestyle in many ways resembles what a fifth- or fourth-century Athenian might regard as *apragmosyne*, and Xenophon for one describes the philosopher in just these terms.[103] Yet, at the same time, those irritated

---

[99] Harvey (1990).

[100] Ar. *Av.* 1423; Harvey (1990), 107. Cf. Epict. *Diss.* 2. 21. 3 for the claim that nobody will own up to being a *periergos*.

[101] See Introduction Sect. 3.

[102] Pl. *Ap.* 31c.

[103] Xen. *Mem.* 3. 11. 16. That the philosophical life can be associated with *apragmosyne* is further apparent from Euripides, *Antiope*. In this play Amphion

34 Polypragmosyne: *Thucydides to Theophrastus*

by his constant interrogation and challenge to their assumptions may indeed feel that Socrates meddles or interferes with their lives and does not mind his own business. Centuries later Epictetus points in this direction as a notional objector asks the philosopher why he is so meddlesome and what concern he has with the actions of those he questions.[104] If his constant questioning of others' lives makes Socrates seem like a rather unwelcome meddler, the elaborate courtesy and ironic self-deprecation on which he trades are rather less confrontational than the approach of another constantly determined to challenge all and sundry: the Cynic. Yet Epictetus at least idealizes much about ancient Cynicism and the account which he offers at *Dissertations* 3. 22 is of great relevance to the matters here at issue.[105] It is indeed true that the Cynic berates all those whom he encounters, but there is no meddling in this. For he has adopted all humanity as his children and approaches them and cares for them in exactly this spirit.[106] The true Cynic must therefore be purer than the sun in his guiding principle,[107] must watch over men and labour on their behalf,[108] and must be in every way as a friend to the gods, as a servant, as a sharer in the power of Zeus.[109] When he watches over the affairs of men, he is no busybody, for these are not the affairs of others but his own. Hence 3. 22. 97 can absolve the philosopher of any charge of meddling; for what he concerns himself with, when he inspects the doings of mortals, are not the affairs proper to another but in fact

praises the philosophical life (Eur. fr. 182 Kannicht = Cic. *Inv. rhet.* 1. 94) and also urges that it is folly to lead an active life when it is possible to abstain and to live as an *apragmon* (Eur. fr. 193 Kannicht = Stob. *Flor.* 4. 16. 2 ὅστις δὲ πράσσει πολλὰ μὴ πράσσειν παρόν, | μῶρος, παρὸν ζῆν ἡδέως ἀπράγμονα). For further praise of quietism, see fr. 194 Kannicht = Stob. *Flor.* 4. 7. 10. For sympathetic reconstruction of the contest between Zethus and Amphion, see L. B. Carter (1986), 163–73.

[104] Epict. *Diss.* 3. 1. 21: οὕτως περίεργος εἶ, ὦ Σώκρατες, καὶ πολυπράγμων; τί δέ σοι μέλει τί ποιοῦμεν;
[105] Kirichenko (2008), 344.
[106] Epict. *Diss.* 3. 22. 81–2: ἄνθρωπε, πάντας ἀνθρώπους πεπαιδοποίηται, τοὺς ἄνδρας υἱοὺς ἔχει, τὰς γυναῖκας θυγατέρας· πᾶσιν οὕτως προσέρχεται, οὕτως πάντων κήδεται. ἢ σὺ δοκεῖς ὑπὸ περιεργίας λοιδορεῖσθαι τοῖς ἀπαντῶσιν; ὡς πατὴρ αὐτὸ ποιεῖ, ὡς ἀδελφὸς καὶ τοῦ κοινοῦ πατρὸς ὑπηρέτης τοῦ Διός.
[107] Epict. *Diss.* 3. 22. 93.
[108] Epict. *Diss.* 3. 22. 95.
[109] Epict. *Diss.* 3. 22. 82, 95.

his own.[110] This is an important formulation and one which will resurface in what I will say in later chapters about licit and illicit modes of investigation.

(8) *POLYPRAGMOSYNE* AND THE INTERVENTIONIST STATE

Herodotus makes but one direct reference to the concept of *polypragmosyne* and then with regards to the political machinations of an individual: had Psammenitus known not to intrigue (πολυπρηγμονέειν), he might have obtained the governorship of Egypt; instead he attempted to rouse the Egyptians to rebellion against Cambyses and was forced to commit suicide by drinking bull's blood.[111] Yet there are other instances where he engages in his own terms with the same problems that later writers will think of as state *polypragmosyne*. This is most clearly the case just a little further on in the same book when the Persian king Cambyses sends an expedition to investigate the land of the Ethiopians.[112] The native king has little trouble identifying their true purposes and asserts that Cambyses cannot be a just man if he desires a country other than his own.[113] The Platonic identification of justice with minding one's own business is already apparent and is here applied to the foreign policies of states and kings.

For the successors of Herodotus, the meddling state par excellence is Athens.[114] This is expressed both through direct reference to *polypragmosyne* and by reference to a number of attributes that go to make up that way of being.[115] Thucydides, for instance, includes

---

[110] Epict. *Diss.* 3. 22. 97: διὰ τοῦτο οὔτε περίεργος οὔτε πολυπράγμων ἐστὶν ὁ οὕτω διακείμενος· οὐ γὰρ τὰ ἀλλότρια πολυπραγμονεῖ, ὅταν τα ἀνθρώπινα ἐπισκοπῆι, ἀλλὰ τὰ ἴδια. Muecke (1993), 135.

[111] Hdt. 3. 15. 2, 4. Note that Hdt. 2. 15 and 3. 46 uses περιεργάζομαι but with the specific sense of doing something superfluous.

[112] Hdt. 3. 17. 2: κατόπτας ... ὀψομένους ... κατοψομένους.

[113] Hdt. 3. 21. 2: οὔτε ἐκεῖνος ἀνήρ ἐστι δίκαιος. εἰ γὰρ ἦν δίκαιος, οὔτ᾽ ἂν ἐπεθύμησε χώρης ἄλλης ἢ τῆς ἑωυτοῦ.

[114] The issue is much studied. See esp. Ehrenberg (1947); De Romilly (1963), 77–8; Kleve (1964); Huart (1968), 385–7; Allison (1979); Harding (1981); Brock (1998); Visentin (1999), 48–50.

[115] Allison (1979) bases her critique of key contributions to this topic on the fact that the abstract noun πολυπραγμοσύνη appears in only two extant 5th-century texts

but one direct reference to *polypragmosyne*, as the Athenian ambassador explains to the people of Camarina that it is best to accept his state's intervention in their affairs: throughout the Greek world the prospect of Athenian intervention offers a warning to the unjust and hope to their victims.[116] Yet what the ambassador refers to by *polypragmosyne* is visible on numerous occasions in the rest of the work as Thucydides brings home the character and the policies of Athens as an imperial power.

Fundamental to Thucydides' conception of Athenian power is the speech of the Corinthians to the Spartans at 1. 68–71 and especially their summary at 1. 70 of what distinguishes the Athenians from their audience.[117] Where the Spartans are concerned to preserve that which they already possess and in action fall short even of what they ought to do, the Athenians seek to do something new, are sharp to form plans and to see them through;[118] where the Spartans are cautious and anxious that they will never escape new troubles, the Athenians are daring beyond their resources, take risks when wisdom dictates that they should not, and are optimistic even in a crisis;[119] where the Spartans delay and stay at home, the Athenians act without fear and head abroad.[120] In short, Athenian expansion is always driven by the thought of what can be gained, not what may

(Thuc. 6. 87. 3; Ar. *Ach.* 833). This, she observes, is scant basis for the modern concept of *polypragmosyne* as a defining feature of late 5th-century Athenian politics. The point is well made, but Allison herself also considers the evidence for the adjective and substantive πολυπράγμων and the verb πολυπραγμονέω, after which the picture is somewhat different. My own approach is rigorously to consider all these terms as well as obvious synonyms such as πολλὰ πράσσειν and to identify which issues they are used to debate and which terms and contentions cluster around them. Allison dubs what emerges a 'family of concepts' (10) and clearly regards it as lazy thinking to gather them all together under the heading of *polypragmosyne* without recognizing how small a part the single substantive πολυπραγμοσύνη plays in that family.

[116] Thuc. 6. 87. 2–4.

[117] Ehrenberg (1947), 47; De Romilly (1963), 77.

[118] Thuc. 1. 70. 2: οἱ μέν γε νεωτεροποιοὶ καὶ ἐπινοῆσαι ὀξεῖς καὶ ἐπιτελέσαι ἔργῳ ἃ ἂν γνῶσιν· ὑμεῖς δὲ τὰ ὑπάρχοντά τε σῴζειν καὶ ἐπιγνῶναι μηδὲν καὶ ἔργῳ οὐδὲ τἀναγκαῖα ἐξικέσθαι.

[119] Thuc. 1. 70. 3: οἱ μὲν καὶ παρὰ δύναμιν τολμηταὶ καὶ παρὰ γνώμην κινδυνευταὶ καὶ ἐν τοῖς δεινοῖς εὐέλπιδες· τὸ δὲ ὑμέτερον τῆς τε δυνάμεως ἐνδεᾶ πρᾶξαι τῆς τε γνώμης μηδὲ τοῖς βεβαίοις πιστεῦσαι τῶν τε δεινῶν μηδέποτε οἴεσθαι ἀπολυθήσεσθαι.

[120] Thuc. 1. 70. 4: ἄοκνοι πρὸς ὑμᾶς μελλητὰς καὶ ἀποδημηταὶ πρὸς ἐνδημοτάτους.

be lost.[121] They are ready to toil in order to achieve this end, and toil (*ponos*) is a hallmark of their character: the Athenians constantly labour with toils and risks to gain something new and regard an inactive peace as no less a sorrow than a toilsome activity.[122] The celebration of Athenian growth through toil is also a feature of Pericles' funeral oration. It was not without toil (οὐκ ἀπόνως) that the previous generation enlarged the Athenian empire and those of Pericles' own time have made it greater still.[123] Urging the Athenians to undertake the Sicilian Expedition, Alcibiades reminds them that what extended their power was their constant readiness to intervene on behalf of those who called on their aid.[124] Conscious surely of the pejorative implications of *polypragmosyne*, Alcibiades instead refers to Athens as a 'not inactive' city and warns that the shift to inactivity proposed by Nicias will be a road to ruin.[125] The only way to preserve the city's former customs is therefore to maintain its constant process of expansion and acquisition.

Thucydides suggests that Sicily is not the limit to Alcibiades' ambitions; once Athens gains control of the island, the next step is to seize Carthage.[126] Plutarch in turn praises Pericles for his restraint of those of his contemporaries who sought to expand into Egypt, Sicily, Etruria, and Carthage, and concentration instead on a policy of conserving that which Athens already held.[127] The expansionist policy is dubbed *polypragmosyne*.[128] The same term is applied by the Oxyrhynchus Historian to those Athenians in 395 BC who favoured a resumption of hostilities with Sparta.[129] Both those who wrote about Athens in the late fifth century and, even more clearly,

---

[121] Thuc. 1. 70. 4: οἴονται γὰρ οἱ μὲν τῇ ἀπουσίᾳ ἄν τι κτᾶσθαι, ὑμεῖς δὲ τῷ ἐπελθεῖν καὶ τὰ ἑτοῖμα ἂν βλάψαι.

[122] Thuc. 1. 70. 8: καὶ ταῦτα μετὰ πόνων πάντα καὶ κινδύνων δι᾽ ὅλου τοῦ αἰῶνος μοχθοῦσι...ξυμφοράν τε οὐχ ἧσσον ἡσυχίαν ἀπράγμονα ἢ ἀσχολίαν ἐπίπονον.

[123] Thuc. 2. 36. 2.

[124] Thuc. 6. 18. 2.

[125] Thuc. 6. 18. 7: παράπαν τε γιγνώσκω πόλιν μὴ ἀπράγμονα τάχιστ᾽ ἄν μοι δοκεῖν ἀπραγμοσύνης μεταβολῇ διαφθαρῆναι; Ehrenberg (1947), 50.

[126] Thuc. 6. 15. 2.

[127] Plut. *Per.* 20. 3 – 21. 1. For this policy, cf. Thuc. 2. 65. 7; Ehrenberg (1947), 48-9.

[128] Plut. *Per.* 21. 1; *Comp. Per. et Fab.* 2. 3.

[129] *P. Oxy.* 842 = *FGrH* 66 F 1. 31–5. The hostility of the author to these politicians is evident from his comment that they favoured such a policy so that they might enrich themselves from the resources of the state (ἵν᾽ αὐτοῖς ἐκ τῶν κοινῶν ἦι χρηματίζεσ[θ]αι).

those who looked back on the history of the Athenian empire in later centuries, clearly thought about her treatment of other states under the heading of *polypragmosyne*.

Perhaps the most sustained engagement with the ideas under discussion is to be found in the 355 BC speech of Isocrates entitled *On The Peace*. The immediate context for this work is the negotiation of a treaty to end the 357–355 BC Social War fought by Athens against her rebellious allies in the Second Athenian Confederation: Chios, Rhodes, Byzantium, and Cos.[130] Yet Isocrates' contribution turns on his conviction that something more is needed if Athens is to secure enduring prosperity. In arguing that the root cause of all her ills is the possession of a maritime empire and the only solution to abandon such aspirations, Isocrates offers a prescription that not only goes well beyond the specific quarrel with the allies but also depends on a historical analysis that looks back all the way to the Persian Wars and perhaps a little further still.[131]

According to the historical analysis presented in *On the Peace*, the last time that Athens followed an appropriate course was during the Persian Wars. The only politicians named with admiration are Miltiades, Themistocles, and Aristeides while those condemned begin with the demagogues Hyperbolus and Cleophon.[132] Yet the policies that Isocrates decries set in a good deal earlier than did the influence of either of these gentlemen: he mentions the overseas missions to Egypt and Cyprus of 460 and the early 450s BC,[133] but suggests that the beginning of all the trouble was precisely the moment that Athens achieved a maritime empire.[134]

Isocrates thus represents the errors of the Second Athenian Confederation as but a repetition of those of the First.[135] Early in the speech, he suggests that Athens can never escape her ills until she

---

[130] Isoc. 8. 15–16. For helpful elucidation of this context and indeed of the speech as a whole, see Mathieu (1925), 12, 113–25; Bringmann (1965), 58–74.

[131] Davidson (1990) is a sympathetic account of Isocrates' historical analysis in this speech. Contrast Wilson (1966), 58–9 for a scathing indictment of Isocrates' inconsistency across his oeuvre and even within individual speeches.

[132] Isoc. 8. 75.

[133] Isoc. 8, 86–9.

[134] Isoc. 8. 101: τότε τὴν ἀρχὴν αὑτοῖς γεγενῆσθαι τῶν συμφορῶν, ὅτε τὴν ἀρχὴν τῆς θαλάττης παρελάμβανον; Davidson (1990), 22–3.

[135] For a similar view, see Phld. *Rhet.* 2. 148. 36 Sudhaus on the *polypragmosyne* of Callistratus.

accepts that quietism is both more beneficial and more profitable than meddling, justice than injustice, the concern for one's own possessions than the desire for those of others.[136] Yet the reason why Athens continues to behave in this way is her failure to learn the lessons of the past. With clear reference to the events of the previous century, Isocrates notes that it was *polypragmosyne* that brought Athens to the most extreme peril while what won her leadership was the observance of an ethical foreign policy, willingness to help the victims of injustice, and a refusal to covet that which belonged to others.[137]

Many of the key terms of the argument are present in the passages just discussed.[138] *Polypragmosyne* itself is the term used with regard to the conduct of the Thebans after their victory at Leuctra in 371. Had they but freed the Peloponnese, decreed the autonomy of the rest of Greece, adopted a policy of quietism (*hesychia*), and left Athens to make the mistakes they themselves made, then Athens would have discovered how much better is temperance than meddling.[139] Sparta too has become an example on a par with Athens of how not to manage power: if the meddling of pro-Athenian parties turned states to sympathy with Sparta, then the arrogance of Sparta's supporters drove them back to Athens.[140] Hand in hand with *polypragmosyne* go injustice,[141] and the pursuit of what belongs to others.[142] The necessary alternatives are *hescyhia* and *sophrosyne*.[143] Should Isocrates' opponents urge that Athens emulate her ancestors, then she must be careful to consider which ones.[144] In Thucydides,

---

[136] Isoc. 8. 26: τὴν μὲν ἡσυχίαν ὠφελιμωτέραν καὶ κερδαλεωτέραν εἶναι τῆς πολυπραγμοσύνης, τὴν δὲ δικαιοσύνην τῆς ἀδικίας, τὴν δὲ τῶν ἰδίων ἐπιμέλειαν τῆς τῶν ἀλλοτρίων ἐπιθυμίας.

[137] Isoc. 8. 30: τὸ πρότερον ἐκ μὲν τῆς τοιαύτης πολυπραγμοσύνης εἰς τοὺς ἐσχάτους κινδύνους κατέστημεν... ἐκ δὲ τοῦ δικαίαν τὴν πόλιν παρέχειν καὶ βοηθεῖν τοῖς ἀδικουμένοις καὶ μὴ τῶν ἀλλοτρίων ἐπιθυμεῖν παρ᾽ ἑκόντων τῶν Ἑλλήνων τὴν ἡγεμονίαν ἐλάβομεν.

[138] Bringmann (1965), 62 likewise cites Isoc. 8. 26 and comments that 'Dies ist die Tendenz der gesamten Rede'.

[139] Isoc. 8. 58: ἡμεῖς τ᾽ ἂν ἔγνωμεν ὅσῳ κρεῖττόν ἐστιν τὸ σωφρονεῖν τοῦ πολυπραγμονεῖν.

[140] Isoc. 8. 108: ἡ μὲν τῶν ἀττικιζόντων πολυπραγμοσύνη... ἡ δὲ τῶν λακωνιζόντων ὕβρις. Bringmann (1965), 63 underlines the Thucydidean character of this formulation.

[141] Isoc. 8. 6, 17, 26, 66, 93.

[142] Isoc. 8. 22, 26, 30, 96.

[143] Isoc. 8. 6, 26 for *hesychia*; 8. 63, 119 for *sophrosyne*.

[144] Isoc. 8. 36–8; Harding (1973), 144–5.

the Corinthian ambassador characterizes the Athenians by their readiness to embrace risk or peril (*kindunos*).[145] Here too Isocrates takes pride in the way that the ancestors exposed themselves to *kindunos* for the sake of Greece,[146] and notes their willingness to risk their own bodies in battle where contemporary Athens turns instead to mercenaries.[147] Yet as we have seen in §30, *kindunos* in the form of extreme peril is also what bad policy can bring and this in turn becomes a recurrent motif of the speech.[148]

In *On The Peace* Isocrates disavows any attempt by Athens to expand at the expense of her fellow Greeks and dubs such a policy *polypragmosyne*. The quietism that he advocates is not, however, to be mistaken for indifference to wrong.[149] For his highest ideal of Athens is that of a city ever ready to go to the aid of the wronged. The same policy was fundamental to Athens' acquisition of leadership over Greece in the past and will underpin her greatness in time to come.[150] To all suppliants of Greece Athens will now be the place to turn.[151] What is striking about this formulation is the way it predicates the city's return to greatness not so much on the historical analysis of what was special about Athens at the time of the Persian Wars as on its appeal to an identity founded in myth. The point I wish to make may be illustrated by reference to the *Plataicus*, a speech in which Isocrates imagines the words of a Plataean appealing to the Athenian assembly for assistance in the aftermath of the Thebans' 373 BC destruction of his city. His first words remind the Athenians that it is their custom eagerly to come to the assistance of the wronged.[152] Yet when he reminds them of the pride that they take in their ancestors, it is with reference not to the recent historical past but rather to the intervention of Theseus to bury the Argive dead from the campaign of the Seven against Thebes.[153] For Athens to vaunt this service in the distant past but to do the opposite with regard to the suppliants of the present would indeed be a source

[145] Thuc. 1. 70. 3, 8.   [146] Isoc. 8. 76.
[147] Isoc. 8. 43, 47; Bringmann (1965), 71.   [148] Isoc. 8. 19, 20, 21, 97.
[149] Bringmann (1965), 72.
[150] Isoc. 8. 30: βοηθεῖν τοῖς ἀδικουμένοις; 8. 137: τοῖς ἀδικουμένοις βοηθεῖν.
[151] Isoc. 8. 138.
[152] Isoc. 14. 1: τοῖς ἀδικουμένοις προθύμως βοηθεῖν εἰθισμένους.
[153] Isoc. 14. 53: φιλοτιμεῖσθαι μὲν ἐν τοῖς τῶν προγόνων ἔργοις; cf. 8. 41: φιλοτιμούμεθα μὲν ἐπὶ τοῖς τῶν προγόνων ἔργοις.

of shame.[154] When Isocrates at the close of *On the Peace* urges Athens, friend of the suppliant and the wronged, to return to her better self and recover the reputation of her ancestors, the ancestors to whom he refers may strike us as belonging to a very distant age indeed.[155] Something unusual is going on at the close of *On the Peace* and it is worth pausing to consider exactly what that is.

Throughout the speech Isocrates has decried the morally corrosive character of maritime empire and has indeed suggested that Athens' relationship to her allies is but that of a tyrant to his subjects.[156] Yet when he offers a prescription for Athens' future conduct and urges her to become the defender of the wronged and the friend to the suppliant, he alludes to myths the propagation of which is closely associated with the very policies he has hitherto deplored. For Athens' succour to Adrastus and the mothers of the Argive dead at Thebes stands alongside her aid to the children of Heracles against the angry Eurystheus as staples of the Athenian funeral oration from the first half of the fifth century onwards, and both serve to offer a positive image of Athens' intervention in the affairs of other Greek states or, to put it another way, her *polypragmosyne*.[157] Isocrates himself, it may be added, is one of the most dedicated exponents of this mode.[158]

The capacity of these myths not only to project a celebratory image of Athenian policy but also to confront and overcome more hostile and suspicious views is less clearly on display in rhetoric than it is in drama. Isocrates may litter his speeches with references to the discomfort or scepticism of an assembly audience that never was, but it is the essence of tragedy to bring on stage representatives of opposed

[154] Isoc. 14. 53: καὶ γὰρ αἰσχρὸν φιλοτιμεῖσθαι μὲν ἐν τοῖς τῶν προγόνων ἔργοις, φαίνεσθαι δ᾽ ἐκείνοις τἀναντία περὶ τῶν ἱκετῶν πράττοντας.

[155] Isoc. 8. 141: τὴν δόξαν τὴν τῶν προγόνων ἀναλαβεῖν.

[156] Davidson (1990), 30–1.

[157] Tzanetou (2011) is a useful account of how deployment of these myths in oratory and drama serves to create a consensual rather than an oppressive image of Athenian power over her allies. Gomme (1956) ad loc. discusses claims that it is just such material that Pericles declines to rehearse at Thuc. 2. 36. 4. See also Grethlein (2003), 109–99, 381–428. For the 5th-century development of the funeral oration, see now Tzanetou (2011), 313. For the 4th century and elsewhere, see also Xen. *Mem.* 3. 5. 10; *Hell.* 6. 5. 46; Pl. *Menex.* 239b; Lys. 2. 7–16; Dem. 18. 186; [Dem.] *Epitaph.* 8, 27; Lycurg. *Leoc.* 98; Arist. *Rh.* 1396a13–14; Dion. Hal. *Ant. Rom.* 5. 17. 4; Loraux (1986), 67–9.

[158] Isoc. 4. 54–60; 5. 34; 6. 42–3; 10. 31; 12. 168–74.

positions and to make them argue these through in the form of the *agon*. When, therefore, Euripides dramatizes the two great myths of intervention in the *Heracleidae* and the *Supplices*, there is no shortage of critics decrying Athenian *polypragmosyne* or of defenders ready to celebrate its aims.[159] Both plays merit closer attention. What connects these two dramas is Athens' intervention to protect the weak against their oppressors.[160] In both instances, however, it is possible for those oppressors to claim that what the Athenians are doing is simply meddling in affairs in which they have no part. In the *Heracleidae*, the Argive herald sent by Eurystheus asserts the rights of Argos to take control of her own subjects,[161] while in the *Supplices* the Theban herald confronting Theseus as he sets off to ensure the burial of the Argive dead objects that the ruler of Athens has nothing to do with the city of Argos.[162] Theseus is undeterred by this observation and the confrontation between the two breaks down into the herald's denunciation of Athenian *polypragmosyne* and Theseus' celebration of a city that grows through virtuous toil:

HER.   ἐν ἀσπίσιν σοι πρῶτα κινδυνευτέον.
TH.   πολλοὺς ἔτλην δὴ χἀτέροις ἄλλους πόνους.
HER.   ἦ πᾶσιν οὖν <σ'> ἔφυσεν ἐξαρκεῖν πατήρ;
TH.   ὅσοι γ' ὑβρισταί· χρηστὰ δ' οὐ κολάζομεν.
HER.   πράσσειν σὺ πόλλ' εἴωθας ἥ τε σὴ πόλις.
TH.   τοιγὰρ πονοῦσα πολλὰ πόλλ' εὐδαιμονεῖ.

HER.   At spear-point must you first face danger.
TH.   Many other toils indeed have I endured and in other situations.
HER.   So did your father beget you to defend all and sundry?
TH.   All men of arrogance do I ward off. The good I do not chastise.
HER.   You and your city are accustomed to interfere.
TH.   By toiling much indeed does it enjoy great prosperity.[163]

---

[159] A key feature of the *Supplices*—and one that underlines the relationship between its subject matter and the funeral oration—is the epitaphic speech given by Adrastus at vv. 857–917. Where Capaneus was seen at vv. 496–9 promising to sack Thebes whether the god desired this or not, he becomes at 860–71 a good man, proud of his simplicity, a true friend and an affable companion. Parthenopaeus at 888–900 is the ideal metic. This is one of the most striking procedures of the entire play. For comment, see Zuntz (1955), 13–16 and 19; Grethlein (2003), 168–89; Tzanetou (2011), 312–16 with full bibliography.

[160] For a wholly positive view of Athens and Theseus in these plays, see De Romilly (1963), 133. Much the most profound and acutely felt interpretation of the *Supplices* that I have found is that of Zuntz (1955), 3–25.

[161] Eur. *Heracl.* 136–43, 175–6, 267.

[162] Eur. *Supp.* 471–2: μηδ' ἀναιρεῖσθαι νεκροὺς | βίαι, προσήκοντ' οὐδὲν Ἀργείων πόλει.

[163] Eur. *Supp.* 572–7; De Romilly (1963), 135; Demont (1990), 160–2.

In the *Heracleidae* the Argive case for possession of a family they themselves drove into exile is a good way short of watertight and is vigorously contested by the aged Iolaus.[164] An argument from kinship is also advanced in that Heracles and Theseus were in fact cousins,[165] and Iolaus reminds Demophon of all that he himself and Heracles did in support of Theseus.[166] Yet it is part of Iolaus' contention that kinship can also be *created* through some new kindness,[167] and both here and in the *Supplices* Athenian intervention finally transcends any question of what is the property of one state or another. Instead the habit of intervention is itself constitutive of the Athenian character and ethics and therefore what the oppressed of Greece can look to her to offer.[168] In both plays, moreover, there is considerable emphasis on Athenian *ponoi* and on growth through toil.[169] Here too the overlap with Pericles' funeral oration is clear to see.[170]

For all that the *Heracleidae* and the *Supplices* give dramatic form to two of Athens' proudest myths, neither offers an uncomplicated view of the values that those myths encode. The former is full of allusions to the failure of the Spartan descendants of the children of Heracles to show due gratitude to Athens for standing by their ancestors in time of peril.[171] This, however, in no sense undermines any admiration for Athens' readiness to do the right thing as she so clearly does in the first half of the play. Much more complicated is the role of the

---

[164] Eur. *Heracl.* 183-8; Wilkins (1993) at Eur. *Heracl.* 142 ff.

[165] Eur. *Heracl.* 205-15. Note v. 214: τοῦ προσήκοντος for kinship.

[166] Eur. *Heracl.* 215-19.

[167] Eur. *Heracl.* 229-31.

[168] Eur. *Heracl.* 191-201, 303-6, 329-32; *Supp.* 184-92, 377-80. Note that in the latter play Athenian insistence on securing burial for the dead is also represented as defence of Panhellenic custom. See Eur. *Supp.* 306-13, 526-7, 537-41, 558-63, 669-72; Zuntz (1955), 8-9 and 17; Vinh (2011), 340-1. For Athenian intervention even in the absence of a prior quarrel with either Eurystheus or Thebes, cf. Lys. 2. 8, 14.

[169] Eur. *Heracl.* 329-32, 503-6; *Supp.* 185, 189, 314-25, 337-45, 373-4, 393-4, 573-7; Ehrenberg (1947), 53-4; De Romilly (1963), 136; Di Benedetto (1971), 112-13.

[170] Note in this context Eur. *Heracl.* 1-11 and the entry speech of Iolaus. The self-interested man may indeed be no use to the city (v. 4 πόλει... ἄχρηστος), but he gains an easier life for himself. Iolaus, by contrast, had the chance to live a quiet life in Argos but chose instead to share the toils of Heracles (vv. 7-8 ἐξὸν κατ' Ἄργος ἡσύχως ναίειν, πόνων | πλείστων μετέσχον εἰς ἀνὴρ Ἡρακλέει) and now must continue to serve the hero's children. One might compare Thuc. 2. 40. 2 and Pericles' disparaging account of citizens who do not involve themselves in public affairs: μόνοι γὰρ τόν τε μηδὲν τῶνδε μετέχοντα οὐκ ἀπράγμονα, ἀλλ' ἀχρεῖον νομίζομεν.

[171] Eur. *Heracl.* 309-15, 333-4, 1034-6; Zuntz (1955), 28; Allan (2001), 217-18.

chorus of Athenians at the drama's close.[172] For Eurystheus may indeed achieve hero-cult at Marathon and resolve to defend Athens against later generations of Heracleidae,[173] but this cannot close our eyes to the complicity of the chorus in Alcmena's plans to execute her prisoner and throw his body to the dogs.[174] In the latter, the crucial feature is perhaps Euripides' decision to make Theseus overcome the Theban resistance to burial of the dead not through diplomacy but rather through force of arms.[175] The result is that celebration of Athens' successful intervention at Thebes sits alongside Argive lament for their own entirely disastrous attempt to involve themselves in the affairs of that city.[176] Where the Athenian characters exalt their own growth through toil, King Adrastus is left to bemoan the consequences of his own adoption of *ponoi* on behalf of Polynices:

ADR. ὦ ταλαίπωροι βροτῶν,
τί κτᾶσθε λόγχας καὶ κατ' ἀλλήλων φόνους
τίθεσθε; παύσασθ', ἀλλὰ λήξαντες πόνων
ἄστη φυλάσσεθ' ἥσυχοι μεθ' ἡσύχων.
σμικρὸν τὸ χρῆμα τοῦ βίου· τοῦτον δὲ χρὴ
ὡς ῥᾶστα καὶ μὴ σὺν πόνοις διεκπερᾶν.

ADR. O wretched mortals, why do you acquire spears and cause death for one another? Stop and, desisting from toil, guard your cities, quiet men in company with quiet. The thing of life is but brief; we must spend it as easily as we may and not in toil.[177]

On one level the difference between the one experience and the other is that between Theseus' orderly consultation of the city before going

---

[172] Zuntz (1955), 37–8, 41–2; Allan (2001), 42–3, 220–5.

[173] Eur. *Heracl.* 1030–6.

[174] Eur. *Heracl.* 1018–21, 1053–5. The chorus attempt at first to persuade Alcmena to release Eurystheus since this is the view of the city, but then agree that it would be best for him to die while she remains obedient to the city. Her resolve at 1050 to throw his body to the dogs receives the assent of the chorus at 1053 and they depart contented that the city's rulers will not regard them as subject to defilement. The attempts of critics to emend away the dogs of 1050 and to identify a lacuna after 1052 are all designed to palliate the shock of this ending. See Allan (2001), 223–4 taking issue with this approach.

[175] Plut. *Thes.* 29. 4 indicates that Aeschylus' *Eleusinians* and the vast majority of ancient sources made this a purely diplomatic achievement. Were Euripides to follow this version, his play would neither be lit up by the splendour of victory nor be overshadowed by awareness of how far defeat could have brought Athens down.

[176] Note how the messenger speech describing the victory of Theseus at Eur. *Supp.* 634–730 immediately precedes the lament of Adrastus at 734–49.

[177] Eur. *Supp.* 949–54. For discussion, see Demont (1990), 164.

to war and the chaos that envelops Argos as the fatal decision to intervene is made.[178] There is indeed some satisfaction to be taken from a king who is also the father of his city's democracy and the prudent decisions that that city's power structures produce.[179] Yet there may also be some suspicion that what differentiates a Theseus from an Adrastus is but the success of the moment. The mothers mourning their dead children, the king repenting of his foolish policy, could as easily be Athenians as Argives.[180] This would be most painfully the case were it established with certainty that the *Supplices* was composed in the aftermath of the defeat at Delion in November 424 BC.[181]

(9) PEISETAIROS, AESOP, AND *POLYPRAGMOSYNE*

The *Birds* of Aristophanes is in many ways a play about *polypragmosyne* and the Athenian spirit.[182] It begins with two countrymen, troubled by their own debts and in flight from the constant litigation of the city, who set out in search of a quiet place to stay.[183] Their distaste for the courts is further represented as coherent with their rural origins.[184] Inasmuch as the quiet place they seek is dubbed a *topos apragmon*, the play appears at this point to be setting up a characteristic opposition of rural quietists and urban busybodies.[185] This is then given a ribald turn as Peisetairos suggests that what they are looking for is a city like a soft blanket to lie in and one where the

---

[178] For Theseus' consultation of the city, see Eur. *Supp.* 349–57, 393–4. For the chaos of the Argive drive to war, see Eur. *Supp.* 155–60, 737–41.

[179] Note the way in which the recurrent phrase 'I/you and the city' conflates the will and destiny of Theseus with that of Athens at Eur. *Supp.* 27–8, 114, 293, 381–2, 1168, 1181, 1233.

[180] Note Nestle (1926), 134 citing Eur. *Supp.* 744–9 and Adrastus' lament for war as a solution to human problems. A case for quietism is also made by the herald at Eur. *Supp.* 506–10.

[181] Thuc. 4. 90–9; Di Benedetto (1971), 156; Collard (1975), i. 8–14.

[182] For sustained discussion of this issue, see Arrowsmith (1973). See also Harding (1981), 41.

[183] Ar. *Av.* 40–1, 108–15.

[184] Ar. *Av.* 109–11.

[185] Cf. Lys. 7. 1 for the defendant representing himself as a rural quietist suddenly prey to sykophants.

greatest troubles (μέγιστα πράγματα) derive from receiving invitations to celebrate a wedding, or, as Euelpides suggests, where the father of a handsome youth will censure you for failing to grope the child's balls.[186] When, moreover, Peisetairos has finally established his city in the clouds, one of the unwelcome visitors he makes haste to expel is a sykophant.[187] Peisetairos dismisses this latest petitioner after wings as a 'poker-about-into-affairs' (πραγματοδίφης) and suggests other morally superior occupations for him to adopt than stitching together lawsuits and engaging in legal chicanery.[188]

Yet quietism and escape from the law are but one aspect of Cloudcuckooland and its founders. For this is a play about getting away and, as has been noted in Section 8, Thucydides' Corinthian speaker identifies the very instinct to leave home and explore more distant lands as typical of the Athenian spirit, while later writers will treat the readiness to travel as a marker of *periergia*.[189] There is a similar overlap between the name Euelpides and the terms in which the same speaker describes that optimistic spirit that fuels the Athenian drive to expand.[190] The name Peisetairos, in turn, suggests that capacity to persuade companions so essential to success in the assembly and the courtroom and is thus better suited to the active than the quietist citizen.[191] Whereas, moreover, Euelpides essentially serves the function of comic buffoon and disappears from the stage after v. 847, the persuasive spirit of Peisetairos, his intellect and imagination, are what transform the kingdom of the birds and drive forward its seemingly relentless growth. Arrowsmith observes the striking presence throughout the play of the language of desire and connects this to the terms in which Thucydides describes the Sicilian Expedition.[192] He also points to the specific claim in Plutarch that the golden shield of Alcibiades was decorated with an image of Eros bearing a thunderbolt.[193] It is further worth noting v. 978 and the allusion to the famous Delphic oracle assuring Athens that with much learning, suffering, and toil she will become an eagle in the sky.[194] To anyone mindful of this promise, the programme of

---

[186] Ar. *Av.* 120–42.   [187] Ar. *Av.* 1410–69.
[188] Ar. *Av.* 1424, 1433–5, 1450, 1468.
[189] Thuc. 1. 70. 4: ἀποδημηταὶ πρὸς ἐνδημοτάτους; Luci. *Ver. hist.* 1. 5.
[190] Thuc. 1. 70. 3; 6. 24. 3: εὐέλπιδες; Arrowsmith (1973), 135; Dunbar (1995), 128.
[191] Dunbar (1995), 128–9.
[192] Arrowsmith (1973), 129–35.
[193] Plut. *Alc.* 16. 2; Arrowsmith (1973), 135.
[194] For the full text of the oracle, see Ar. fr. 241 K-A = Schol. Ar. *Eq.* 1013.

Peisetairos will seem all the more apt a symbol of his nation's expansion overseas. What makes Peisetairos so impressive and at times so alarming to the birds is his command of words.[195] He comes from Greece the clever, and it was a proud boast of Athens that she had taught her fellow Greeks cleverness by introducing them to the art of persuasive speech.[196] The acquisition of power through superior intellect and greater power of persuasion is therefore a major theme of the play and is nowhere better seen than in Peisetairos' efforts to convince the birds that they once enjoyed far greater power and prestige than at present. These efforts, moreover, involve the one explicit reference to *polypragmosyne* in the course of the play, but one which requires some elucidation. I refer to vv. 465–70, where the chorus are surprised by Peisetairos' claims for their former dominion. He, however, has an easy explanation for their difficulties: they are unlearned and incurious, and have not thumbed Aesop, who tells of how the lark was the first of all creation.[197] What makes these lines hard to integrate into an account such as that of Arrowsmith is that, while the play as a whole may offer a surreal commentary on the state as *polypragmon*, what is here at issue is the energetic information-gathering of the individual *polypragmon*. In many cases the type of research to which a *polypragmon* will devote himself will be that of the malicious prosecutor hunting out the misdeeds of his fellow citizens or of the compulsive gossip haunting the barbers' shops and perfume-sellers, the port and the marketplace, in search of the latest salacious titbit. Yet here for the first time we see that energy devoted instead to literature. Reading Aesop may not be classed as the most challenging mode of scholarship, but the point Peisetairos makes is that the birds have failed themselves by their ignorance and lack of the drive to acquire learning. This positive conception of *polypragmosyne* will be of no little importance for the Hellenistic Greek usage of the term, be it in Polybius' account of historical research or Plutarch's injunction to redirect potentially destructive impulses and focus instead on the great questions of science.

---

[195] Ar. *Av.* 317, 428–30, 627–37.

[196] Ar. *Av.* 409; Isoc. 4. 50; 15. 295–6.

[197] Ar. *Av.* 471–2: ἀμαθὴς γὰρ ἔφυς κοὐ πολυπράγμων, οὐδ᾽ Αἴσωπον πεπάτηκας, | ὃς ἔφασκε λέγων κορυδὸν πάντων πρώτην ὄρνιθα γενέσθαι. Dunbar (1995) ad loc. comments intelligently on the problem. See also Dover (1974), 189. Allison (1979), 18 puzzles over but does not really know what to do with this passage.

(10) DEMOSTHENES, ARISTOMEDES, AND LEVELS OF *PERIERGIA*

The fourth *Philippic* of Demosthenes is no easy text to work with. Its authenticity is intermittently questioned; its contents overlap significantly with those of other speeches; and its somewhat disparate elements cohere uncertainly.[198] Yet it also presents one passage that anyone interested in the issues addressed in this chapter can ill afford to overlook.[199] I refer to §§70–4 and the assault on the otherwise somewhat obscure figure of Aristomedes. For in vindicating his own demands for an activist foreign policy against the objections of the meddlesome Aristomedes, Demosthenes brings together levels of personal and collective conduct that hitherto have appeared to run in parallel to each other, and he does so to devastating effect.

There is no place at all in the extant works of Demosthenes for *polypragmosyne* or any of its related forms. Where such concepts are present, they are expressed through the synonyms *philopragmosyne* or—as here—*periergia*.[200] In this instance, Demosthenes' achievement is to show that what Aristomedes calls meddling on the part of Athens is rather the upholding of a noble civic tradition, and that what he would pass off as an honourable display of personal ambition is in fact no more than meddling and the continuation of the dishonourable traditions of his family.

Demosthenes begins with the observation that some men appear to apply different counsel to the community as a whole from that which they apply to themselves.[201] For they call on the community to remain quiet even if someone does it wrong but are themselves unable to adopt the same attitude even when the victim of no injustice whatsoever.[202] He then turns to Aristomedes and asks him how he would respond should someone ask him why he chooses the

[198] All three issues are clearly interrelated. Note that Dilts (2002) and Hajdu (2002) both regard the speech as authentic. For specific problems relative to the authenticity of Dem. 10. 70–4, see Hajdu (2002), 426–7.

[199] Brief discussion at Ehrenberg (1947), 59.

[200] For *philopragmosyne*, see Dem. 1. 14; 4. 42; 21. 137; 39. 1; cf. Isae. 4. 30; Lycurg. *Leoc.* 3. For *periergia*, see Dem. 18. 72; 32. 28; [Dem.] 13. 7; 26. 15.

[201] Dem. 10. 70: οὐ τὸν αὐτὸν δὲ τρόπον περί θ' ὑμῶν καὶ περὶ αὐτῶν ἐνίους τῶν λεγόντων ὁρῶ βουλευομένους.

[202] Dem. 10. 70: ὑμᾶς μὲν γὰρ ἡσυχίαν ἄγειν φασὶ δεῖν, κἄν τις ὑμᾶς ἀδικῇ, αὐτοὶ δ' οὐ δύνανται παρ' ὑμῖν ἡσυχίαν ἄγειν οὐδενὸς αὐτοὺς ἀδικοῦντος.

life of the politician even though he knows that it is exposed to censure and full of hazards rather than that of the private citizen which is secure, untroubled, and free from danger.[203] Should Aristomedes be able to give the best possible answer, and imagining this to be true, that he does so out of a love of ambition and for repute,[204] Demosthenes wonders why he should regard himself as obliged to act and toil and face danger all for this end while advising the city calmly to abandon all such concerns.[205] Demosthenes has begun the process of reeling his opponent in. He now declines to believe that Aristomedes would regard it as proper that he himself should have standing in the city while Athens itself is held as worthless amongst the Greeks.[206] Nor can he see why it should bring security to the city to mind its own business but danger to Aristomedes himself should he cease to meddle in the affairs of others.[207] Indeed the opposite is surely the case: that the meddling of Aristomedes exposes him to the greatest danger while what imperils the city is instead the life of inaction.[208] Finally there arises the question of ancestral tradition. For sure Aristomedes has the reputation of his father and grandfather to maintain while Athens' inheritance is miserable and obscure.[209] Or so he would say. But the truth is quite the opposite. For if the father of Aristomedes was anything like his son, he must have been a thief, while the Greeks whom they saved from the greatest dangers know exactly what the forefathers of the Athenians were like.[210]

In all this we can already see a weaving together of themes and terms examined at earlier stages of this analysis. The ideal of tran-

[203] Dem. 10. 70: τί δὴ γιγνώσκων ἀκριβῶς ... τὸν μὲν τῶν ἰδιωτῶν βίον ἀσφαλῆ καὶ ἀπράγμονα καὶ ἀκίνδυνον ὄντα, τὸν δὲ τῶν πολιτευομένων φιλαίτιον καὶ σφαλερὸν καὶ καθ' ἑκάστην ἡμέραν ἀγώνων καὶ κακῶν μεστόν, οὐ τὸν ἡσύχιον, ἀλλὰ τὸν ἐν τοῖς κινδύνοις αἱρεῖ;
[204] Dem. 10. 71: ὑπὲρ φιλοτιμίας καὶ δόξης.
[205] Dem. 10. 71: θαυμάζω τί δήποτε σαυτῷ μὲν ὑπὲρ τούτων ἅπαντα ποιητέον εἶναι νομίζεις καὶ πονητέον καὶ κινδυνευτέον, τῇ πόλει δὲ προέσθαι ταῦτα μετὰ ῥαθυμίας συμβουλεύεις.
[206] Dem. 10. 71: οὐ γὰρ ἐκεῖνό γ' ἂν εἴποις, ὡς σὲ μὲν ἐν τῇ πόλει δεῖ τινὰ φαίνεσθαι, τὴν πόλιν δ' ἐν τοῖς Ἕλλησι μηδενὸς ἀξίαν εἶναι.
[207] Dem. 10. 72: τὸ τὰ αὑτῆς πράττειν ... εἰ μηδὲν τῶν ἄλλων πλέον περιεργάσει.
[208] Dem. 10. 72: σοὶ μὲν ἐξ ὧν ἐργάζει καὶ περιεργάζει τοὺς ἐσχάτους ὄντας κινδύνους, τῇ πόλει δ' ἐκ τῆς ἡσυχίας.
[209] Dem. 10. 73: ἀλλὰ νὴ Δία παππῴα σοι καὶ πατρῷα δόξ' ὑπάρχει, ἣν αἰσχρόν ἐστιν ἐν σοὶ καταλῦσαι· τῇ πόλει δ' ὑπῆρξεν ἀνώνυμα καὶ φαῦλα τὰ τῶν προγόνων.
[210] Dem. 10. 73: οὓς πάντες ἴσασιν οἱ Ἕλληνες ἐκ τῶν μεγίστων κινδύνων σεσωσμένοι.

quillity (*hesychia*), the concept of quietism (*apragmosyne*), and the obligation to mind one's own business all stand as the opposite of the frenetic activity both of individual and state (*polypragmosyne* or *periergia*). The association of an active citizen life with ambition or the love of honour (*philotimia*) and the claim to follow in the tradition of one's ancestors recall precisely that which Lysias' Mantitheus says in his own defence.[211] No less does the ready embrace of danger (*kindunos*) and toil (*ponos*) mirror what the Athenians of the *Supplices* and *Heracleidae* take pride in just as others accuse them of meddling. These benefactions are, moreover, no more than the projection onto the mythological plane of Athens' role in saving Greece in the time of the Persian Wars, a role to which Demosthenes must refer in his vindication of ancestral tradition and the obligations that it imposes. Now Aristomedes reserves all the toil and danger for himself while urging the city to adopt a quiet life, but what he calls toil is in turn no more than the lowest form of meddling (*periergia*). It cannot be allowed.

What makes this attack so brilliant is the manner in which it first allows Aristomedes to set out his thoroughly debased understanding of Athens' duties and absurdly self-serving account of his own role in civic life. Only when this has been done does Demosthenes turn the tables on him, and he does so through critical engagement with the very terms that Aristomedes has been made to use. What he calls the meddling of the state is but the maintenance of a noble tradition; what he presents as selfless acceptance of toil and danger out of devotion to the state is in fact the self-interested meddling of a thief and the son of a family of thieves. Nowhere in this period are the two levels of meddlesome behaviour brought so closely into relation with each other or to such devastating effect.

(11) THEOPHRASTUS AND THE *PERIERGOS*

The *Characters* of Theophrastus are where the stock figures of Greek New Comedy meet the ethology of Aristotle. The thirty types described in this work are different sorts of man to be seen on the streets of late fourth-century Athens. Inasmuch as they also

---

[211] Lys. 16. 20–1; Bearzot (2007), 126–8.

embody moral categories set out in the *Nicomachean Ethics*, they are evidently the work of a philosopher and indeed of the direct inheritor of Aristotle's school. Inasmuch as they depict figures also to be seen in the masks of Menander, Diphilus, Philemon, and their peers, and indeed are themselves rather funny, their connection to New Comedy is clear. In the case of the boastful man or *alazon* of *Characters* 23, we may as easily refer to the discussion of *alazoneia* at *Nicomachean Ethics* 1127b9–22 as to the boastful chef and vainglorious warrior of the comic stage.[212]

The busybody is also a stock type of New Comedy. Pollux lists him as the *polypragmon* and describes his curly hair, elongated chin, and permanently raised eyebrow.[213] The same figure is perhaps even more commonly described as a *periergos* and is examined in detail in the next chapter. The problem in this context is that the *periergos* of comedy and the *periergos* of Theophrastus have markedly little in common. Where the comic figure expresses his *periergia* through unwarranted curiosity about and meddling in the affairs of others, his Theophrastan counterpart does so by going too far: he promises more than he can deliver,[214] orders more wine to be served than his guests can drink,[215] so overstates a clearly just case that he alienates his audience,[216] and constantly offers too much information.[217] He may perhaps be said to meddle when he intervenes to stop a brawl even when he does not know the combatants, when he asks the general to outline his plan of campaign, or when he decides to give a sick man wine as an experiment though told not to do so by his doctor.[218] Yet the common thread in his behaviour cannot be meddling because, as often as not, it is his own business that he minds. What is truly significant is what Rusten and Diggle see as the 'overzealous' and Stein as the 'übereifrig' character of everything that he does.[219] Instead of looking to the comic *periergos*, it may

---

[212] Note Theophr. *Char.* 23. 3 for the *alazon* claiming to have served with Alexander in Asia when in truth he has never left the city. For the boastful soldier and his lies about his campaigns, see Plaut. *Mil.* 35; *Truc.* 484–6.

[213] Poll. *Onom.* 4. 145: ὁ δὲ Λυκομήδειος οὐλόκομος, μακρογένειος, ἀνατείνει τὴν ἑτέραν ὀφρύν, πολυπραγμοσύνην παρενδείκνυται.

[214] Theophr. *Char.* 13. 2, 6.

[215] Theophr. *Char.* 13. 4.

[216] Theophr. *Char.* 13. 3.

[217] Theophr. *Char.* 13. 8, 10–11.

[218] Theophr. *Char.* 13. 5, 7, 9.

[219] Stein (1992), 194; Diggle (2004), 105, 327.

therefore be more helpful to consider another sense of the adjective that is amply attested both in the works of Theophrastus himself and in the literature of the fourth century in general. For at *On the Causes of Plants* 3. 7. 8 Theophrastus decrees it superfluous (*periergon*) to keep pruning from fresh wood in slower-growing trees and at *Historia Plantarum* 1. 1. 4 employs the same adjective for futile modes of investigation.[220] The orators likewise draw away from discussing issues superfluous to the matter in hand and state that to go further would be *periergon*, while the rhetorical teachers use the same term as they warn against straying into unnecessary fields.[221] Isocrates, in particular, warns that private citizens representing themselves in court should state their case and retire or risk seeming to stray into superfluity (*periergazdesthai*).[222] This, as we have seen, is exactly what Theophrastus' *periergos* does—and to disastrous effect—when pleading a case, but he does it everywhere else as well. He is a man unable to observe limits and constantly offering more than is feasible, needful, or in good taste. He has no malice but no judgement either.[223]

(12) CONCLUSION

My stated aim at the outset of this chapter was twofold: to identify the most important patterns of thought in the fifth and fourth centuries BC in which the concept of *polypragmosyne* was active and to highlight the earliest manifestations of motifs that would

---

[220] See also Theophr. *Metaph.* 8a22.

[221] Andoc. 3. 33; [Dem.] 43. 21; Hyp. 6. 7; Isae. 1. 17, 31; Anaxim. *Rhet.* 29. 7; 35. 8. Ussher (1960), 121 is heading in a similar direction when he connects the use of περίεργος in Theophr. *Char.* 13 to the description of stylistic elaboration or over-elaboration at Dion. Hal. *Vett. Cens.* 3. 2. For this concept, see Ch. 5 Sect. 2.

[222] Isoc. 15. 104.

[223] The benevolence of the *periergos* even as he goes astray is underlined at Theophr. *Char.* 13. 1: ἀμέλει <ἡ> περιεργία δόξει<εν ἂν> εἶναι προσποίησίς τις λόγων καὶ πράξεων μετὰ εὐνοίας. I am unable to regard προσποίησίς here as other than corrupt and would commend Herwerden's emendation περιττότης as coming much closer to describing the superfluous effort that the description details. That Theophr. *Char.* 1. 1 employs προσποίησις does not so much defend the authenticity of the transmitted text of 13. 1 as suggest the origin of the corruption: while Theophr. *Char.* 1. 5 says of the *eiron* that he ἀκούσας τι μὴ προσποιεῖσθαι, no equivalent point is made with regard to the *periergos*. Note that Theophr. *Char.* 23. 1 προσποίησις is an emendation of the transmitted προσδοκία. Both Stein and Diggle regard all introductory definitions in the *Characters* as spurious.

take a central position in the more thematic later chapters of this study. I then began that survey with a definition of justice quoted by Socrates in the *Republic* as one that both he and others had often deployed. That definition was shown to overlap closely with the ancient wisdom quoted by Gyges in the first book of Herodotus and to apophthegms associated with figures such as Pittacus and Chilon. This basic association of *polypragmosyne* with the failure to distinguish between that which is proper to oneself and that which is proper to others will indeed resurface in a variety of contexts across the coming centuries: on the comic stage of Terence; in the theological reflections of Seneca; even in the foreign policy of the emperor Vespasian. Here, above all else, can be traced a continuity of thought from the earliest period onwards.

Yet through the chapters that follow it may also become apparent just how much of what has been studied in this chapter is specific to a single place and time. Towards the end of Menander's *Epitrepontes*, the slave Onesimos turns to Smikrines, his master, and reflects that 'There are, to put it roughly, a thousand cities all in all'.[224] It is hard to imagine any Athenian of the fifth century uttering these words. There are other cities out there, and indeed it may be helpful to define what is distinctively Athenian by reference to what goes on in Sparta or in Thebes, but to treat Athens as but one among a thousand polities is almost unthinkable. The language of *polypragmosyne* as found in the texts of the fifth and fourth centuries is so much to do with the civic institutions that made Athens unique: the law courts with their call to the individual citizen to launch a prosecution where he saw fit; the funeral orations where the city's war dead were collectively praised and myths spun of Athens' virtuous intervention in the affairs of other states; the extravagant civic festivals where tragic drama could stage those same myths and debate their contradictions, or where the comic poets could satirize the very figures whose ceaseless activity was essential to the working of the institutions of the state. Precious little of this was reproduced in the new Greek states of the Hellenistic world or at Rome. If talk of *polypragmosyne* and *periergia* was to endure—and it did—it would be by reference to subtly different fields and themes. The remaining chapters of this study set out to show what those were.

---

[224] Men. *Epit.* 1087–8: εἰσὶν αἱ πᾶσαι πόλεις, ὅμοιον εἰπεῖν, χίλιαι.

2

Translating *Polypragmosyne*

(1) INTRODUCTION

The previous chapter surveyed the semantic range of *polypragmon* and *periergos* in the Greek literature of the fifth and fourth centuries BC. In doing so it also identified the first examples of a number of motifs that will be central to later explorations of how this language is deployed in ancient discussions of the world of knowledge revealed by empire, of the proper limits of mortal investigation of the divine, and finally of the useful and useless knowledge to which our curiosity can be directed. One body of material, however, was reserved for this chapter and that was the Greek New Comedy of the fourth and third centuries BC. For what these works reveal is of interest not only in and of itself but also for what it can tell us about the earliest stage of the Roman writers' search for equivalents within their own language for the concepts that their Greek predecessors express through the terms *polypragmosyne* and *periergia*.

No one Latin term more often or more exactly renders the Greek concepts at issue than does the adjective *curiosus*.[1] Throughout this chapter and repeatedly in the more thematic investigations that follow, specific uses of *curiosus* will be elucidated by reference to how Greek writers employ *polypragmon* and *periergos*. Before entering into this body of material, it is important to offer two cautionary observations: first, not every employment of *curiosus* in Latin corresponds to the semantic range of *polypragmon* and *periergos* and it can often mean no more than 'careful' or 'precise'; second, it is not as obvious to every Latin author as it may seem to us that the best way

---

[1] Labhardt (1960) and Bös (1995) offer valuable surveys of Latin usage but are much more superficial on the Greek concepts that the Roman authors translate.

to translate either of the key Greek terms is by *curiosus*. These issues are addressed in the next two sections of this chapter.

(2) *CURIOSUS* AND CARE

The connection between the adjective *curiosus* and the Latin term for care (*cura*) is evident.[2] To Varro what *curiosus* indicates is an excessive disposition to *cura* and this basic notion is essential to many adjectives ending in the suffix -*osus*.[3] Yet the suffix does not carry the same implications in all cases and *curiosus* itself is striking for its ability to carry neutral, even positive associations as well as the bad.[4] This is evident from the number of occasions on which Latin authors employ *curiosus* and *curiose* as synonyms for *diligens* and *diligenter*, running forms of each word together within the same sentence.[5] This application of *curiosus* is particularly common with regard to the careful conduct of technical work and craft, be it building,[6] agriculture,[7] pharmacy,[8] or even the production of papyrus.[9] When such work is not done to the proper standard, it is done *incuriose* or *parum curiose*.[10] What is true for craft is also true

---

[2] This, however, does not justify the claim of Bös (1995), 79 and Keulen (2007), 102 that the 'root sense' of *curiosus* is 'careful'. Such a view relegates the suffix to a secondary semantic role when, in the first extant appearances of the adjective in Plautus and Terence, it seems in fact to be of primary importance.

[3] Varro, *Ling.* 6. 46; Ernout (1949), 7.

[4] Gell. *NA* 4. 9. 2 and 12 attributes to Nigidius Figulus the view that adjectives ending in -*osus* always carry an indication of excess, but Gell. *NA* 4. 9. 12–14 contests this view: Figulus' claim may be true for *uinosus, mulierosus, morosus, uerbosus* but is not for *ingeniosus, formosus,* and *officiosus* (12). That *curiosus* is not of itself always sufficient to express the idea of excess is evident from Cic. *Nat. D.* 1.10: 'curiosius... quam necesse est'; Quint. *Inst.* 11. 3. 143: 'paene etiam nimium curiosi'; Quint. *Decl. Min.* 328. 11: 'filio nimium curioso'.

[5] Sen. *Brev.* 12. 5: 'quam diligenter...quam curiose'; Petron. *Sat.* 29. 4: 'omnia diligenter curiosus pictor...reddiderat'; Plin. *HN* 18. 19; Columella, *Rust.* 2. 2. 21; 11. 2. 18; 12. 57. 2; Scrib. Larg. 94.

[6] Vitr. *De arch.* 5. 3. 1; 7. 1. 1, 7; 7. 2. 2; 7. 4. 2.

[7] Columella, *Arb.* 7. 4; *Rust.* 2. 2. 21; 3. 10. 7; 5. 6. 7; 11. 2. 19; 12. 16. 4; 12. 57. 2; Plin. *HN* 18. 19.

[8] Scrib. Larg. 21, 37, 63, 74, 78, 94, 111, 209, 270. Note that *curiose* is particularly used in these passages for grinding or sieving meticulously.

[9] Plin. *HN* 13. 75.

[10] Plin. *HN* 13. 81: 'incuriose' for careless damping of papyrus; Val. Max. 1. 1. 4: 'parum curiose' for insufficient care in conducting sacrifice.

for more elevated occupations and it is possible to describe one performing public responsibilities with due care as *curiosus*.[11] There is here relatively little overlap with the semantic fields of *polypragmon* and *periergos*.[12] We are much closer here to what Greek expresses through the noun *epimeleia* and its related forms.[13]

What is distinctive about the uses of *curiosus* just surveyed emerges clearly from consideration of its antonyms. Work that is done carelessly (*incuriose*) or with insufficient care (*parum curiose*) fails to reach a basic minimum standard. It is, in other words, expected that a craftsman as much as a scholar should exercise due care in the performance of his tasks, but it is possible to do so without that supererogatory energy and devotion that distinguishes so many of the figures to be surveyed in this study. It has been observed that *polypragmosyne* and *apragmosyne* in Greek represent departures at either extreme from a median standard of activity for which no agreed term exists.[14] In Latin, by contrast, *curiosus* can stand both for a proper degree of care and for action that goes a good deal further. The former category will necessarily stand at the margins of this study though we will have reason to consider what Tacitus means when he describes Tiberius as *incuriosus* to expand the boundaries of the empire and to note how different senses of *curiosus* shade into each other in the *Metamorphoses* of Apuleius.

(3) *PRAGMA, NEGOTIUM, CURA*

The second problem with which I wish to engage may be illustrated by reference to a famous anecdote from the works of the grammarian

---

[11] Sen. *Cons. Marc.* 12. 3 describes the deceased son of Marcia as 'omnis officii curiosus'. The context is wholly laudatory.

[12] For a possible parallel, see Luci. *Alex.* 49 on scrolls sealed with particular care (περιεργότερον), Luci. *Alex.* 53 for a question sealed carefully (περιέργως). Note also Arist. *Mete.* 369b27: καὶ γὰρ οὗτος ὁ λόγος ἀπραγμόνως εἴρηται λίαν on insufficient care to substantiate a claim as a parallel for *incuriose*. This, however, is far from the field of craft.

[13] This observation is supported by the late antique bilingual glossaries. See *CGL* ii. 49, 309.

[14] Kleve (1964). Perhaps the most common term for that which does the job without going into undue elaboration is ἀπερίεργος. M. Aur. 1. 5 ἀπολυπράγμων has no broader currency.

Aulus Gellius.[15] At *Attic Nights* 11. 16, Gellius describes the recent
arrival of a copy of Plutarch's essay *Peri Polypragmosynes* and the
difficulty in which he finds himself when asked by a companion
ignorant of Greek literature and the Greek language to explain what
the title means.[16] Some thought is given to the otherwise unparalleled
formation *negotiositas*;[17] but the real sticking point is the want of any
word which will express both the sense of multiplicity in the Greek
prefix *poly-* and the affairs (*pragmata*) implied in *-pragmosyne*.[18] In
the end only a full sentence can explain that *polypragmosyne* implies
engagement in many different matters,[19] and even then it proves
necessary to explain that this is a fault because the matters with
which one engages are indiscriminate and superfluous.[20]

The Renaissance Latin title given to the *Peri Polypragmosynes* is *De
Curiositate*, but two points may be made with respect to this term
and to Gellius' failure to take it into consideration at this point. First,
it must be noted that where the abstract nouns *polypragmosyne* and
periergia appear in Greek as early as do the adjectives to which they
relate, the Latin noun *curiositas*—one usage in Cicero apart[21]—is
remarkable for its invisibility in extant Latin literature prior to its
emergence as a key concept in the *Metamorphoses* of Apuleius.[22]
Gellius may be of the same century as Apuleius, but he has no room
for this term in his vocabulary, and it is reasonable to assume that,
had he known of it at all, he would have regarded the term as a rather
dubious neologism. Second, attention must also be paid to the sense
applied elsewhere by Gellius to *curiosus* itself. For this is a recurrent

[15] Labhardt (1960), 210; Walsh (1988), 75–6.
[16] Gell. *NA* 11. 16. 2.
[17] Gell. *NA* 11. 16. 3.
[18] Gell. *NA* 11. 16. 4: 'nihil erat prorsus...quod non insigniter asperum absur-
dumque esset, si ex multitudine et negotio uerbum unum compingerem'.
[19] Gell. *NA* 11. 16. 6: 'ad multas igitur res adgressio earumque omnium rerum
actio πολυπραγμοσύνη...Graece dicitur'.
[20] Gell. *NA* 11. 16. 8: 'deterret enim nos hoc quidem in libro, quam potest maxime,
a uaria promiscaque et non necessaria rerum cuiuscemodi plurimarum et cogitatione
et petitione'.
[21] Cic. *Att.* 2. 12. 2. Labhardt (1960), 209 describes this usage as 'une création du
moment, un de ces néologismes sans lendemain que l'on risque dans une conversation familière, pour l'oublier aussitôt'.
[22] Apul. *Met.* 3. 14; 5. 6; 5. 19; 6. 20; 6. 21; 9. 12; 9. 13; 9. 15; 11. 15; 11. 22; 11. 23. A
similar distribution may be observed for the noun *formositas*, which appears once in
Cic. *Off.* 1. 126, then nowhere else before being used 11 times by Apuleius in the
Metamorphoses.

term in the *Attic Nights* but one used only to describe care or precision in scholarship.[23] For all his familiarity with the Latin writers of earlier centuries, he does not in this instance carry over their usage into his own work.

The above considerations are undoubtedly important, but what most cries out for attention here is the fact that Gellius' first instinct is to render the Greek term *pragma* not by *cura* but rather by *negotium*. There is in this a salutary warning against any casual assumption of isometry between *polypragmon* and *curiosus*, and it could come from few better sources than one as devoted to the study of the Greek and Latin languages as Gellius himself. And what is true of Gellius is true of a number of other Latin writers as well. Brief examination of one area of debate should illustrate the point well.

The gods of Epicurus famously exist but only in such a way as to ensure that one would never be aware of their existence: perched on the outer edge of the universe and never concerned to intervene in any of the affairs of men, they bear more than a passing resemblance to the quietist philosopher lurking in his garden in the deme of Gargettus and aspiring to make good the injunction: do not let them notice that you lived.[24] This observation would certainly not be lost on Plutarch: he identifies the Epicurean lifestyle with *apragmosyne*,[25] suggests that the gods of Epicurus are represented as living in precisely this way,[26] and makes the actual *apragmosyne* of the gods and potential *apragmosyne* of the king and general an important theme in his *Life of Pyrrhus*.[27] The same point underscores the

---

[23] Gell. *NA* 1. 4. 1; 1. 25 pref.; 2. 17. 1; 3. 3. 1; 12. 14. 4; 13. 1 pref.; 16. 12. 1; 17. 9. 5; 18. 15 pref.; 19. 13. 1; cf. 6. 7 pref.; 7. 5. 1; 12. 14. 4; 17. 2. 11; 19. 9. 7; 20. 11. 1 for *non incuriosus* or *non incuriose*. For *incuriosus* and *incuriose* applied to those who read, write, or conduct scholarly work without due care: Gell. *NA* 1. 7. 6; 2. 6. 1; 2. 28. 5; 2. 30. 6; 13. 25. 31. See also Holford-Strevens (2003), 229 n. 226.

[24] Epicurus fr. 551 Usener. For this interpreted as a call to *apragmosyne*, see the passages cited at Usener (1887), 326–7.

[25] Plut. *Mor.* 789B–C argues that it is reasonable to tell a quietist to stay a quietist in old age: οὕτως ἔχει τινὰ λόγον τὸ προσιόντα δήμωι πρεσβύτην, ἢ Χλίδωνα τὸν γεωργὸν ἢ Λάμπωνα τὸν ναύκληρον ἤ τινα τῶν ἐκ τοῦ κήπου φιλοσόφων, νουθετῆσαι καὶ καταχεῖν ἐπὶ τῆς συνήθους ἀπραγμοσύνης.

[26] Plut. *Mor.* 1043 B: τῶι Ἐπικούρωι τὴν πρόνοιαν ἀναιροῦντι διὰ τῆς ἀπραγμοσύνης τῆς περὶ τὸν θεόν.

[27] Plut. *Pyrrh.* 20. 3 describes the dinner-time conversations of Cineas and Fabricius: ἐν δὲ τῶι δείπνωι λόγων παντοδαπῶν γενομένων, πλείστων δὲ περὶ τῆς Ἑλλάδος καὶ τῶν φιλοσοφούντων, ἔτυχέ πως ὁ Κινέας ἐπιμνησθεὶς τοῦ Ἐπικούρου, καὶ διῆλθεν ἃ λέγουσι περὶ θεῶν καὶ πολιτείας καὶ τέλους, τὸ μὲν ἐν ἡδονῆι τιθέμενοι, πολιτείαν δὲ

much-quoted Epicurean dictum, that that which is blessed and eternal, i.e. a god, neither has troubles (*pragmata*) nor inflicts them on anyone else.[28] An important parallel for the Gellian translation of *pragma* by *negotium* is therefore provided by Cicero's translation of the Epicurean dictum at *De Natura Deorum* 1. 45.[29] Yet only a little later on, at *De Natura Deorum* 1. 54, Cicero's exponent of Epicurean theology, the senator C. Velleius, rejects the Stoic gods as constant meddlers, and this time the adjective *curiosus* and the noun *negotium* come together to express the same idea.[30] Seneca in turn will express the same ideas through *curiosus*: a polemical account of Epicurean theology closes with the suggestion that the philosopher leaves his gods entirely isolated, untouched even by the collapse of the heavens, deaf to prayers, and indifferent to humanity.[31] When he comes to

φεύγοντες ὡς βλάβην καὶ σύγχυσιν τοῦ μακαρίου, τὸ δὲ θεῖον ἀπωτάτω χάριτος καὶ ὀργῆς καὶ τοῦ μέλειν ἡμῶν εἰς ἀπράγμονα βίον καὶ μεστὸν εὐπαθειῶν ἀποικίζοντες. This passage coheres with Plut. *Pyrrh.* 13. 1 and 14. 7, where Plutarch describes the character of Pyrrhus and the efforts of Cineas to persuade him that ceaseless activity and intervention are unnecessary in the pursuit of happiness. Note esp. Plut. *Pyrrh.* 13. 1 for Pyrrhus permitted to χρῆσθαι τοῖς παροῦσιν ἀπραγμόνως καὶ ζῆν ἐν εἰρήνηι, βασιλεύοντα τῶν οἰκείων, but deeply suspicious of τὸ μὴ παρέχειν ἑτέροις κακὰ μηδ' ἔχειν ὑφ' ἑτέρων and finally fashioning plans for πραγμάτων καινῶν.

[28] Epicurus *KD* 1 = Diog. Laert. 10. 139. See Usener (1887), 394 for numerous ancient citations of this formula, including Sen. *Apocol.* 8. 1 joking that Claudius Ἐπικούρειος θεὸς non potest esse: οὔτε αὐτὸς πρᾶγμα ἔχει τι οὔτε ἄλλοις παρέχει', and Sallustius, *De Diis* 9: τὸ γὰρ θεῖόν φασιν οὐδὲ αὐτὸ πράγματα ἔχειν οὐδὲ ἄλλοις παρέχειν. Phld. *De Piet.* 529–33 with Obbink (1996) ad loc. is also relevant in this context. For πράγματα παρέχειν as a common set phrase, cf. Thuc. 8. 48. 6; Ar. *Plut.* 20, 102; Isoc. 15. 15, 39, 148, 163, 241; 18. 7; Xen. *Hell.* 2. 4. 28; *Mem.* 1. 3. 14; *Anab.* 1. 1. 11; Philemon fr. 92. 11 K-A; Long. 2. 39. 3; Ach. Tat. 5. 12. 2. For πράγματα ἔχειν, cf. Ar. *Nub.* 1216; Pl. *Resp.* 549c; Isoc. 7. 33; Ath. 49A; Long. 3. 6. 2.

[29] Cic. *Nat. D.* 1. 45: 'quod beatum aeternumque sit id nec habere ipsum negoti quicquam nec exhibere alteri'. See also Cic. *Div.* 2. 40: 'illius enim deus nihil habens nec sui nec alieni negotii'; *Off.* 2. 36: 'qui deum nihil habere ipsum negotii dicunt, nihil exhibere alteri'. For *negotium exhibere* as a set phrase in Latin, see Plaut. *Amph.* 894–5; *Men.* 1072; *Merc.* 273; *Most.* 565; *Per.* 315; *Poen.* 239; *Rud.* 473, 556; Cic. *Off.* 3. 112; Plin. *HN* 26. 43.

[30] Cic. *Nat. D.* 1. 54: 'quis enim non timeat omnia prouidentem et cogitantem et animaduertentem et omnia ad se pertinere putantem curiosum et plenum negotii deum?' See also Cic. *Div.* 2. 104: 'Epicurus…qui negat quicquam deos nec alieni curare nec sui'; *Leg.* 1. 21: 'nihil curare deum nec sui nec alieni'. Note also Lucr. 5. 82: 'nam bene qui didicere deos securum agere aeuum'; cf. Hor. *Sat.* 1. 5. 101–3: 'namque deos didici securum agere aeuum, | nec si quid miri faciat natura, deos id | tristis ex alto caeli demittere tecto'. In both cases *securus* may translate the Greek ἀπράγμων. For discussion of Cic. *Nat. D.* 1. 54 and Epicurean physics, see Blumenberg (1983), 263–5.

[31] Sen. *Ben.* 4. 19. 1-2: 'in medio interuallo huius et alterius caeli desertus sine animali, sine homine, sine re ruinas mundorum supra se circaque se cadentium euitat non exaudiens uota nec nostri curiosus'.

state his own Stoic providentialist creed, Seneca asserts that the gods preside over the universe, temper everything with their own force, watch over the well-being of the human race, and occasionally show concern for individuals.[32]

Aulus Gellius had good reason to suspect that *negotiositas* was unlikely to catch on as a translation for *polypragmosyne*. Yet the evidence surveyed in these pages would suggest that *negotium* and *cura* are almost interchangeable as Latin writers seek an equivalent in their language for what the Greeks called *pragma*.[33]

(4) THE COMIC BUSYBODY FROM GREECE TO ROME

The previous chapter noted the status of the busybody as one of the set characters of Greek New Comedy and the permanently raised eyebrow that was the distinctive feature of his mask.[34] We may think of just such a figure when Plutarch, *Moralia* 469B quotes lines addressed to a *polypragmon* asking why, acutely envious as he is, he has so sharp an eye for the ills of others but somehow fails to spot his own.[35] Yet it would seem likely that *polypragmosyne* and *periergia* are attributes more widely displayed than by just one character type.[36] In the

---

[32] Sen. *Ep.* 95. 50: 'illos esse qui praesident mundo, qui uniuersa ui sua temperant, qui humani generis tutelam gerunt interdum curiosi singulorum'. Both Madvig and Reynolds emend *curiosi* to *incuriosi* as if Seneca apologizes for the fact that the gods occasionally do not provide individuals with their moral deserts. Yet the obvious contrast is between the gods' watchfulness over the entire human race and their only occasional concern for its individual members. This is coherent with the following sentence, where Seneca states that the gods chastise *some* people and *occasionally* exact punishment: 'hi nec dant malum nec habent; ceterum castigant quosdam et coercent et inrogant poenas et aliquando specie boni puniunt'. For further criticism of Madvig's reasoning, see Bellincioni (1979), 293–4.

[33] See also Hor. *Sat.* 2. 3. 18–20: 'postquam omnis res mea Ianum | ad medium fracta est, *aliena negotia curo*, | excussis propriis'. Muecke (1993), 135 is alert to the Greek concepts being translated.

[34] See Ch. 1 Sect. 11. For the busybody of Greek New Comedy, see esp. Mette (1962).

[35] com. adesp. fr. 725 K-A = Plut. *Mor.* 469B, 515D: τί τἀλλότριον, ἄνθρωπε βασκανώτατε, | κακὸν ὀξυδορκεῖς τὸ δ' ἴδιον παραβλέπεις;

[36] The concepts can also take on different senses, see esp. Alexis fr. 145. 1 K-A = Ath. 123F–124B, where the claim that man is a περίεργον...φυτόν introduces a critique of perverse and contradictory behaviour. Likewise Philemon fr. 92. 3 K-A = Stob. *Flor.* 4. 34. 16.

Epitrepontes of Menander, for instance, the cook Karion recognizes in the slave Onesimos the same curiosity that he himself displays and states that he likes him for it.[37] What Karion understands by *periergia* is surely revealed when he adds that there is nothing sweeter than to know everything.[38] Onesimos himself, meanwhile, in a soliloquy delivered just after he and Habrotonon have hatched the plan by which she will pretend to have been raped by Charisios at the Tauropolia, resolves in future to renounce all meddlesome behaviour and chatter.[39] Finally we may consider the parallel case of the slave Parmenon in the *Samia* of whom Demeas, seeking information on the origins of the baby, comments that nothing escapes his observation and that he is a busybody or man of curiosity par excellence.[40]

To the Roman comic writers, the busybody is a *curiosus*. According to Festus p. 384 L, Livius Andronicus offers the formulation *sollicuria* and translates this as 'curious in every matter' (*in omni re curiosa*).[41] Yet this coinage is otherwise unattested. By contrast, Plautus, Terence, and Afranius all have their characters refer to busybodies as *curiosi* and in a manner that recalls the *polypragmones* and *periergoi* of the Greek stage.[42] The earliest example is that of the impecunious Plautine parasite Gelasimus at *Stichus* 198–208:

GE. sed curiosi sunt hic complures mali,
alienas res qui curant studio maxumo,
quibus ipsis nullast res quam procurent sua:
i quando quem auctionem facturum sciunt,

---

[37] Men. *Epit.* fr. 2a Arnott: φιλῶ σ᾿, ᾿Ονήσιμε· | καὶ σὺ περίεργος εἶ.

[38] Men. *Epit.* fr. 2b Arnott: οὐδέν ἐστι γὰρ | γλυκύτερον ἢ πάντ᾿ εἰδέναι. Crucial here is Cic. *Att.* 4. 11. 2, where Cicero first describes the time he has spent in literary study with the scholar Dionysius, then offers a slight misquotation of Karion's words (οὐδὲν γλυκύτερον ἢ πάντ᾿ εἰδέναι), and follows this with the exhortation to write to him as a man of curiosity (*ut homini curioso*) with all the latest news of political life in the capital.

[39] Men. *Epit.* 573–6 Arnott: χαιρέ[τω | τὸ πολλὰ πράττειν. ἂν δέ τις λάβηι μ[έ τι | περιεργασάμενον ἢ λαλήσαντ᾿, ἐκτεμεῖν | δίδωμ᾿ ἐμαυτοῦ τὰς γονάς.

[40] Men. *Sam.* 299–300 Arnott: ἔστι γὰρ | περίεργος, εἴ τις ἄλλος.

[41] Lenchantin de Gubernatis (1937), 44 prints the form *sollicularia* and posits that this is a fragment of an unnamed comedy, perhaps describing a busybody old woman.

[42] Afran. fr. 189–91 Ribbeck 3rd edn. is clearly spoken by a paterfamilias faced with an alliance between his son and a meddlesome slave: 'seruus est mihi Nicasio, | sceleratus curiosus, is cum filio | coiecerat nescio quid de ratiuncula'. Afran. fr. 250 Ribbeck 3rd edn. is from a speech in which one character uses the abstract noun *caries* in order to refer pejoratively to another: 'nemo illa uiuit carie curiosior'.

adeunt, perquirunt quid siet caussae ilico:
alienum aes cogat an pararit praedium,
uxorin sit reddenda dos diuortio.
eos omnis tam etsi hercle haud indignos iudico
qui multum miseri sint, laborent, nil moror:
dicam auctionis caussam, ut damno gaudeant;
nam curiosus nemo est quin sit maliuolus.

GE. But here there are masses of wicked busybodies, who concern themselves with the utmost zeal for the affairs of others, who have no property of their own to take care of. When they hear that someone is going to hold an auction, immediately they sidle up and ask the reason why: is debt bearing down on him or has he acquired an estate or is he getting divorced and bound to give his wife her dowry back? Though—by Hercules!—I judge them all worthy to be thoroughly wretched and to struggle, I don't care a jot for them. I shall state the cause of my auction so that they may rejoice at my loss; for there is no busybody who is not malicious.

These lines begin with a run of terms denoting different forms of care (*curiosi... curant... procurent*). What the busybodies care for is the affairs of others and the Latin *alienas res* corresponds precisely to what Greek expresses as τὰ ἀλλότρια.[43] They have a particular interest in the misfortunes of others and, whenever a man is obliged to sell off his property, will do all that they can to find out whether the cause is debt, over-optimistic investment, or divorce. Plutarch likewise identifies *polypragmosyne* as a fascination with the sorrows of others.[44] The malevolence attributed to all *curiosi* in v. 208 may in turn be connected with the delight in the sufferings of others (*epichairekakia*) that Plutarch associates with *polypragmosyne*.[45]

Two passages of Terence may be quoted in this context. The first is from the *Eunuchus* and represents the moment at vv. 553-6 that young Chaerea emerges from the house of Thais after carrying out the rape of Pamphila. He is still disguised as a eunuch and has no wish to answer questions on his actions or his dress:

[43] For the Greek categories translated by Plautus, see Labhardt (1960), 206-7. Petersmann (1973) at v. 198 offers some parallels for Gelasimus' claim that Athens is a hotbed of meddlers. To these may be added Char. *Call.* 1. 11. 6.
[44] Plut. *Mor.* 515D: οἷον εὐθὺς ἡ πολυπραγμοσύνη φιλομάθειά τίς ἐστιν ἀλλοτρίων κακῶν.
[45] Plut. *Mor.* 518C: ἐπιχαιρεκακία δ' ἡδονὴ ἐπ' ἀλλοτρίοις κακοῖς.

CH. sed neminemne curiosum interuenire nunc mihi
qui me sequatur quoquo eam, rogitando obtundat enicet
quid gestiam aut quid laetu' sim, quo pergam, unde emergam, ubi
   siem
uestitum hunc nanctu', quid mi quaeram, sanu' sim anne insaniam.

CH. To think that there is no busybody to bump into me now,
follow me wherever I go, and belabour me half to death with questions about what I'm excited about, why happy, where I'm off to,
where I'm coming from, where I got these clothes, what I'm aiming
at, whether I'm sane or mad.

In this instance Chaerea has every reason to avoid detailed interrogation about his activities. The relentless pursuit and ceaseless questioning he fears from a *curiosus* may remind us of the pest of Horace,
Satires 1. 9. Yet when at vv. 557–61 he is in fact met by his fellow
ephebe Antipho, and is asked all the questions he has only just
expressed a burning desire to avoid, he is more than happy to
encounter him:

AN. adibo atque ab eo gratiam hanc, quam uideo uelle, inibo.
Chaerea, quid est quod sic gestis? quid sibi hic uestitu' quaerit?
quid est quod laetus es? quid tibi uis? satine sanu's? quid me adspec-
   tas?
quid taces?
CH. o festu' dies hominis! amice, salue:
nemost hominum quem ego nunc magis cuperem uidere quam te.

AN. I'll go up and I'll do him the favour that I can see that he wants.
   Chaerea, why are you so excited? What does this clothing mean?
Why are you happy? What are you aiming at? Are you quite sane?
   Why are you looking at me? Why are you silent?
CH. O you one-man festival! Greetings, friend: there is no man I
   would sooner see now than you.

The very interrogation that in a *curiosus* would seem the height of
impertinence, when launched by a trusted friend, prompts at vv. 562–
606 the long and gloating narrative of the rape that many readers
find so very distasteful. The audience have neither buttonholed
Chaerea and demanded his story in the manner of a *curiosus* nor
are they the bosom friends on whom the young man can count for

the complaisant attention of an Antipho. It is precisely this detached position that allows a critical assessment of his words.

The *Eunuchus* is a conflation of two plays of Menander: the *Eunouchos* and the *Kolax*.[46] When therefore Chaerea expresses apprehension at the possibility of encountering *curiosi*, it may be reasonable to assume that any corresponding speech in the *Eunouchos* would have referred to them as *polypragmones* or *periergoi*. Inasmuch, however, as Antipho is identified by Donatus as a Terentian invention, it must be concluded that the comic responsion between the questions Chaerea seeks to avoid and Antipho then goes on to put is the original work of the Roman dramatist.[47]

The second passage of Terence is also to be found in a work translated from Menander: the *Self-Tormentor*.[48] As the play opens the elderly Menedemus is busy punishing himself through strenuous labour on his estate at Halae in the Attic countryside. The neighbouring landowner Chremes is puzzled by such conduct and seeks an explanation.[49] Hence the following exchange at vv. 75–7:

MEN. Chreme, tantumne ab re tuast oti tibi
aliena ut cures ea quae nil ad te attinent?
CHR. homo sum: humani nil a me alienum puto.

MEN. Chremes, do your own affairs allow you so much free time that you can meddle with those things which have nothing to do with you?
CHR. I am a man. I consider nothing in the world of man as outside my proper realm.

Chremes' words at v. 77 have taken on a life of their own and are often evoked as an encapsulation of scholarly *humanitas*.[50] Quoted out of context in an ancient florilegium, they could even suggest the standpoint attributed to the philosopher by Epictetus.[51] Yet in the context of the play as a whole what they betray is precisely his status

---

[46] Ter. *Eun.* 19–34.
[47] Donat. at Ter. *Eun.* 593.
[48] The *didascalia* to the play states 'Graeca est Menandru'. Ter. *Haut.* 7–9 assumes that the large majority of the audience have no need to be told as much.
[49] Note how Chremes' questions at Ter. *Haut.* 61–2 echo those Chaerea seeks to avoid at Ter. *Eun.* 555–6: 'quid tibi uis aut | quid quaeris?'
[50] Jocelyn (1973); Lefèvre (1994), 26–57.
[51] Epict. *Diss.* 3. 22. 97: διὰ τοῦτο οὔτε περίεργος οὔτε πολυπράγμων ἐστὶν ὁ οὕτω διακείμενος· οὐ γὰρ τὰ ἀλλότρια πολυπραγμονεῖ, ὅταν τα ἀνθρώπινα ἐπισκοπῆι, ἀλλὰ τὰ ἴδια.

as a busybody. As does Gelasimus in the *Stichus*, Menedemus deprecates any tendency to meddle with that which is proper to someone
else and none of one's own business (*aliena . . . quae nil ad te attinent*), but such distinctions mean nothing to Chremes who proclaims
himself a man and nothing in the world of men to be other than
proper to him (*a me alienum*).[52] The self-assurance he displays in
this scene is that of a man being set up for a fall. For all that he feels
confident to censure Menedemus for the errors that he made in
raising his son Clinia, he is blind to the rebellion of his own child
Clitipho and will end the play taking drastic action to restore the
well-being of his own household.[53] He is a classic comic *polypragmon*
and one who must learn to mind his own business.[54]

(5) THE CAREWORN LAMB OF THE *AULULARIA*

One particular use of *curiosus* in Plautus stands out as requiring
careful evaluation. It comes from the *Aulularia* and is to be found in
an exchange between the miser Euclio and his wealthy neighbour
Megadorus, who proposes not only to marry the daughter of Euclio
without a dowry but to furnish the wedding feast himself. When,
however, his slave Strobilus returns from market with two lambs and
two flute-girls, the fat lamb and the slender flute-girl are sent to the
house of Strobilus but the scrawny lamb and the chubby flute-girl to
that of Euclio.[55]

In the passage at issue, the paranoid and avaricious Euclio has just
complained of being asked to play host to cooks, who require constant observation lest they ransack the contents of the house, and to a
flute-girl who could happily drink a whole fountain of wine.[56] Now
he turns to the provisions:

EUCL. tum opsonium autem—
MEG. pol uel legioni sat est.

[52] For Chremes invited to mind his own business, cf. Ter. *Haut*. 80: 'mihi sic est
usu'; tibi ut opu' factost face'.
[53] Note Ter. *Haut*. 922–3 for Menedemus' rebuke to his neighbour: 'nonne id
flagitiumst te aliis consilium dare, | foris sapere, tibi non posse te auxiliarier?'
[54] Labhardt (1960), 207; Mette (1962), 399–405; Jocelyn (1973), 23–4; Lefèvre
(1994), 70 with exhaustive bibliography.
[55] Plaut. *Aul*. 327–34.   [56] Plaut. *Aul*. 551–9.

etiam agnum misi.
EUCL. quo quidem agno sat scio
magi' curiosam nusquam esse ullam beluam.
MEG. uolo ego ex te scire qui sit agnus curio.
EUCL. quia ossa ac pellis totust, ita cura macet.
quin exta inspicere in sole ei uiuo licet:
ita is pellucet quasi lanterna Punica.
EUCL. Then as for the provisions—
MEG. By Pollux they're enough even for a legion. I even sent a lamb.
EUCL. I know full well that there isn't anywhere any beast more
curiosus than that lamb.
MEG. I'd like you to tell me how a lamb can be a *curio*.
EUCL. Because it's all skin and bones, it's so wasting away with *cura*.
You can even look at its guts while it's still alive in the sunlight. It's
as pellucid as a Punic lantern.[57]

Few jokes benefit from explication and most puns are untranslatable.
This has not deterred scholars from attempting to elucidate this
exchange and, in particular, the play on *curiosam*, *curio*, and *cura*.
The problems posed have also led to two radically different textual
proposals. These too require careful attention.

What makes this exchange complicated is the intervention of
Megadorus at v. 563. Were Euclio to state that he had never seen a
beast more *curiosus*, then immediately add the punchline 'it's all skin
and bones, it's so wasting away with *cura*', then we would have little
trouble recognizing a playful misapplication or *catachresis* of an
adjective (*curiosus*) which the Latin of Plautus and Terence otherwise
uses only to mean 'meddling' or 'nosy'.[58] This, however, is less
obvious once Megadorus has asked how a lamb can be a *curio*,
which is a Latin term for a priest presiding over a quarter or *curia*.
Hence both textual interventions.

The first solution to the problems posed by the text is that
of Gulielmius and is accepted among others by Ussing, Leo, and
Ernout.[59] This is to emend *curiosam* in v. 562 to *curionem*. Euclio

---

[57] Plaut. *Aul.* 560–6.
[58] I have found no instance of *curiosus* in the sense of 'careworn' before Varro,
Ling. 6. 46; Sen. *Ep.* 56. 12. Stockert (1983), 155: 'Vielleicht ist die Stelle unter jene
plautinischen Witze zu zählen, bei denen um scherzhafter Wortverdrehung willen
vom Sinne abgesehen wird'.
[59] Ussing (1878), 336 argues the case for emendation.

thus states that he has never seen a beast more of a *curio* than the lamb; Megadorus asks in what sense a lamb can be a *curio*; and Euclio replies that it is because it is shrunken with care (*cura*). The principal objection to this interpretation is that the reading *curiosam* is attested not only by the manuscripts of Plautus but also by Nonius, and the alleged false reading must therefore have entered the tradition at a relatively early stage.[60]

The second solution was proposed over a century ago by Prescott and has recently been revived by Fontaine.[61] It too presupposes textual corruption but of a more radical sort. For both scholars argue that, where the manuscripts offer *curiosam* and *curio*, Plautus actually wrote κουριῶσαν and κουριῶν, that is to say the feminine accusative singular and masculine nominative singular present participles from the Greek verb κουριάω meaning 'to be in need of shearing'. Fontaine further suggests that *cura* in v. 564 suggests κουρᾷ, that is to say the dative singular of the noun κουρά meaning 'shearing'.

What underpins Prescott and Fontaine's suggestion of play on κουριάω is the observation that a lamb (*agnus*) is technically a lamb only until its first shearing, and that we may therefore infer not only that the beast in question is scrawny but also that its salad days are well behind it.[62] This is an engaging idea and one that makes good sense of v. 563. However, it is rather undermined by vv. 565–6 and the suggestion that the animal is as pellucid as a Punic lantern. This is entirely intelligible for a lamb that has been shorn and thus reveals quite how little flesh is left on the bone, but rather less for one still in need of shearing. To get around this problem, it is therefore necessary to assume that the participles in vv. 562–3 refer to the state of the lamb when it arrived in the kitchen while the noun κουρᾷ at v. 564 implies that the necessary haircut has now been applied and the true state of the beast beneath made clear.[63]

Both suggested emendations are born out of disquiet at the flow between *curiosam*, *curio*, and *cura* and the former certainly creates an

---

[60] Non. 86 and 455M; Stockert (1983), 155.

[61] Prescott (1907); Fontaine (2004). Fontaine develops Prescott's idea, takes *qui* in v. 563 to be an interrogative pronoun, suggests emendation of *quia* to *qui* in v. 564, and argues for the pun on *cura* / κουρᾷ. For intrigued scepticism towards Prescott's approach, see Comfort (1933); Stockert (1983), 155–6.

[62] Alf. *Dig.* 32. 60 pr. states that a lamb remains a lamb 'dumtaxat sex mensium' while Marcian. *Dig.* 32. 65. 7 states that 'ouium numero sunt, cum ad tonsuram uenerint'.

[63] Inasmuch as Fontaine (2004), 152 does not translate κουριῶσαν and κουριῶν, it is unclear how he means to get around this problem.

entirely intelligible comic routine. Yet closer attention to the transmitted text, and particularly to v. 563, may suggest a means by which to come to its defence. It has been indicated that, but for the interjection of Megadorus at v. 563, there would be no problem here in perceiving a punning misuse or *catachresis* of the adjective *curiosus*. What makes the reply of Megadorus complicated is that he does not so much ask Euclio to explain the *catachresis* as introduce another of his own, suggesting that *curiosus* connects directly to the actions of a *curio*. Yet the question 'How can a lamb be a *curio*?' has a humorous point of its own because of the category confusion on which it turns; for a *curio* is a priest with responsibility *inter alia* for conducting sacrifice and the lamb, by contrast, very much a sacrificial victim.[64] If Euclio in response pays no attention to the implications of Megadorus' pun and instead develops that which he himself had set up at vv. 561–2, this is nothing unusual in comic cross-talk. Moreover, there is now no contradiction with vv. 565–6, which can progress smoothly from the suggestion of careworn emaciation in v. 564 without raising questions about whether the sheep has been shorn or remains in need of the clippers.

(6) CURIOSITY AND THE IMPULSE TO RESEARCH

Some categories of Greek thought carry over into Latin more readily than others. In the previous chapter much attention was paid to the concept of the sykophant and to the tendency to level charges of *polypragmosyne* against those who took it on themselves to launch a prosecution. In Roman comedy, by contrast, the *sycophanta* is no more than a trickster and *sycophantia* a term for tricksterism.[65] In the language of the Roman courts, the classic way to defame a prosecutor is to dub him a *quadruplator*, but I have found no instance of anyone being called a *quadruplator* and a *curiosus*.[66] In the imperial age, Suetonius criticizes Augustus for ordering the summary execution of the knight Pinarius as a meddler and a spy (*curiosum ac*

[64] For the *curio* as sacrificer, see *CIL* VIII. 1174 and XI. 6955. For the lamb as sacrificial victim, see Plaut. *Capt.* 862; *Poen.* 453; *Rud.* 1208; *St.* 251; Cato, *Agr.* 141. 4; *TLL* i. 1363. 45–1364. 2.

[65] *OLD* p. 1895 s.v. *sycophanta* 2 and s.v. *sycophantia*.

[66] *OLD* p. 1532 s.v. *quadruplator* 1. Note esp. *Rhet. Her.* 2. 41: 'quadruplator est...improbus et pestifer ciuis'.

speculatorem) after he noticed Pinarius taking notes during an address of the emperor to the troops.[67] Yet it is not until the early third-century AD jurist Ulpian that we find the notorious malicious pro-secutors of this age—the *delatores*—described in terms of *curiositas*.[68]

Sykophancy and delation are perhaps the least palatable products of the thirst for knowledge. What though if that same basic impulse is turned to more innocent, indeed more scholarly, ends? This must be what is implied at *Tusculan Disputations* 1. 108 as Cicero describes the energy devoted by Chrysippus to the study of how different cultures dispose of the dead:

> permulta alia colligit Chrysippus, ut est in omni historia curiosus, sed ita taetra sunt quaedam, ut ea fugiat et reformidet oratio.

> Chrysippus collects very many other methods, vigorous as he is in every field of inquiry, but so ghastly are some that words shun and fear them.[69]

Dougan's note on this passage is right to gloss *curiosus* as *polyprag-mon*.[70] Yet what sort of *polypragmosyne* is here at issue? The answer is not hard to find. For Cicero's phrase 'vigorous as he is in every field of inquiry' is introduced with reference to Chrysippus' collection of 'very many' other ways of disposing of the dead. The suggestion is thus that he has thrown himself into this particular cross-cultural investigation just as he does in every other topic that he takes up. If there is any criticism here, it is that he offers 'too much information', that the principle of cultural relativism could be established—as it is at Herodotus 3. 38—by considering the burial practices of two and not two hundred different peoples. This certainly corresponds to some of what is said elsewhere of the literary production of the great Stoic, not least the claim of his housekeeper, as reported by Diocles, that he would happily write up to 500 lines a day.[71]

The sense that Cicero applies to *curiosus* corresponds to that first given to *polypragmon* in the *Birds* as Peisetairos blames the ignorance

---

[67] Suet. *Aug.* 27. 3; cf. Sen. *Con. ex.* 6. 2. For the spy as *polypragmon*, cf. Joseph *AJ* 5. 6; 15. 285.

[68] Justinian, *Dig.* 22. 6. 6 = Ulpian book 18 *ad legem Iuliam et Papiam*: 'delatoria curiositas'.

[69] *SVF* iii. 322. Cf. Sil. *Pun.* 13. 466–87, where Scipio Africanus treats the ghost of Appius Claudius to an extended catalogue of different methods of disposing of the dead around the world. For the possibility that Silius draws here on Chrysippus, see Bassett (1963); Reitz (1982), 40–1; Spaltenstein (1990) at Sil. *Pun.* 13. 468.

[70] Dougan (1905), i. 143. The remainder of the note is positively misleading.

[71] *SVF* ii. 1 = Diog. Laert. 7. 181.

regarding their origins of his avian friends on their failure to study the works of Aesop. If the association of *polypragmosyne* with the impulse to research is but rarely made in the fifth and fourth centuries, it becomes increasingly prominent in the Greek of the Hellenistic period and thereafter. One interesting example is that offered by the hypothesis to the *Rhesus*, which argues that the 'keen interest' in matters astronomical testifies to the play's authenticity as a work of Euripides.[72] The hypothesis in the form that we have it derives from the Byzantine period, but Ritchie is surely right to argue that its content derives from the scholarly inquiry of the three centuries between Aristotle and Didymus.[73] A clear parallel is offered by Polybius, who uses *polypragmosyne* to describe the activities of those scientists who study the stars or measure the height of an object standing straight on a flat surface.[74] Nor does Polybius restrict this usage to natural science, for *polypragmosyne* and its cognate forms are used repeatedly in his works to describe historical and geographical research as well.[75]

Of Polybius and those writers such as Posidonius, Diodorus, and Strabo, who wrote in his tradition, there will be a great deal more to say in a later chapter.[76] Yet what he and the unknown critic of the *Rhesus* illustrate is a significant stage in the developing understanding of *polypragmosyne*. In the imperial period this usage is to be found in a number of authors. In the *Peri Polypragmosynes* itself, Plutarch opines that the very curiosity which is offensive when directed at the private affairs of others is laudable when it is rather Nature's secrets into which one inquires.[77] Lucian in turn appears to pick up on Plutarch's claim that Nature will never take umbrage at being examined as he evokes the indignation of the moon at her constant molestation by

---

[72] Eur. *Rhes.* Hyp. 1: καὶ ἡ περὶ τὰ μετάρσια δὲ ἐν αὐτῶι πολυπραγμοσύνη τὸν Εὐριπίδην ὁμολογεῖ. 'Keen interest' is the felicitous translation of Ritchie (1964), 28–9.
[73] Ritchie (1964), 4.
[74] Polyb. 9. 15. 7; 9. 19. 5, 9. For astronomical investigation and *polypragmosyne*, see also Paus. 9. 20. 3 on Atlas.
[75] Polyb. 3. 59. 4; 5. 75. 6; 12. 25c. 2; 12. 25e. 1; 12. 25i. 2; 12. 26. 9; 12. 26e. 3; 12. 27. 1–3, 4–6; 12. 28a. 2–4; 14. 1a. 4; 15. 36. 3; 36. 1. 6–7. This usage may be connected to Polyb. 1. 1. 4; 1. 3. 1; etc. describing the *Histories* as a *pragmateia*. For this term, see now *P. Artemid.* Col. i. 5 with the passages cited by Gallazzi et al. (2008), i. 198–9, but note that that listed as Diod. Sic. 39. 8. 8 is actually from Polybius.
[76] See Ch. 3.
[77] Plut. *Mor.* 517C–E, 518D. For similar associations, see Plut. *Mor.* 647 A–B on botany, fr. 191. 8 Sandbach. See also Tasinato (1994), 46–7.

scientists of every sort.[78] In the same writer's *Alexander*, the many
intellectual gifts abused by the wicked false-prophet include his *periergia*, and the clear implication is that this quality, as much as any
other, could have been put to virtuous ends had he chosen to do so.[79]
Pausanias, meanwhile, describes investigation of everything from the
ages of Homer and Hesiod to the source of the Arcadian river Lymax
in terms of *polypragmosyne*.[80]

Later sections of this work will look in detail at how Cicero and
Seneca in particular apply the term *curiosus* to various modes of
scholarly investigation and to their practitioners. Here, however, we
may close with two further examples of how this adjective can be
used to express what Greeks of the same period would have understood by *polypragmon* or *periergos*. The first comes from book 25 of
Pliny's *Natural History* and its tribute to the scientific interests first
of the mythical Orpheus, then of Rome's great foe, Mithridates VI of
Pontus. Of Orpheus Pliny remarks that he was the first to offer more
detailed or precise information on plants.[81] As for Mithridates, Pliny
describes him as a man of immense intellect and scholarly interest
and as a formidable linguist who never addressed a subject through
an interpreter.[82] Yet amidst all these remarkable accomplishments,
Mithridates was particularly interested in medicine and compiled
works on poisons which his conqueror Pompey gave to his freedman
Pompeius Lenaeus to translate.[83] As ever Rome was more than ready
to learn from the talents of her foe.[84]

The second example to be considered refers to a quite different
field of knowledge. In his note on *Aeneid* 1. 44, where the poet
describes the piercing of the breast of Ajax Oileus, Servius Auctus
records Probus' reading *tempore* in place of *pectore* and suggestion

[78] Luci. *Icar.* 20–1; cf. Plut. *Mor.* 517D.

[79] Luci. *Alex.* 4: συνέσει μὲν γὰρ καὶ ἀγχινοίαι καὶ δριμύτητι πάμπολυ τῶν ἄλλων
διέφερεν, καὶ τό τε περίεργον καὶ εὐμαθὲς καὶ μνημονικὸν καὶ πρὸς τὰ μαθήματα
εὐφυές, πάντα ταῦτα εἰς ὑπερβολὴν ἑκασταχοῦ ὑπῆρχεν αὐτῶι. Cf. Herennius Philo of
Byblos *FGrH* 790 F1 = Euseb. *Praep. evang.* 1. 9. 19–29 praising the Phoenician
scholar Sanchuniathon. Note esp. §§23–4 on the proem and Philo's admiring ἀνὴρ
πολυμαθὴς καὶ πολυπράγμων.

[80] Paus. 1. 28. 7; 5. 20. 2; 6. 19. 9; 8. 41. 10; 9. 20. 3; 9. 30. 3, 12.

[81] Plin. *HN* 25. 12: 'Orpheus de herbis curiosius aliqua prodidit'.

[82] Plin. *HN* 25. 5–7.

[83] Plin. *HN* 25. 7: 'in reliqua ingenii magnitudine medicinae peculiariter curiosus'.

[84] An obvious parallel is Plin. *HN* 18. 22–3, which discusses the senatorial
commission established to translate the works of the Punic agronomist Mago.

that the body-part at issue is actually the temple. This the grammarian connects to an image of Capaneus on the visitor's left as he enters the temple of Castor and Pollux at Ardea, and attributes to Vergil knowledge of the particular local tradition this involves (*topica historia*). Servius treats this as proof of Vergil's manifold and ardent interest in all of Italy and there is no sense that he regards this attitude with anything but admiration.[85] Such attention to local traditions may bring to mind the scholarly pursuits of Pausanias, and indeed we may refer to what he says in book 6 about those who have given particular care to the cities of Italy.[86] No less relevant in this context are what the scholia to Pindar's second *Isthmian Ode* say in tribute to the work of Artemon on the peoples of Sicily.[87] When the *polypragmosyne* driving such local investigations next comes into focus in this context in this study, it will be with reference to those like Polybius who condemn the trivial and profitless entertainment that it offers. For now it is useful to have observed that a less censorious view could also be held.[88]

(7) CICERO ON BEING *CURIOSUS*

If Cicero applies a remarkable range of meanings to the adjective *curiosus*, it is because he is more aware than any other extant Latin writer of the full semantic range of *polypragmon* and *periergos* in the writings of the Greeks. Even before we turned to his account of the writings of Chrysippus, this had already been illustrated with reference to *ad Atticum* 4. 11. 2 and the indirect evidence that it offers for the characterization of the meddlesome cook Karion in the *Epitrepontes*.[89] The association made between the *curiosus* and an unquenchable thirst for political gossip is one that recurs through

---

[85] Serv. at Verg. *Aen.* 1. 44: 'totius autem Italiae curiosissimum fuisse Vergilium multifariam apparet'.

[86] Paus. 6. 19. 9: ὁπόσοι δὲ περὶ Ἰταλίας καὶ πόλεων ἐπολυπραγμόνησαν τῶν ἐν αὐτῆι.

[87] Artemon *FGrH* 569 F6 = Schol. Pind. *Isthm.* 2. inscr. a: ὁ δὲ ' Ἀρτέμων σφόδρα τὰ περὶ τοὺς Σικελιώτας πεπολυπραγμονηκὼς αὐτὸν μόνον συγγενῆ φησιν εἶναι Θήρωνος.

[88] See Ch. 5 Sect. 5.

[89] See Sect. 4.

the letters,[90] and it is in this context that Cicero first coins the term *curiositas*.[91] In the chapters that follow, Cicero will again take a prominent position whether through his association of the *curiosus* with prying inquiry into the realm of the divine or through his critique of the indiscriminate pursuit of knowledge.[92] For now I seek merely to illustrate some of that range of signification and to explore the writer's constant engagement with the categories and language of Greek thought.

An appropriate point of departure may be offered by *De Finibus* 1. 3. This work as a whole has much to say about what it is to be in love with knowledge and what it means to be *curiosus* and will therefore be considered in detail in a later chapter.[93] In this instance, however, Cicero takes issue with those who would deter him from the writing of philosophy and does so by striking reference to a scene from the *Self-Tormentor* of Terence that has already taken a prominent role in the discussion of the busybody of comedy. The end of philosophy is, he asserts, a thing most lovely.[94] If, therefore, its pursuit gives him pleasure, who is so malign as to try to draw him away? If it becomes a source of toil, who is to put a limit on another man's industry?[95] In Terence, he adds, Chremes displays no want of humanity when he urges his new neighbour no longer to dig and plough and lug things around; for he deters him not from industry but from ungentlemanly labour. Yet those men are busybodies (*curiosi*) who take umbrage at a form of labour that Cicero finds the opposite of unpleasant.[96] This is not the last occasion in the *De Finibus* when Cicero will demonstrate his interest in the opening

---

[90] Cic. *Att.* 2. 4. 4; 2. 12. 2; 5. 14. 3; 6. 1. 25; 15. 26. 5; cf. *Fam.* 8. 1. 1 where Caelius makes clear his familiarity with Cicero's interest in gossip; Bös (1995), 40–1. See also Plin. *Ep.* 9. 32, where Pliny confesses to Titianus that the leisure he enjoys makes him all the more *curiosus* for gossip.

[91] Cic. *Att.* 2. 12. 2: 'sum in curiositate ὀξύπεινος'.

[92] See Ch. 4 Sect. 2 and Ch. 5 Sect. 5.

[93] See Ch. 5 Sect. 5.

[94] Cic. *Fin.* 1. 3: 'cum id, quod quaeritur, sit pulcherrimum'.

[95] Cic. *Fin.* 1. 3: 'etenim si delectamur, cum scribimus, quis est tam inuidus, qui ab eo nos abducat? sin laboramus, quis est, qui alienae modum statuat industriae?'

[96] Cic. *Fin.* 1. 3: 'nam ut Terentianus Chremes non inhumanus, qui nouum uicinum non uult "fodere aut arare aut aliquid ferre denique" (non enim illum ab industria, sed ab inliberali labore deterret) sic isti curiosi, quos offendit noster minime nobis iniucundus labor.'

scene of the *Self-Tormentor*.[97] Yet what makes this passage so very interesting is the way that it sets Chremes up as the benevolent alternative to the *curiosi* who now gnaw away at Cicero. In Terence he belongs to the group to which he is now opposed, but Cicero would appear to regard his intervention in the life of Menedemus as less vicious than that of the detractors of philosophy in his own.

The commentaries of both Madvig and Reid are alert to the relationship between the *curiosi* of *De Finibus* 1. 3 and the *polypragmones* and *periergoi* of Greek thought.[98] Reid does no more than gloss the Latin term with the Greek, but Madvig offers a number of parallels from Cicero, Suetonius, and Quintilian though with the prudent observation that the last employs the term in a significantly different sense.[99] This concern to distinguish the variety of meanings that *curiosus* can take on might also usefully be displayed at *De Finibus* 2. 28, where Cicero imagines himself in dialogue with an increasingly tetchy Epicurus over whether pleasure (*uoluptas*) is truly identical with the state of not feeling pain (*non dolendi status*). Epicurus declines to get into a fight about terminology (*non laboro... de nomine*) and states that he can find many, indeed innumerable, men neither so bothersome (*curiosos*) nor so irritating (*molestos*) as Cicero whom he can easily convince of whatever he wishes.[100] Here Madvig is again absolutely right to gloss *curiosos* as *polypragmones* and to describe them as those who engage in subtle investigation of unnecessary or superfluous matters (*qui non necessaria subtiliter exquirunt*), but he is less helpful when he directs the reader back to the material already collected at 1. 3. For there the *curiosi* are those who try to tell others how to live their own lives, and none of the passages cited properly parallels Epicurus' evident irritation here at those who reduce philosophy to mere terminological argument. More exact parallels for this usage are furnished by Philo, who rails at those who argue over names or terms (*onomata*)

---

[97] Cic. *Fin.* 3. 63: 'ex hoc nascitur ut etiam communis hominum inter homines naturalis sit commendatio, *ut oporteat hominem ab homine ob id ipsum quod homo sit non alienum uideri*' must echo the dictum of Chremes at Ter. *Haut.* 77. Thus also Lefèvre (1994), 27.

[98] Madvig (1876); Reid (1925).

[99] For what *curiosus* means at Quint. *Inst.* 8. 3. 55, see Ch. 5 Sect. 2.

[100] Cic. *Fin.* 2. 28: 'reperiam multos, uel innumerabilis potius, non tam curiosos nec tam molestos quam uos estis, quibus quicquid uelim facile persuadeam'.

and by Numenius, who decries the excessive subtleties of the Stoic logicians.[101] The number of ways in which Cicero can use *curiosus* in order to translate *polypragmon* and *periergos* is not yet exhausted. This may be illustrated by reference to two of the passages adduced by Madvig as parallels for Cicero's usage at *De Finibus* 1. 3. Perhaps the closest is *De Natura Deorum* 1. 10, where Cicero responds to those who demand an explicit statement of his own conviction and introduces his defence of the Academic denial of absolute certainty. Those who ask what he himself thinks on any given matter display a needless curiosity which perhaps borders on the prying.[102] Cicero himself disavows the unquestioned authority of a Pythagoras and would not have anyone assent to his views just because he himself has uttered them.[103] This passage may also be related to the dialogue format of *De Natura Deorum* and to Cicero's ability to shelter behind the views that he attributes to his speakers.[104] In another work, the *Brutus*, where the voice of Cicero himself is dominant, the only way to frustrate unwelcome attempts to elicit his views on the oratorical talents of those still alive is to limit discussion to the achievements of the dead.[105] In both these cases, therefore, Cicero carefully polices what is his own and insists on his right to maintain some secrets. It is to be assumed that the commander does much the same when the *periergos* of Theophrastus interrogates him on his plan

---

[101] Philo *Congr.* 53 criticizes philosophical quibblers who argue ὥσπερ τῆς εὐδαιμονίας ἐπ' ὀνομάτων καὶ ῥημάτων [καὶ] ἀπεράντωι καὶ ἀνηνύτωι περιεργίαι κειμένης. Philo *Quod Omn. Prob.* 88 praises the Essenes and their virtue based on action, not the futility of Greek talk: τοιούτους ἡ δίχα περιεργίας Ἑλληνικῶν ὀνομάτων ἀθλητὰς ἀρετῆς ἀπεργάζεται φιλοσοφία, γυμνάσματα προτιθεῖσα τὰς ἐπαινετὰς πράξεις, ἐξ ὧν ἡ ἀδούλωτος ἐλευθερία βεβαιοῦται. For criticism of Stoic logic-chopping, see Numen. ap. Euseb. *Praep. evang.* 728a = *SVF* ii. 20: αὐτοὶ γὰρ οὗτοι τοὺς ἑτέρους ὑπερβαλλόμενοι τῇ τε πολυπραγμοσύνῃ τοῖς τε σκαρ <ι>φηθμοῖς ἐπετίμων θᾶττον.

[102] Cic. *Nat. D.* 1. 10: 'qui autem requirunt quid quaque de re ipsi sentiamus, curiosius id faciunt quam necesse est'.

[103] Cic. *Nat. D.* 1. 10.

[104] Cic. *Nat. D.* 3. 95 gives some indication of the author's sympathies, but even here this is couched in terms only of what then seemed to him to be closer to the truth.

[105] Cic. *Brut.* 231: 'quoniam hoc sermone nostro statui neminem eorum qui uiuerent nominare, ne uos curiosius eliceretis ex me quid de quoque iudicarem, eos qui iam sunt mortui nominabo'. Contrast Cic. *Brut.* 133, where Brutus confesses to prior ignorance of the works of Catulus and Scaurus and resolves to hunt them out 'curiosius' in future. Here, unlike at 231, the comparative adverb has none of the implied sense of doing something to excess.

of campaign.[106] By contrast, Madvig introduces a rather different category when he cites *De Officiis* 1. 125 and the proper limits to the political activities of foreigners and immigrants.[107] For here we are some way from the simple bossiness of a Chremes telling his neighbour how to live or a critic telling Cicero what to write. The point is more specific and the obligation imposed on incomers to Rome identical to the conditioned quietism of the Athenian metic as already observed in the speeches of Lysias.[108]

(8) TRANSLATING *POLYPRAGMOSYNE* AND THE INTERVENTIONIST STATE

Rome was, if anything, even more inclined to intervene in the affairs of neighbouring states than was Athens and its chosen mode was conquest. National myth knows no equivalent to the rescue of the children of Heracles or the burial of the dead at Thebes. The essence of the stories Athens tells of herself is the combination of temporary action to bring her neighbours back to a proper course and enduring respect for the autonomy they previously enjoyed. When Euripides' Theseus returns having secured the burial of the Argive dead, Creon lies slain before his city but the Theban state endures. When Hersilia and the Sabine women intervene to prevent battle between the country of their birth and Rome, the enduring result is the fusion of the two peoples under the Roman citizenship.[109] The *Sabinae* of Ennius dramatized just this myth.[110]

From the letter of Mithridates in Sallust's *Histories* to the speech of Calgacus in the *Agricola*, Roman historians offer bravura imaginings of what their opponents have to say about them.[111] Yet brute force

---

[106] Theophr. *Char.* 13. 7.

[107] Cic. *Off.* 1. 125: 'peregrini autem atque incolae officium est nihil praeter suum negotium agere, nihil de alio anquirere minimeque esse in in aliena republica curiosum'.

[108] See Ch. 1 Sect. 5. The comments of Dyck (1996) ad loc. are largely to the point, but the citation of Pl. *Leg.* 952d1 is of limited relevance since it does not concern metics.

[109] Livy 1. 13. 4–5.

[110] Enn. *Praet.* 5–6 Ribbeck, 3rd edn. It is perhaps significant that the appeal of the Sabine women in this fragment borrows a motif from Jocasta at Eur. *Phoen.* 571–7, hence from the Theban crisis. For sensible discussion and exhaustive bibliography, see Manuwald (2001), 178–9.

[111] Sall. *Hist.* 4. 69M; Tac. *Agr.* 30–2; Ogilvie and Richmond (1967), 253–4.

and greed for plunder are here the central accusations and there is no obvious conceptual equivalent for *polypragmosyne*. In order to see how Latin writers responded to such language in their Greek sources, we must therefore look to Livy and to those passages in which he recasts diplomatic debates between Rome and Antiochus as reported in Polybius and those who drew on him.

In book 18 of the *Histories*, Polybius describes the 196 BC meeting at Lysimachia between Antiochus III and the Roman commissioners led by L. Cornelius. The Romans express displeasure at Antiochus' retention of Greek cities in Asia previously held by Ptolemy and at his advance into Europe. Antiochus replies as follows:

> ὁ δὲ βασιλεὺς πρῶτον μὲν διαπορεῖν ἔφη κατὰ τίνα λόγον ἀμφισβητοῦσι πρὸς αὐτὸν ὑπὲρ τῶν ἐπὶ τῆς Ἀσίας πόλεων· πᾶσι γὰρ μᾶλλον ἐπιβάλλειν τοῦτο ποιεῖν ἢ Ῥωμαίοις. δεύτερον δ᾽ ἠξίου μηδὲν αὐτοὺς πολυπραγμονεῖν καθόλου τῶν κατὰ τὴν Ἀσίαν· οὐδὲ γὰρ αὐτὸς περιεργάζεσθαι τῶν κατὰ τὴν Ἰταλίαν ἁπλῶς οὐδέν.

> The king first stated that he could not understand on what grounds they were entering into dispute with him about the cities in Asia. For to do this was nobody's business less than it was Rome's. Second, he demanded that they intervene not one jot in the affairs of Asia; for he himself was in no way meddling with the affairs of Italy.[112]

Livy in turn offers his own version of this response in book 33 of the *Ab Urbe Condita*:

> aduersus ea Antiochus mirari se dixit Romanos tam diligenter inquir-ere quid regi Antiocho faciundum aut quousque terra marique progre-diundum fuerit, ipsos non cogitare Asiam nihil ad se pertinere nec magis illis inquirendum esse quid Antiochus in Asia quam Antiocho quid in Italia populus Romanus faciat.

> In response to this Antiochus stated that he was amazed that the Romans were so carefully inquiring into what Antiochus should be doing or how far he should advance by land and sea, but were not themselves reflecting that Asia was none of their business and that they had no more right to inquire into what Antiochus was doing in Asia than Antiochus had to inquire what the Roman people was doing in Italy.[113]

If this is an attempt to communicate to a Latin audience what Livy has found in Polybius, it is only a rather approximate one. Both

---

[112] Polyb. 18. 51. 1–2.
[113] Livy 33. 40. 1–2.

passages certainly reflect the attempt to dictate spheres of influence
and to question why Rome bothers herself with the affairs of Asia
when Antiochus does nothing of the sort in Italy. When Livy's
Antiochus reminds the Romans that Asia is none of their business
(*Asiam nihil ad se pertinere*), the contention will be familiar from
the Greek debates of the fifth and fourth centuries sampled in the
previous chapter. Yet when he does so he is responding to the sentence
which I have translated as 'For to do this was nobody's business less
than it was Rome's' (πᾶσι γὰρ μᾶλλον ἐπιβάλλειν τοῦτο ποιεῖν ἢ
'Ρωμαίοις). This then leaves the twofold employment of the verb 'to
inquire' (*inquirere... inquirendum*) in order to render what Antiochus
has expressed through three separate verbs (ἀμφισβητοῦσι...
πολυπραγμονεῖν... περιεργάζεσθαι). For much of the work of Polybius, as has already been indicated and will be discussed in detail
later on, the second of these verbs does indeed have the principal
meaning of 'inquire', and it would appear that Livy has erroneously
read the same sense into this passage as well.[114] Nowhere, it may
be added, does he use either the verb *curare* or any of its cognate forms.

This is not the end of the debate with Antiochus and an important
passage from book 34 of Livy turns on many of the same motifs.[115]
Here, however, the original version as found in Polybius is no longer
extant and it is necessary instead to turn to Diodorus Siculus for some
idea of the Greek concepts that Livy attempts to render in Latin.[116] The
context is the 193 BC embassy sent by Antiochus to the Roman senate
and the passage describes both the representations made on behalf of
the king by Menippus and the singularly frosty response delivered by
Titus Quinctius Flaminius. In Diodorus, therefore, Menippus expresses the king's inability to understand why the Romans should tell
him not to meddle with specific parts of Europe, to stay away from
certain cities, and not to take from some the levies owed to him.[117]

[114] For Livy's mistranslations and misunderstandings of Polybius, see Tränkle
(1977), 178–91 with examples and bibliography.
[115] Livy 34. 57–9.
[116] Diod. Sic. 28. 15. 2–4. Comparison of the close overlap in content and phrasing
between Diod. Sic. 28. 12 and Polyb. 18. 50–2 is instructive. For Diodorus' dependence on Polybius in 28. 15, see Briscoe (1981), 2 and 137.
[117] Diod. Sic. 28. 15. 2: ἔφησε δὲ θαυμάζειν τὸν βασιλέα διὰ τίνα ποτ' αἰτίαν
προστάττουσιν αὐτῷ 'Ρωμαῖοι τινὰ μὲν τῶν κατὰ τὴν Εὐρώπην μὴ πολυπραγμονεῖν,
τινῶν δὲ τῶν πόλεων ἀφίστασθαι καὶ παρ' ἐνίων τοὺς ὀφειλομένους φόρους μὴ
λαμβάνειν.

In Livy Menippus reports Antiochus' amazement that the Romans
should think it right to impose terms on him, stating which cities
they wish to be free and untaxed, which ones subject to the levy.[118]
In Diodorus Flaminius replies that, should Antiochus quit Europe,
the Romans are willing not to intervene in Asia,[119] while in Livy Flaminius
states that, if Antiochus wishes the Romans not to concern themselves
with Asia, he himself should depart from Europe.[120] Finally, where the
senate in Diodorus states before all the gathered Greeks that any
meddling by Antiochus with Europe will result in their taking energetic
action to liberate the cities of Asia,[121] in Livy it urges them all to report
to their states that, should he not leave Europe, the Romans will
vindicate their liberty with the same fidelity and valour as previously
they did when faced with Philip.[122] Three times Diodorus employs the
verbs *polypragmonein* or *periergazdesthai* but only in the second instance does Livy take up this language when Flaminius employs the
verb *curare*. Here at least the historian demonstrates a more accurate
understanding of *polypragmonein* than he does in book 33, but it
appears overall that he is happier to sidestep than to translate terms
with which he is somewhat ill at ease.

(9) THE *CURIOSI* OF CATULLUS, HORACE, AND MARTIAL

The first three syllables of *curiosus* are by nature long–short–long.
The term therefore has no place in any work composed in hexameters or pentameters, which is to say in the large part of surviving
Latin verse. The same problem does not, however, hold for the
hendecasyllables of Catullus 7 and Martial 11. 63 or the iambic

---

[118] Livy 34. 57. 10: 'mirari se quod Romani aequum censeant leges ei dicere quas
Asiae urbium liberas et immunes, quas stipendiarias esse uelint'.
[119] Diod. Sic. 28. 15. 3: εἰ μὲν βούλεται τῆς Εὐρώπης ἀπέχεσθαι, μηδὲν
πολυπραγμονεῖν Ῥωμαίους τῶν κατὰ τὴν Ἀσίαν.
[120] Livy 34. 58. 2: 'si nos nihil quod ad urbes Asiae attinet curare uelit, ut et ipse
omni Europa abstineat'.
[121] Diod. Sic. 28. 15. 4: ἐὰν Ἀντίοχος περιεργάζηταί τι τῶν κατὰ τὴν Εὐρώπην,
Ῥωμαῖοι μετὰ πολλῆς σπουδῆς τοὺς κατὰ τὴν Ἀσίαν Ἕλληνας ἐλευθερώσουσιν.
[122] Livy 34. 59. 5: 'renuntiarent ciuitatibus suis populum Romanum, qua uirtute
quaque fide libertatem eorum a Philippo uindicauerit, eadem ab Antiocho, nisi
decedat Europa, uindicaturum'.

trimeters of Horace, *Epode* 17. There is, moreover, no little degree of continuity between the *curiosi* of each of these poems, in particular between Catullus and Martial. The themes that predominate will also be relevant to the ensuing examination of the *curiosi* of Petronius.

Horace, *Epode* 17 is a pendant to *Epode* 5. In the former poem, Horace describes a ghastly exercise in love magic conducted by the witch Canidia and her sidekicks Sagana, Veia, and Folia.[123] The aim is to restore Canidia's former lover Varus to her and the centrepoint of the rite is the sacrifice of an unknown child, who closes the poem with a Thyestean curse against the witch. By *Epode* 17, the final poem of the collection, Canidia has decided to take her revenge on Horace for profaning her rites and the first fifty-two lines consist of a speech in which he pleads with her to treat him more gently. The appeal is in vain and Canidia's ears deaf to any such blandishments. This much we learn from the first three lines of her response. There then follows the crucial statement of Horace's crime:

> 'inultus ut tu riseris Cotyttia
> uulgata, sacrum liberi Cupidinis,
> et Esquilini pontifex uenefici
> impune ut Urbem nomine impleris meo?'

'Are you to laugh unavenged at the profanation of the rites of Cotys, and the sacred ceremony of free Love, and as the priest of the Esquiline poisoning with impunity to have filled the City with my name?'[124]

The rites that Canidia accuses Horace of profaning do not correspond precisely to those described in *Epode* 5. She and Sagana have already featured in *Satire* 1. 8 and Watson is probably right to suggest that Horace here invents other stages in their entanglement of which we are otherwise uninformed.[125] Yet what Horace has done in both poems is to fill the city with the name of Canidia and to expose to common knowledge the grisly rites that she performs.[126] His crime is thus twofold: he has spied on that which he has no right to see and he

---

[123] Hor. *Epod.* 5. 41–6 perhaps falls some way short of asserting that Folia was actually present.

[124] Hor. *Epod.* 17. 56–9.

[125] Watson (2003) at Hor. *Epod.* 17. 57.

[126] Cf. Prop. 2. 5. 1–2 as a comment on the reception of the *monobiblos*: 'hoc uerum est tota te ferri, Cynthia, Roma | et non ignota uiuere nequitia?'

has shared with others the secrets that he learned. Hence the final lines of Canidia's response, of the poem, and of the whole collection:

> 'an quae mouere cereas imagines,
> ut ipse nosti curiosus, et polo
> deripere lunam uocibus possim meis,
> possim crematos excitare mortuos
> desiderique temperare pocula,
> plorem artis in te nil agentis exitus?'

'Or am I, who can, as you know, meddler that you are, move wax images, and draw the moon down from heaven by my words, who can rouse the cremated dead and mix the cups of desire, am I to weep over arts that have no effect on you?'[127]

In these lines, therefore, we see a first instance of motifs that will be examined in depth in my analysis of *polypragmosyne* and the divine.[128] For curiosity and the impulse to chatter are intimately linked, and those who seek to witness that which is forbidden to them are rarely satisfied to keep those secrets to themselves.[129] Without anticipating discussion of how these issues play themselves out in the *Metamorphoses* of Apuleius, we may at least compare what drives the vengeful Canidia of the *Epodes* with the determination of Apuleius' witch Meroe to prevent Aristomenes from telling any more tales on her and to take vengeance on him for his past talkativeness and current curiosity.[130]

Catullus 7 is also a pendant to a prior poem, in this case poem 5 and its playful appeal to Lesbia to live, to love, and to value the rumours of over-censorious old men at but one penny. Yet the style of the second poem is strikingly different from that of the first.[131] In poem 5 Catullus urges Lesbia to kiss him a hundred, then a thousand, then a hundred times again. When finally many thousands of kisses have been

---

[127] Hor. *Epod.* 17. 76–81.

[128] See Ch. 4. Watson (2003) at v. 77 has an excellent note on *curiosus*.

[129] Plut. *Mor.* 508C, 519C; Diod. Sic. 18. 62. 4; Philo *Abr.* 20; *Sobr.* 32; Luci. *Icar.* 20–1; Stob. *Flor.* 1. 49. 44; Ael. *Ep. Rust.* 14; Porphyrio at Hor. *Epist.* 1. 16. 4. For the mystic quality of silence, see Plut. *Mor.* 504A, 505F, 510E; Merkelbach (1962), 19–20. The juxtaposition of Plutarch's essays on loquacity and curiosity is no accident.

[130] Apul. *Met.* 1. 12: 'impune se relaturum meas contumelias putat...et praecedentis dicacitatis et instantis curiositatis'.

[131] Kroll (1980), 14; Syndikus (1984), 99: 'Das Gedicht ist ein Zwillingsstück zu c. 5: mit neuen Bildern und in einem anderen Ton verfolgt es das dort angeschlagene Motiv weiter'.

exchanged, they will jumble their accounts lest they themselves know
the true figure or any ill-wisher envy them when he knows how many
kisses there have been.[132] This is a strikingly direct poem and one that
includes very little beyond the accountancy metaphor that requires
any learned elucidation.[133] Poem 7 is a great deal more elaborate:

> quaeris quot mihi basiationes
> tuae, Lesbia, sint satis superque.
> quam magnus numerus Libyssae harenae
> lasarpiciferis iacet Cyrenis
> oraclum Iouis inter aestuosi
> et Batti ueteris sacrum sepulcrum;
> aut quam sidera multa, cum tacet nox,
> furtiuos hominum uident amores:
> tam te basia multa basiare
> uesano satis et super Catullo est,
> quae nec pernumerare curiosi
> possint nec mala fascinare lingua.

You ask, Lesbia, how many kissifications from you are enough and
beyond for me. As many as there are grains of sand in the Libyan desert
at silphium-bearing Cyrene between the oracle of boiling Jupiter and the
sacred tomb of ancient Battus; or as many as there are stars, when night
falls silent, that espy the secret loves of men: it is enough and beyond for
demented Catullus to kiss you so many kisses that busybodies are
unable to count them or to bewitch them with malign tongue.

The poem opens by reporting a question from Lesbia who is a
perhaps a little tired of her lover's exuberance: precisely how many
kisses will be enough and more for him? There follows a succession of figures of innumerability—the grains of sand in the desert,
the number of stars in the sky—which are expressed in such a way
as to presuppose knowledge of the silphium trade of Libyan Cyrene,[134] the oracle of Jupiter at Ammon,[135] Callimachus' account of
Battus the founder of Cyrene,[136] and even perhaps the work of the

---

[132] Catull. 5. 11–13: 'conturbabimus illa, ne sciamus, | aut ne quis inuidere possit, |
cum tantum sciat esse basiorum'.

[133] For *conturbare* as a technical term implying intentional confusion or falsifica-
tion of the balance, see Syndikus (1984), 96 n. 19; *TLL* iv. 808. 6–20.

[134] *lasarpicifer* is a neologism equating to Str. 2. 5. 37 σιλφιοφόρος.

[135] Prop. 4. 1. 103; Str. 17. 1. 42–3; Luc. 9. 511–86; Plin. *HN* 5. 31.

[136] Callim. *Hymn.* 2. 65. For Battus as mythical founder of Cyrene, see also Pind.
Pyth. 4 and 5; Hdt. 4. 150–5; Str 17. 3. 21: λέγεται δὲ ἡ Κυρήνη κτίσμα Βάττου·
πρόγονον δὲ τοῦτον ἑαυτοῦ φάσκει Καλλίμαχος. For a more recent Battus as father of
Callimachus, see Suda s.v. Καλλίμαχος who refers to the poet as son of Battus and

mathematician Archimedes entitled *Psammites* or *Sand-Reckoner*,[137] and the efforts of Hipparchus to catalogue and to count the stars.[138]

When at the close of the poem Catullus suggests that he requires so many kisses that busybodies (*curiosi*) can neither count nor bewitch them with a malign tongue, those he seeks to frustrate correspond to the ill-wishers (*mali*) of poem 5.[139] These unwelcome witnesses to Catullus' activities also anticipate the *curiosi* of Martial 11. 63. This poem opens with the accusation that Philomusus watches Martial every time he goes to the baths and asks him why he has such well-hung and smooth-skinned boys for company. The question receives a straightforward response: they shaft busybodies (*curiosos*).[140]

Martial thus responds to an essential feature of the *curiosi* of poem 7 and by extension of the censorious old men and ill-wishers of poem 5: their unwelcome interest in the sexual proclivities of others. This, however, may not exhaust the significance of the term *curiosi* for poem 7. Two points may be made. First, the extravagantly learned style adopted here by Catullus is one that a Greek writer might well call *periergos* and a Latin author *curiosus*.[141] The close of the poem may thus include a sly acknowledgement of what differentiates it from the less flamboyantly phrased poem 5. Second, the activity with which Catullus first associates the *curiosi* is the precise calculation of the number of kisses that he and Lesbia will share. In this context it may therefore be helpful to compare a very different writer—Philo of Alexandria—who notes that the number of sheaves stored up by Joseph in the seven years of plenty was so great that not even those assigned to the task could apply their *periergia* and count them.[142]

Mesatma. For Battiades as a way of naming Callimachus, see Callim. *Epigr.* 35 Pfeiffer; Catull. 65. 16 and 116. 2; Ov. *Am.* 1. 15. 13; *Ib.* 55; *Tr.* 2. 367; Stat. *Silv.* 5. 3. 157.

[137] For this work, see the Teubner edition of Archim. ii. 216–59; Heath (1921), ii. 81–5; Netz (2009), 30–3, 56–8, 105–6, 166–7.

[138] For Hipparchus, see Heath (1921), ii. 255; Netz (2009), 33. For the figures of innumerability in this poem as a whole, see Syndikus (1984), 100–1 and nn. 6–9. For such figures in ancient and modern literature, see the material collected in McCartney (1960).

[139] Kroll (1980), ad loc.

[140] Mart. 11. 63: 'spectas nos, Philomuse, cum lauamur, | et quare mihi tam mutuniati | sint leues pueri subinde quaeris. | dicam simpliciter tibi roganti: | pedicant, Philomuse, curiosos'.

[141] Quint. *Inst.* 8. 3. 55. For more on such terminology, see Ch. 5 Sect. 2.

[142] Philo *Jos.* 158: πίστις δὲ σαφεστάτη τὸ μηδ' ἀριθμηθῆναι δύνασθαι, καίτοι μυρία τινων πονηθέντων, οἷς ἐπιμελές, περιεργίαι διαριθμήσασθαι. Perhaps even closer to Catullus is August. *Conf.* 5. 3. 3–4: 'nec inueniris a superbis, nec si illi *curiosa peritia* numerent stellas et harenam et dimetiantur sidereas plagas et uestigent uias astrorum'.

When Catullus returns to kissing and counting in poem 48, he tells Iuventius that he could not be sated even if the crop of their kisses should be thicker than the dry heads of grain.[143]

(10) *POLYPRAGMONES, PERIERGOI,* AND *CURIOSI* IN THE ANCIENT NOVEL

The unwelcome interest in the love life of others displayed by the *curiosi* of Catullus and Martial is also a recurrent motif in the *Satyrica* of Petronius. This motif is first to be found on the occasion of the defloration of Pannychis by Giton.[144] In what is represented as a form of wedding, the young couple are enclosed in the marriage chamber while Encolpius, Quartilla, and the rest take up positions by the threshold. Quartilla in particular applies her curious eye to a chink in the door and watches their youthful play with a lustful concentration.[145] Encolpius himself is soon drawn to join her and as their cheeks brush against each other, Quartilla takes the opportunity to plant kisses on him.[146]

Where here Encolpius plays the *curiosus* spying on others as they make love, in his later encounter with Circe he has to be assured that there is no need to fear interference and that his 'brother' Giton is far away.[147] Elsewhere the context is slightly different. Of particular importance is a passage that follows on directly from the reunion of Encolpius and Giton and their taking up residence in the house of Eumolpus.[148] A knock on the door is now followed by the entry into the room of their host, who immediately looks at Giton and comments 'I like your Ganymede. Things should go well today'.[149]

---

[143] Catull. 48. 5–6. For the heads of grain as a figure of innumerability, cf. Ov. *Met.* 11. 613–15; *Tr.* 4. 1. 57; *Pont.* 2. 7. 25.

[144] Petron. *Sat.* 25. 1 – 26. 5.

[145] Petron. *Sat.* 26. 4: 'per rimam improbe diductam adplicuerat oculum curiosum, lusumque puerilem libidinosa speculabatur diligentia'.

[146] Petron. *Sat.* 26. 5. For spying on others as they meet to make love as *polypragmosyne*, see also Phlegon F. 1. 11 Giannini, where Philinnion returns from the dead to be with her beloved Machates until spied on by her parents Demostratus and Charito. This episode contains many features typical of the Greek novel.

[147] Petron. *Sat.* 127. 7: 'neque est quod curiosum aliquem extimescas: longe ab hoc loco frater est'.

[148] Petron. *Sat.* 91.

[149] Petron. *Sat.* 92. 3: 'laudo…Ganymedem. oportet hodie bene sit'.

Encolpius, who has just seen in the gallery a painting of Ganymede taken off to heaven by the eagle, has some reason to fear that Eumolpus takes himself for a Jupiter.[150] He comments that he did not like this meddling opening and feared that he had found another Ascyltos, that is to say another rival for Giton's affections.[151] In no time at all, Eumolpus is indeed flirting with the boy.[152]

The extant remains of the *Satyrica* apply *curiosus* and *curiose* to a wide range of activities: to the meticulous work of a painter,[153] to the compositional practices of the poet Horace,[154] to a teacher not learned but painstaking,[155] to the wrapping or washing of hands,[156] even to the shelling of beans.[157] In all this, *curiosus* is no more than a synonym for *diligens*, itself another of Petronius' favourite words.[158] Whereas in Apuleius it will be suggested that the different meanings of *curiosus* shade into each other and create an overall atmosphere of overcharged mental and physical activity, in Petronius this only properly occurs in the case of the lustful concentration (*libidinosa...diligentia*) with which Quartilla spies on Giton and Pannychis as they make love.

When *curiositas* and *periergia* are such dominant categories in the *Metamorphoses* and in the Greek *Onos* to which it so closely relates, it is tempting to assume that the same will be the case in other ancient novels as well.[159] In the case of Chariton's *Callirhoe*, moreover, the curiosity of individual characters and of groups can drive the plot

---

[150] Petron. *Sat.* 83. 3.

[151] Petron. *Sat.* 92. 4: 'non delectavit me tam curiosum principium, timuique ne in contubernium recepissem Ascylti parem'. For a parallel, compare Petron. *Sat.* 13. 1 'nam adhuc ne suturae quidem attulerat rusticus curiosas manus'. Had the country-man who bought the tunic applied 'meddling' hands to it, he would have discovered the gold coins sewn up inside; instead he is selling it off with distaste as if spoil taken from a beggar (*tanquam mendici spolium etiam fastidiose uenditabat*). *TLL* iv. 1494. 6–7 suggests that 92. 4 is an otherwise unparalleled instance of object-oriented curiosity, implying that Encolpius finds his host's words 'peculiar'. For the reasons given I do not believe this to be correct. The erroneous interpretation of the passage is perpetuated by Kenny (1998), 37 and by Habermehl (2006) ad loc.

[152] Petron. *Sat.* 94. 1–2. The lacunose state of the text makes it unclear exactly how much time has passed, but Eumolpus does not seem the sort to hang around.

[153] Petron. *Sat.* 29. 4.

[154] Petron. *Sat.* 118. 5.

[155] Petron. *Sat.* 46. 6.

[156] Petron. *Sat.* 63. 6; 135. 2.

[157] Petron. *Sat.* 135. 5.

[158] Petron. *Sat.* 6. 1; 6. 3; 12. 3; 14. 5; 20. 2; etc.

[159] Whitmarsh (2011), 185–91 does what he can with the available evidence. I have also learned a lot from Hunter (2009).

forward in significant ways. We see this in the first book of the novel as the garlands and torches abandoned by the unseen komasts of the night before gather a crowd all subject to the same curiosity.[160] This in turn fires the returning Chaireas with anxiety and prompts an angry outburst against his wife.[161] If disaster is for now averted, the happiness of the married couple is not destined to last. Chaireas' Agrigentine rival suborns a friend to pretend that Callirhoe is engaged in an affair and fills him with hope, fear, and curiosity.[162] This time the plot works only too well and Chaireas, rushing into the bedroom, delivers a kick to her diaphragm from which she appears to die.[163] Callirhoe's subsequent burial, the intervention of the tomb-robbers, and her transportation to Ionia are all now set in motion. As the novel develops, other changes will also be driven by curiosity. Theron the pirate, for instance, vetoes any attempt to sell Callirhoe in Athens on account of the *periergia* and *polypragmosyne* of the city's population and the risk of falling prey to sykophants.[164] In a later episode the plans of Mithridates the Carian are undone when the people of Priene, a city of small dimensions and full of Greek curiosity, are intrigued by the wealth of the men he has sent there.[165] This interest in group psychology is also reflected in the scene of the return of hero and heroine to Syracuse and the gathering of the crowd to greet their trireme as it enters port; Chariton observes that a mob is by nature a curious thing.[166]

The role of curiosity in driving forward the plot is evident from the simple statistic that all but one of twelve references in *Callirhoe* to *polypragmosyne* or *periergia* occur in the first four books of the novel. In this respect, at least, we must observe some overlap between the narrative strategies of a rather banal Greek fiction and the eminently more sophisticated work of Apuleius. Yet to turn *Callirhoe* into another but less effective novel of curiosity and its consequences would be wrong. For the further the novel progresses, the more it identifies its true motor as jealousy (*zelotypia*) and the more Chaireas comes to repent the various mistakes that his jealous disposition led

---

[160] Char. *Call.* 1 3. 3: καὶ πᾶς ὁ παριὼν εἰστήκει κοινῷ τινι πολυπραγμοσύνης πάθει.
[161] Char. *Call.* 1. 3. 3–6.
[162] Char. *Call.* 1. 4. 4: ἐλπίδος καὶ φόβου καὶ πολυπραγμοσύνης.
[163] Char. *Call.* 1. 4. 12.
[164] Char. *Call.* 1. 11. 6.
[165] Char. *Call.* 4. 5. 4: πόλει δὲ μικρᾷ καὶ περιεργίας Ἑλληνικῆς πλήρει.
[166] Char. *Call.* 8. 6. 5: φύσει μὲν γὰρ ὄχλος ἐστὶ περίεργόν τι χρῆμα.

him to commit.[167] As Homer's Odysseus suffers for the offence he has caused to Poseidon and the Petronian Encolpius falls victim to the anger of Priapus, so Chaireas discovers that his wanderings have been due to the wrath of Aphrodite at his untimely jealousy.[168] This combination of an angry god and a central psychological or moral category around which the novel can turn is also evident in the work of Xenophon of Ephesus, where the pride in his purity of the asexual Habrocomes displeases Eros, and the girl for whom he is made to fall must endure every torment before she returns home, her own *sophrosyne* intact.[169]

In Xenophon of Ephesus, the verb *polypragmonein* refers only to the energy which one character expends in hunting after another.[170] Achilles Tatius uses the same verb for the efforts of his father to locate Clitiphon and Leucippe,[171] and the pattern holds also for the *Aethiopica* of Heliodorus.[172] More interesting, and a significant parallel for the erotic associations of *curiosus* in Petronius, is the connection between *periergia* and sex. In Longus the springtime mating of the flocks proves an inspiration for Daphnis and Chloe and he, in particular, becomes more urgent and more bold in all that they do.[173] Likewise in Achilles Tatius the effect of wine and desire on Leucippe is to embolden her to gaze more urgently at Clitiphon.[174] All that

---

[167] Char. *Call.* 1. 2. 5, 6; 1. 5. 4; 2. 5. 5; 4. 4. 9; 5. 1. 1; 5. 9. 9; 6. 6. 5; 8. 1. 3, 15; 8. 4. 4; 8. 5. 15; 8. 7. 6. For the jealousy of Dionysius, see Char. *Call.* 2. 10. 1; 3. 7. 6; 3. 9. 4; 5. 9. 9; 8. 5. 15. For the jealousy of the queen, see Char. *Call.* 6. 6. 5.

[168] Hom. *Od.* 11. 100–3; Petron. *Sat.* 139. 2; Char. *Call.* 8. 1. 3.

[169] For the anger of Eros, see Xen. Ephes. 1. 1. 5 - 1. 2. 1. For the pride of the young Habrocomes in his own *sophrosyne*, see Xen. Ephes. 1. 4. 4; 3. 12. 4. For the imperilled *sophrosyne* of Anthia, see Xen. Ephes. 5. 4. 6; 5. 5. 5; 5. 7. 2; 5. 14. 2.

[170] Xen. Ephes. 3. 9. 2; 4. 1. 2.

[171] Ach. Tat. 5. 10. 7.

[172] Heliod. *Aeth.* 2. 17. 4; 2. 20. 1; 8. 3. 5; cf. 4. 12. 2.

[173] Long. 3. 13. 4: ἐς πᾶν ἔργον περιεργότερος καὶ θρασύτερος. See also 3. 18. 4: τὸ δὲ ἐντεῦθεν οὐδὲν περιειργάζετο ξένον for Lycaenium needing to offer no further instructions in sex to Daphnis.

[174] Ach. Tat. 2. 3. 3: ἤδη δὲ καὶ αὐτὴ περιεργότερον εἰς ἐμὲ βλέπειν ἐθρασύνετο. The phrasing of this sentence reflects Ach. Tat. 1. 2. 1 and the first of the novel's ecphrases. Here the narrator describes how he was particularly drawn to that part of the picture depicting Eros as he leads the bull (ἐγὼ δὲ καὶ τὰ ἄλλα μὲν ἐπῄνουν τῆς γραφῆς, ἅτε δὲ ὢν ἐρωτικὸς περιεργότερον ἔβλεπον τὸν ἄγοντα τὸν βοῦν Ἔρωτα). For sex and *periergia*, see also Ach. Tat. 2. 38. 1–2 and 5, where Menelaos prefers the natural pleasure of sex with boys to the *periergia* and *polypragmosyne* that women bring to the act, and 5. 27. 3–4, where Clitiphon and Melite make love then and there in the cell where he has been imprisoned and he claims to prefer the *aperiergon* to the *polypragmon* in matters of sex.

now stands in the way of the lovers is the slave Conops whom Clitiphon describes as a busybody, a chatterer, and appetitive and who watches keenly over her bedchamber.[175]

(11) CONCLUSION

Across a striking range of genres, a close correspondence may be observed between the way that Latin writers employ the term *curiosus* and their Greek counterparts employ *polypragmon* and *periergos*. It did not have to be this way. When Aulus Gellius is asked to translate *polypragmosyne* and therefore ponders the closest Latin equivalent for the Greek term *pragma*, he reaches not for *cura* but for *negotium*. The free movement between the two Latin alternatives is also evident from the way that Cicero, Seneca, and others set about translating the first of Epicurus' *Kyriai Doxai*. When, moreover, *curiosus* is used as a synonym for *diligens*, the intensifying, often pejorative force commonly associated with the suffix *-osus* is lost and the meaning of the Latin adjective is far closer to the Greek *epimeles* than it is to *polypragmon* and *periergos*.

In the light of these factors, it is perhaps the more remarkable how frequently *curiosus* does indeed equate to the Greek terms at the heart of this inquiry. This is true as early as Plautus and remains so into the writers of late antiquity. Now the problem for the scholar is not just to identify this relationship but also to express the precise sense in which words as polysemous as *polypragmon* and *periergos* are being used each time that a Latin writer renders them as *curiosus*. How easy it is to go wrong is evident from the repeated tendency of scholars on Ciceronian philosophy to refer back to Madvig's original note on *curiosus* at *De Finibus* 1. 3. For though the Greek parallels adduced by Madvig correspond well enough with the sense of 'busybody' or 'meddler' that Cicero associates with *curiosus* in this particular passage, they are quite inadequate when used by the same author to elucidate *curiosus* at *De Finibus* 2. 28 or by Dougan to do

---

[175] Ach. Tat. 2. 20. 1: πολυπράγμων καὶ λάλος καὶ λίχνος. Cf. Cic. *Clu.* 175, where Nicostratus, the loyal slave of Oppianicus, reports on the attempts of his master's wife to enter into an affair and is described as 'percuriosus et minime mendax'.

the same at *Tusculan Disputations* 1. 108. In each case I have therefore attempted not only to suggest an appropriate English translation but also to propose the best possible Greek literary parallel. When it is in fact Philo of Alexandria whose use of *periergos* actually comes closest to what Cicero and maybe even Catullus means by *curiosus*, this is a reminder that linguistic usage is not the same thing as literary allusion. It can as easily have been in conversation as through reading that Cicero became acquainted with the tendency of some Greeks to associate *periergia* with quibbling argument over terminology. What Philo, writing perhaps a century later, makes clear is that the association was current in his own time and probably had been for a good while before that.

Where it was possible for the previous chapter to explicate the different meanings attributed to *polypragmon* and *periergos* in the literature of fifth- and fourth-century Greece without any reference to later Latin usage, it becomes increasingly advantageous to consider the usage of the subsequent centuries through constant cross-reference between Greek and Latin. Perhaps the most striking development in the Greek understanding of the terms in the Hellenistic period and beyond is their increasing association with the impulse to, and conduct of, scholarly research. This is also part of how Latin writers understand *curiosus* from Cicero onwards if not before. I am quite sure here, as so often elsewhere, that this is an instance of a Roman thinking in Greek but writing in Latin, and that Cicero's broadening of the semantic range of *curiosus* is on the model of the recent broadening of the range of the key Greek terms as well. Yet I would hesitate to insist that the process always was and had to be one of translation from Greek to Latin and not vice versa.

The ensuing chapters consider some of the same problems through more sustained investigations of three themes to which the concepts of *polypragmosyne* and *periergia* most frequently speak. Where the issue is the Roman empire and the world of knowledge opened up by its restless aggression, the central issue will be the capacity of *polypragmosyne* from the fifth century onwards to describe the meddlesome or interventionst state and the developing association of the same word with the process of scholarly research. *Curiosus*, by contrast, will be found to have very little to contribute to Roman reflections on the same issue. Where, however, the debate is over which branches of knowledge are either licit or illicit, useful or useless, the Latin term will be quite as prominent as its Greek equivalents. Be the issue man's thirst for knowledge of the cosmos and the divine, the desirability of a sober or an ornate style, or even the historian's choice between offering erudite entertainment and a true education for aspiring statesmen, *curiosus* will contribute quite as much as either *polypragmon* or *periergos*.

3

Polypragmosyne and Empire

(1) INTRODUCTION

This chapter brings together two versions of *polypragmosyne* that often seem to run on parallel lines: that of the individual hungry for knowledge and that of the expansionist state intervening beyond its own boundaries. It begins with consideration of the scholar as traveller and of his self-identification with the curious voyager par excellence, the Odysseus of Homer. It then turns to a writer whose Odyssean aspirations depend for their fulfilment on the agency and patronage of the very Roman state that first imposed the role of traveller on him. Where Polybius marks the end of Ehrenberg's classic study of *polypragmosyne* and the Athenian empire, where indeed his employment of the term illustrates the final sterility of this key category of earlier Athenian thought, here he points the way forward and suggests the new significance of the concept in thinking about Rome.[1] In the pages that follow on from my analysis of Polybius I therefore study geographers and historians alike for reflections on the co-dependence of conquerors and scholars in opening up and mapping new fields of knowledge. I also consider the central importance granted to the ruler as motive force in the expansion of empire and of the knowledge that it brings, and finally look to the thoroughly Thucydidean speeches of Cassius Dio and ask what is at issue when the historian weaves into Caesar's speech at Vesontio themes and phrases drawn directly from those classic expressions of Athenian imperial *polypragmosyne*: Pericles' funeral oration and the speech of Alcibiades in favour of the Sicilian Expedition.

---

[1] Ehrenberg (1947), 62 and n. 46.

(2) *APODEMIA* AND THE PURSUIT OF WISDOM

At Thucydides 1. 70 the ambassador of the Corinthians regales his Spartan audience with an account of what differentiates their collective psychology from that of the Athenians. This passage is of fundamental importance for any account of the *polypragmosyne* of the Athenian state and has already been addressed in the first chapter of this study. Yet more remains to be said about the categories introduced and in particular with regard to the Corinthian's observation that the Athenians are fearless where the Spartans delay and are ready to travel abroad where the Spartans are strongly inclined to stay at home.[2]

The contrast between the two peoples' attitudes to travel abroad effects an interesting inversion of the characteristic account of their early histories. According to Herodotus, when Croesus of Lydia began to investigate which of the Greek states he should seek as allies, he was informed that the Spartans were much-travelled while the Athenians had never quit their own land.[3] The distinction drawn is that between the Dorian origins of the Spartans and subsequent migration south and the autochthony of the Athenians, born out of the very land they still inhabit. Yet once established in the Peloponnese the Spartans demonstrate a notable reluctance to resume their travels or to take action abroad while it is the Athenians who actually intervene in support of the Ionian revolt and send the twenty ships identified by Herodotus as the start of all the trouble between Greece and Persia.[4] In Thucydides, meanwhile, the Corinthian's emphasis on Athens' openness to action outside their own realm reflects their conduct across the fifty years between the defeat of the Persian invasion and the outbreak of the Peloponnesian War, events which Thucydides narrates in the *pentekontaetia* of 1. 89–117. It also prepares the ground for the disastrous Sicilian Expedition of 415 BC to which the historian devotes books 6–7 of his work.[5]

---

[2] Thuc. 1. 70. 4: καὶ μὴν καὶ ἄοκνοι πρὸς ὑμᾶς μελλητὰς καὶ ἀποδημηταὶ πρὸς ἐνδημοτάτους. For Spartan resistance to ἀποδημία, see also Xen. *Lac.* 14. 4; Arist. fr. 543 Rose; Plut. *Lyc.* 27. 3; *Mor.* 238E. Hornblower (1991) ad loc. points to Xen. *Hell.* 4. 3. 2 for Derkyllidas, apparently atypical among the Spartans because φιλαπόδημος.

[3] Hdt. 1. 56. 2: καὶ τὸ μὲν οὐδαμῇ κω ἐξεχώρησε, τὸ δὲ πολυπλάνητον κάρτα.

[4] Hdt. 5. 97. 3.

[5] For the *pentekontaetia*, see e.g. Thuc. 1. 100. 1 for the Athenians in Pamphylia; 1. 104. 2 for Cyprus and Egypt; 1. 109–10 for Egypt again; 1. 112. 2–4 for Cyprus and

From the fifth century onwards, the language of *polypragmosyne* and *periergia* is as readily applied to the individual in relation to his fellow citizens as it is to the actions of the state, of the citizen-body as a whole. This is essential to any analysis of the concepts and has already been addressed in my first chapter. That the same point may be made with regard to travel as an expression of curiosity emerges most clearly from analysis of a text of relatively late date but which takes as its target a mode of writing rooted in the very earliest stages of Greek culture. I refer to the *True Histories* of Lucian of Samosata, a travel narrative which bases its claim to truth purely on the initial statement that everything it contains is in fact false.[6] For this is introduced as a response to others' tales of wanderings and trips abroad,[7] and what drives our narrator to leave home is precisely the spirit of curiosity and the aspiration after novelty.[8] Lucian thus couples two key concepts for this chapter: *periergia* and *apodemia*. The formulation is significant. So too is that at *True Histories* 2. 10, when the travellers reach the Islands of the Blest but are made to understand that their presence is not entirely welcome. For among those who try their case is Aristeides the Just, and he decrees that in the afterlife they must pay the penalty for their meddling and their travels.[9] Curiosity has clearly pushed these voyagers to lands where they do not belong and the censure of their conduct could scarcely come from any more authoritative source.

The tradition parodied in the *True Histories* is that of travellers' tales and paradoxography. Lucian opens his work with reference to two noted exponents of this mode: Iamboulos, whose journey south from Ethiopia as far as an island paradise is recorded at Diodorus Siculus 2. 55–60,[10] and Ctesias of Cnidus, the fifth–fourth-century

---

Egypt again; 1. 115–17 for Samos. Note also the treatment of Athens' expeditions to Cyprus and Egypt at Isoc. 8. 86–9.

[6] Luci. *Ver. hist.* 1. 4: ἐν γὰρ δὴ τοῦτο ἀληθεύσω λέγων ὅτι ψεύδομαι.

[7] Luci. *Ver. hist.* 1. 3: πλάνας τε καὶ ἀποδημίας.

[8] Luci. *Ver. hist.* 1. 5: αἰτία δέ μοι τῆς ἀποδημίας καὶ ὑπόθεσις ἡ τῆς διανοίας περιεργία καὶ πραγμάτων καινῶν ἐπιθυμία. For more on this theme, see Mette (1956), 228 nn. 1–2.

[9] Luci. *Ver. hist.* 2. 10: τῆς μὲν φιλοπραγμοσύνης καὶ τῆς ἀποδημίας, ἐπειδὰν ἀποθάνωμεν, δοῦναι τὰς εὐθύνας. This passage surely plays on Pl. *Grg.* 526c. See von Möllendorff (2000), 314.

[10] For the paradoxographical character of this narrative, note esp. Diod. Sic. 2. 55. 1: παραδοξολογουμένων, 2. 59. 4: παράδοξον. For discussion, see von Möllendorff (2000), 54 n. 64.

medic who studied Persian life and history at first hand and also wrote a multi-volume study of Indian affairs. Ctesias himself took pride in the scholarly curiosity he devoted to the study of the Persian archives,[11] but to others he was a byword for the fabulous and unreliable.[12] However, the father of such nonsense is Homer's Odysseus and the tales he tells the Phaeacians of the enslavement of the winds; of one-eyed, man-eating savages; of beasts with many heads; and of comrades changing shape under the influence of potions.[13] Odysseus then has a lot to answer for. Yet his place within the ancient history of travel and of curiosity is by no means as uniformly dishonourable as Lucian would imply. He is also the standard-bearer for a long tradition of scholar-travellers who expose themselves to the strangeness of the world beyond their shores and who seek to bring back to their readers a more comprehensive understanding of what the world can offer.[14]

Ancient celebrations of Odysseus the explorer habitually refer back to the proem to the *Odyssey* and to his description as the man who 'saw the cities of many men and got to know their minds'.[15] As we shall see in the course of this chapter, more than one scholar and historian casts himself on the basis of this line as the new Odysseus, but the first among them must be Herodotus, who points at the outset of his work to his intention to advance with his text through the cities of men.[16] And when Herodotus himself is not conducting such investigations, key figures from within his cast of characters certainly are. The first such is surely Solon, who quits Athens in order to ensure the maintenance of his laws but also with a view to

---

[11] Ctesias *FGrH* 688 F5 = Diod. Sic. 2. 32. 4: πολυπραγμονῆσαι τὰ καθ᾽ ἕκαστον καὶ συνταξάμενος τὴν ἱστορίαν εἰς τοὺς Ἕλληνας ἐξενεγκεῖν. For sceptical discussion of Ctesias' claim, see Lenfant (2004), pp. xxxvi–xxxix. See also von Möllendorff (2000), 53 n. 62.

[12] Ctesias *FGrH* 688 T11 is a collection of ancient judgements questioning the veracity of his work.

[13] Luci. *Ver. hist.* 1. 3.

[14] Marincola (2007) is now a fundamental point of reference on this topic.

[15] Hom. *Od.* 1. 3: πολλῶν δ᾽ ἀνθρώπων ἴδεν ἄστεα καὶ νόον ἔγνω; Marincola (2007), 2.

[16] Hdt. 1. 5. 3: ἐγὼ δὲ περὶ μὲν τούτων οὐκ ἔρχομαι ἐρέων ὡς οὕτως ἢ ἄλλως κως ταῦτα ἐγένετο, τὸν δὲ οἶδα αὐτὸς πρῶτον ὑπάρξαντα ἀδίκων ἔργων ἐς τοὺς Ἕλληνας, τοῦτον σημήνας προβήσομαι ἐς τὸ πρόσω τοῦ λόγου, ὁμοίως σμικρὰ καὶ μεγάλα ἄστεα ἀνθρώπων ἐπεξίων. For discussion, see Moles (1993), 96; Clarke (1999), 101 n. 55; Marincola (2007), 13–14.

scholarly inspection.[17] He travels first to Egypt and then to Lydia, where he is greeted by Croesus as one who, through devotion to wisdom and for the purpose of scholarly investigation, has travelled over much of the world.[18] What I have here translated as 'scholarly inspection', Linforth calls 'sight-seeing' and Redfield 'tourism'.[19] The essence of *theoria* is, for sure, the Greek concept of looking or watching, but there is some distance between the love of wisdom acknowledged by Croesus and the gawping wonder of the tour party.[20]

If the investigations of Solon are a surrogate for those of Herodotus himself, so too must be those of Anacharsis the Scythian.[21] Here, however, we encounter some problems. For though Anacharsis inspects great portions of the world and gains no little wisdom along the way,[22] he does not win the sympathy of his native land. On returning to Scythia, and in fulfilment of a vow taken in the course of his travels, he performs the Cyzicene rites of the Great Mother, is overseen, and promptly slain.[23] Even now, adds Herodotus, the Scythians are so troubled by his example that they routinely deny any knowledge of him.[24] This acute hostility to contamination by alien cultures is clearly a trait peculiarly associated with the Scythians, but it may also offer a warning to anyone who chooses to stand outside the modes of his own world and to learn from others. It brings to mind a passage already examined in a previous chapter: Gyges' initial refusal to gaze on the naked form of Candaules' wife

[17] Hdt. 1. 30. 1: αὐτῶν δὴ ὧν τούτων καὶ τῆς θεωρίης ἐκδημήσας ὁ Σόλων εἴνεκεν. For Solon as a surrogate for Herodotus, see Redfield (1985), 102; Montiglio (2005), 133.

[18] Hdt. 1. 30. 2: ὡς φιλοσοφέων γῆν πολλὴν θεωρίης εἴνεκεν ἐπελήλυθας.

[19] Linforth (1919), 297–8; Redfield (1985); Montiglio (2005), 119, 131–2.

[20] For the journeys of Solon, see also Arist. [*Ath. Pol.*] 11. 1; Plut. *Sol.* 2. 1: καίτοι φασὶν ἔνιοι πολυπειρίας ἕνεκα μᾶλλον καὶ ἱστορίας ἢ χρηματισμοῦ πλανηθῆναι τὸν Σόλωνα. σοφίας μὲν γὰρ ἦν ὁμολογουμένως ἐραστής; 25. 5–26. 1.

[21] That Solon and Anacharsis are equivalent figures within their own cultures is underpinned by those stories that bring them together. See esp. Diog. Laert. 1. 101–2 and Luci. *Scyth.* 4–7. When Toxaris introduces the two to each other at Luci. *Scyth.* 7, he assures Anacharsis that, in meeting Solon, he has achieved the aim of his journey, namely to see the best of Greece: ἔχεις τῆς ἀποδημίας τὰ ἆθλα, τοῦ ἔρωτος τὸ τέλος. For what sets Herodotus and Anacharsis apart, see Montiglio (2005), 129–33.

[22] Hdt. 4. 76. 2: γῆν πολλὴν θεωρήσας καὶ ἀποδεξάμενος κατ' αὐτὴν σοφίην πολλήν.

[23] Hdt. 4. 76. 5.

[24] Hdt. 4. 76. 5: καὶ νῦν ἤν τις εἴρηται περὶ Ἀναχάρσιος, οὗ φασί μιν Σκύθαι γινώσκειν, διὰ τοῦτο ὅτι ἐξεδήμησέ τε ἐς τὴν Ἑλλάδα καὶ ξεινικοῖσι ἔθεσι διεχρήσατο.

because to do so would violate the wisdom of the ancients, that every man should look at that which is proper to him.[25] What matters here is the proverbial nature of the wisdom and the manner in which it transcends the immediate context to which it is applied. It is clear, moreover, that this is a rule to which not only Lucian's Aristeides, displeased to be visited by one who has no right to do so, and the home-loving Scythian, indignant at any adulteration of inherited culture, would readily subscribe.

Asheri's note on this passage of Herodotus traces this ancient wisdom back to Pittacus of Mytilene, one of the Seven Sages.[26] Yet here we must note a certain tension. For all that such thinkers may urge us to look to what is our own, it is a commonplace of the ancient lives of the philosophers that they themselves leave home in pursuit of wisdom.[27] The technical term for such journeys is *apodemia* and Diogenes Laertius finds it distinctive in the life of Socrates that he required no *apodemia* save for the purposes of military service.[28] He is the exception who proves the rule. For those engaging on such a venture there is, moreover, no destination more compelling than the land of Egypt. It is to Egypt that Solon heads in book 1 of Herodotus; it is Egypt that Herodotus himself studies in depth in book 2; and it is to Egypt that Greeks have flocked—for trade, as mercenaries, and just to inspect the land—when Cambyses launches his invasion in book 3.[29] Centuries later, looking back on Herodotus' visit and in particular on his investigation of the sources of the Nile, Diodorus Siculus will dub him a 'man of curiosity like no other and experienced in many branches of investigation'.[30] In the ensuing sections of

---

[25] Hdt. 1. 8. 4: πάλαι δὲ τὰ καλὰ ἀνθρώποισι ἐξεύρηται, ἐκ τῶν μανθάνειν δεῖ· ἐν τοῖσι ἓν τόδε ἐστί, σκοπέειν τινὰ τὰ ἑωυτοῦ.

[26] Asheri (2007) ad loc. cites, inter alia, the wisdom of Pittacus as recorded at *Anth. Pal.* 7. 89.

[27] Plut. *Sol.* 2. 4 on Thales, Hippocrates, and Plato; Diog. Laert. 4. 29 on Arcesilaus; 8. 2 on Pythagoras; 9. 35 and 39 on Democritus; 9. 109 on Timon; Cic. *Fin.* 5. 50 on Plato, Democritus, and Pythagoras. See also Montiglio (2005), 123, 125–6; Marincola (2007), 6–8 for the pride in their travels of Democritus, Parmenides, and Hecataeus.

[28] Diog. Laert. 2. 22. The claim derives from Pl. *Cri.* 52b.

[29] Hdt. 3. 139. 1: αὐτῆς τῆς χώρης θεηταί.

[30] Diod. Sic. 1. 37. 4: Ἡρόδοτος δὲ ὁ πολυπράγμων, εἰ καί τις ἄλλος, γεγονὼς καὶ πολλῆς ἱστορίας ἔμπειρος. Note that Diod. Sic. 1. 32–41 is given in its entirety as Agatharchides *FGrH* 86 F 19 though explicit citation of Agatharchides only begins at 1. 41. 4.

this chapter, I will consider the fortunes of other Odyssean travellers
and seekers after wisdom and will attempt to trace some of the stages
in the emergence of what Diodorus here exemplifies: the very positive interpretation of *polypragmosyne* and its contribution to the
world of learning.

(3) POLYBIUS, ODYSSEUS, AND THE PURSUIT OF LEARNING

Next in line after Herodotus among the great Greek traveller-
historians and sons of Odysseus must be Polybius of Megalopolis.[31]
Already a significant figure in his homeland, Polybius was one of
many Achaean statesmen transported to Rome in 167 BC and
detained there until the senate finally agreed to their release sixteen
years later.[32] Yet if Rome initially forced travel on Polybius, it later
facilitated it for him as well, and his subsequent investigations are
inextricably linked with the expansion of the power that held him in
its thrall.

That Polybius saw himself as a latter-day Odysseus is suggested by
much within and without the text of his *Histories*. Pausanias, for
instance, describes the monument to the historian in his native
Megalopolis paying tribute to him as one who wandered over all
the land and sea.[33] Plutarch, in turn, records a witticism on the part
of Cato the Elder that is all the more effective if we presuppose the
historian's heroic self-image: when in 150 BC, even after the senate
had finally conceded the return of the Achaean exiles, Polybius
wished to resume negotiations and request that they should be
restored to the honours they had enjoyed before their imprisonment,
Cato quipped that this would be rather like Odysseus wanting to re-
enter the Cyclops' cave in order to ask for his cap and his belt.[34]
These anecdotes may in turn be related to what Polybius himself

[31] For Polybius and Odysseus, see von Scala (1890), 66–72; Walbank (1972), 125–7, and (2002), 31–52, esp. 42–4; Clarke (1999), 100–1; Marincola (2007), 16–20.
[32] Polyb. 30. 13 and 30. 32. 1–12; Paus. 7. 10. 11–12; Livy 45. 31. 9.
[33] Paus. 8. 30. 8–9, esp. 8. 30. 8: ὡς ἐπὶ γῆν καὶ θάλασσαν πᾶσαν πλανηθείη.
[34] Plut. *Cat. Mai.* 9. 3 = Polyb. 35. 6 with Walbank (1957–79) ad loc. For scholarship on this topic, see von Scala (1890), 66–72; Walbank (1972), 125–7, and (2002), 31–52, esp. 42–4; Clarke (1999), 100–1.

states in the *Histories*. For in book 9 he describes Odysseus as the man most blessed with the qualities of leadership and again in book 12 as the ideal picture of the *pragmatikos*, the man of affairs.[35] What makes him such is then underlined by citation of *Odyssey* 1. 1–3 and 8. 183: the man of affairs, we infer, must travel and learn and endure.

What Polybius here says of Odysseus aligns interestingly with a scholion to *Odyssey* 1. 3 in which the mind (νοῦς) is subjected to a threefold division into the contemplative, physical, and pragmatic (θεωρητικὸς, φυσικὸς, πραγματικός). The first of these categories relates to the philosopher's contemplation of the universe; the second is no more than that which we all possess by virtue of being alive; but the third—now restated as the practical (πρακτικός)—refers to whenever someone, having seen many cities and lands and gained experience of them, gathers together knowledge from them; for knowledge is gathered together from experience.[36] What is striking here is the scholion's employment of the term 'pragmatic'. For this is essential to Polybius' definition of his own work and the distinctions he draws between it and that of other writers of history. I refer to the opening of book 9 of the *Histories* and the definition of pragmatic history as that which concerns the deeds of peoples and cities and rulers (τὰς πράξεις τῶν ἐθνῶν καὶ πόλεων καὶ δυναστῶν) and which will be of particular interest to the statesman (πολιτικός).[37] Walbank notes that reference to 'peoples and cities and rulers' parallels the language not only of other Hellenistic historians but also of the official decrees of the Greek cities.[38] Inasmuch, however, as a key component of such a theme is the readiness of the traveller-historian actually to visit the cities and the peoples that he studies, it may be argued that this phrase alludes at a distance to that Odyssean mode of investigation to which Polybius so strongly adheres.

---

[35] Polyb. 9. 16. 1: τὸν ἡγεμονικώτατον ἄνδρα; 12. 27. 10–11: οἷον δεῖ τὸν ἄνδρα τὸν πραγματικὸν εἶναι.

[36] Schol. Hom. *Od.* 1. 3: ὡς ὅταν τις ἰδὼν πολλὰς πόλεις καὶ χώρας κἀκείνων γενόμενος ἔμπειρος ἐξ ἐκείνων γνῶσιν συνάξῃ. ἐκ γὰρ τῆς ἐμπειρίας ἡ γνῶσις συνάγεται. The term πρακτικός is also one familiar to Polybius. For its application to an effective commander, see esp. Polyb. 1. 80. 5; 2. 47. 4; 5. 18. 7; 5. 55. 2; 7. 10. 5; 11. 25. 8; 24. 7. 1; 27. 13. 2; 28. 18. 1. See also 3. 59. 4, where Paton's translation 'men of action' might be replaced with 'men capable of effective action'. Elsewhere in Polybius, πρακτικός is used for weapons, stratagems, and the like which prove effective.

[37] Polyb. 9. 1. 4.

[38] Walbank (1972), 55–6, esp. 56 and n. 145 citing Diod. Sic. 19. 57. 3; *OGIS* 229 l. 11; *Syll.* 590, ll. 121–4 ; *OGIS* 441, l. 132; *Syll.* 760; Rostovtzeff (1941), 502–3, 1347, 1439–40.

The division of modes of investigation drawn by Polybius at *Histories* 9. 1–2 also offers crucial, if potentially misleading, evidence for his concept of *polypragmosyne*. For the category of pragmatic history is contrasted first with that dealing in genealogies, which will attract those who care to listen to a story (*philekoos*), and secondly with that giving an account of colonies, foundations, and kinship, which will appeal to those of active curiosity and a taste for the recondite (*polypragmon kai perittos*). Read on its own, this passage might suggest that *polypragmosyne* in historical research is no better than what a modern historian might disdain as antiquarianism.[39] When, however, the same passage is considered in conjunction with others in which Polybius reflects on the process and the purpose of historical investigation, the historian's insistence on the taste for the recondite (*perittos*) plays a larger role; a productive distinction may thus be drawn between the end-state of being a *polypragmon kai perittos*, that is to say a man of energetic curiosity who expends it on the recondite and insignificant, and the raw curiosity of *polypragmosyne*, which can be harnessed to more serious ends. For Polybius regularly uses *polypragmosyne* and its cognate forms to describe the process of research,[40] and also describes the ill-informed man as *apragmon*.[41] There is much criticism here of the energy which Timaeus in particular devotes to maligning his predecessors,[42] and of his predilection for documentary sources over travel and autopsy,[43] but this is juxtaposed with that mode of investigation which Polybius himself favours,[44] and *polypragmosyne* when applied to appropriate ends will furnish the practical *empeiria* which pragmatic history offers the politician.[45]

The manner in which Polybius applies *polypragmosyne* and its cognates to the field of scholarly research is suggestive of a significant rehabilitation of a concept that the fifth and fourth centuries treated with suspicion and disdain. This process is also visible in his

---

[39] I return to this issue in Ch. 5 Sect. 5.

[40] Polyb. 5. 75. 6; 12. 25c. 2; 12. 25e. 1; 12. 25i. 2; 12. 26. 9; 12. 26e. 3; 12. 27. 1–3, 4–6; 12. 28. 2–4; 14. 1a. 4; 15. 36. 3; 36. 1. 6–7.

[41] Polyb. 9. 29. 2. Cf. Arist. *Mete.* 369b27 ἀπραγμόνως for claims made with insufficient scholarly rigour.

[42] Polyb. 12. 25c. 2.

[43] Polyb. 12. 25e. 1; 12. 25i. 2; 12. 26. 9; 12. 26e. 3; 12. 27. 1–6; 12. 28. 2–4.

[44] Polyb. 12. 27. 1–11; 12. 28a. 2–4.

[45] Polyb. 5. 75. 6; cf. 1. 1. 6; 9. 2. 5.

employment of the concept in relation to the reconnaissance under-
taken by a state or a general,[46] or to the activities of those scientists
who study the stars[47] or measure the height of an object standing
straight on a flat surface.[48] Yet these usages must be set against those
instances where he visibly maintains the categories of earlier centuries, and this is particularly true with regard to inter-state relations
and the intervention of one nation in the affairs of another. When,
for instance, he comes to describe the resistance of Aratus of Sicyon
to Antigonus Gonatas and the Aetolians, he dubs their intervention
in Achaean affairs *polypragmosyne* and *pleonexia*,[49] and treats it as
manifestly unjust behaviour.[50] The negative understanding of the
concept is also evident in the claim of Antiochus that the Romans
have no business intervening (*polypragmonein*) in the affairs of the
Greek cities of Asia at a time when he in no way meddles (*periergazdesthai*) with the cities of Italy.[51] Only when describing the
Roman decision to intervene in the affairs of Spain in response to
the alarming growth of the power of Hasdrubal, does Polybius use
the verb *polypragmonein* in potentially a more neutral sense.[52]

It is one thing to identify the range of meanings attributed by
Polybius to *polypragmosyne* and its cognates but quite another to
consider how they relate to each other. What do the pejorative
implications of their usage when applied to the state have to do
with the essentially positive account of the individual scholar and
his activities? Do they stand apart in the well-policed subheadings of
the dictionary entry or do they run together in potentially more
intriguing ways? This is a question which the historian at once
addresses and evades.

[46] Polyb. 3. 80. 2; 5. 109. 5; 8. 24. 10; 31. 1. 8.
[47] Polyb. 9. 15. 7; 9. 19. 5.
[48] Polyb. 9. 19. 9.
[49] Polyb. 2. 43. 9; 2. 45. 6.
[50] Polyb. 2. 43. 10; 2. 45. 6; cf. 2. 56. 14. For the Achaean Polybius' consistent
hostility to Aetolia, see Walbank (1957–79) at Polyb. 2. 43. 9.
[51] Polyb. 18. 51. 2. Cf. App. *Syr.* 13, 23; Diod. Sic. 28. 12. 1; 28. 15. 2; Livy 33. 40. 1–2.
[52] Polyb. 2. 13. 3. Cf. App. *Hisp.* 9, which follows on directly from the 1–8
description of the *situs* of Spain, and attributes the first act of interventionist *polypragmosyne* to the Carthaginians. All other references to *polypragmosyne* in Appian
save *Mac.* 1 regard such interventionism and expansionism (*Lib.* 135; *Syr.* 13, 23; *Celt.*
fr. 2. 3). Note also App. *B Civ.* 2. 89 for the temporary quietism of Caesar in
Alexandria described as *apragmosyne*.

The problems posed may be encapsulated in a passage found at Pliny, *Natural History* 5. 9 and attributed by Büttner-Wobst to the entirely geographical book 34 of the *Histories*.[53] What Pliny here describes is how, at the time that Scipio Aemilianus was conducting operations in Africa, that is to say in 146 BC and towards the close of the Third Punic War, Polybius received from him a fleet with which to examine the westward coastline of that region as far as Mount Atlas and beyond.[54] Polybius here was sailing seas that he himself assures us were once sailed by his hero Odysseus,[55] but it may properly be asked how much the fleet furnished for him by his patron had in common with the twelve scarlet-cheeked ships of the man of Ithaca.[56] If these are both state fleets, the one state is a poor, craggy island off the coast of Acarnania, the other the mistress of the Mediterranean world.

If Rome was now the mistress of the world, she was also capable of revealing herself a very cruel mistress indeed. The resumption of hostilities against Carthage in 149 BC had provoked unhappy commentary around the Greek world, commentary which Polybius himself records.[57] There is, moreover, no more anguished portion of the work of Polybius than his description of the events surrounding the 146 BC destruction of Corinth and of Carthage. The historian himself is a witness to events and is seen at one moment hastening to the side of Scipio, at another pleading with Mummius for the preservation of the statues of Philopoemen or groaning over the thuggish squaddies who throw to the ground Aristeides' portrait of Dionysus and use it as a draughtsboard.[58] Yet without Rome Polybius would surely have

---

[53] Although book 34 is itself entirely devoted to geography, it is somewhat arbitrary to place in it any fragment of a geographical nature quoted without reference to the specific book in which it first appeared. For Polyb. 12. 25 d–e treats an understanding of geography (or more accurately chorography) as a prerequisite for effective historical analysis, and such matters are therefore handled throughout his narrative. On this point, see van Paassen (1957), 290–313, esp. 292–4 and 304–5; Clarke (1999) 77–128.

[54] Polyb. 34. 15. 7. For more data garnered from this voyage, see Polyb. 34. 15. 8–9; 34. 16. 1–3. Note Polyb. 34. 16. 2 = Plin. *HN* 8. 47 for the historian described as 'Aemiliani comes'.

[55] Polyb. 1. 39. 1–4 identifies the island of Meninx off the coast of Libya with the land of the Lotus-eaters.

[56] Hom. *Il.* 2. 637; *Od.* 9. 159.

[57] Polyb. 36. 9 gives a range of Greek responses—positive and negative—to Rome's renewal of this conflict.

[58] Polyb. 38. 14. 3; 38. 19–22; 39. 2–3.

been much worse placed to conduct his voyage of exploration: Carthaginian resistance to the navigation and exploration of these seas was noted.[59] For all the pathos and indignation generated by the fall of Carthage, her elimination did wonders for the development of Graeco-Roman geography. It is to Polybius that we look both for the narrative of her fall and for the charting of the coast of Africa that that fall allowed.[60]

The pattern suggested by the North African voyages of Polybius leaves its mark on his understanding of *polypragmosyne*. This emerges most clearly at *Histories* 3. 58–9, where he first celebrates the opportunities for geographical *polypragmosyne* enjoyed by his own age,[61] and then admits that these are to be put down to the fact that the dominance first of Alexander, then of the Romans has made it possible to travel almost anywhere by land and sea.[62] It is even thanks to Rome that the men of action of Greece have been freed from any practical involvement in politics and can devote themselves to scientific work instead.[63] Just like Polybius himself.

This is a crucial formulation and one in which the different senses of *polypragmosyne* all but bleed into each other. Hence my suggestion that Polybius actually addresses the implications of the way that he uses this term. No less significant, however, are his evasions. In book 12 of the *Histories*, Polybius launches an extended assault on the third-century Greek historian Timaeus of Tauromenium. Among the many faults attributed to this scholar is his frank confession that he spent fifty years at work in Athens but never enjoyed any

---

[59] That this is Pliny's understanding is confirmed by Plin. *HN* 5. 11–15, where a further stage of expansion of Roman knowledge of Africa is identified: the Mauretanian campaign of Suetonius Paulinus in AD 42. For the specific seas sailed by Polybius, cf. Eratosthenes ap. Str. 17. 1. 19 and his complaint that the Carthaginian tendency to sink any ships making for Sardinia or the pillars of Hercules renders most geographical accounts of the western region unreliable. For Polybius and the fleet of Scipio, see Walbank (1948), 160; Momigliano (1979), 66; Nicolet (1991), 30; Cotta Ramosino (2001), 221–2; Woolf (2011), 59, 61.

[60] Momigliano (1980), 125–7 is eloquent on the discomfort of Polybius' position.

[61] See esp. Polyb. 3. 58. 5; cf. 3. 59. 4.

[62] Polyb. 3. 59. 3: ἐν δὲ τοῖς καθ' ἡμᾶς τῶν μὲν κατὰ τὴν Ἀσίαν διὰ τὴν Ἀλεξάνδρου δυναστείαν τῶν δὲ λοιπῶν τόπων διὰ τὴν Ῥωμαίων ὑπεροχὴν σχεδὸν ἁπάντων πλωτῶν καὶ πορευτῶν γεγονότων. The importance of this formulation is noted by Nicolet (1991), 30, 64–5, 85.

[63] Polyb. 3. 59. 3–4: ἀπολελυμένων δὲ καὶ τῶν πρακτικῶν ἀνδρῶν τῆς περὶ τὰς πολεμικὰς καὶ πολιτικὰς πράξεις φιλοτιμίας, ἐκ δὲ τούτων πολλὰς καὶ μεγάλας ἀφορμὰς εἰληφότων εἰς τὸ πολυπραγμονεῖν καὶ φιλομαθεῖν.

active experience of warfare or visited the places that he describes.[64] Polybius' scorn for this approach reaches its greatest height when he records the determination of Timaeus to track down manuscript sources on the Celts and the Ligurians when he would have done better to visit them in person.[65] Yet what he does not add at this point is that his own acquaintance with the same peoples, much like the arduous travels to Libya, Spain, and Gaul proclaimed at 3. 59. 7, were all conducted in concert with those Roman governors and commanders who took him under their wing.[66]

Polybius may see himself as a latter-day Odysseus, but it is reasonable to suggest that this role is better fulfilled by men such as the great privateer navigator Pytheas of Massilia.[67] Yet Polybius is consistent in his disparagement of Pytheas and refuses to believe that a private citizen, let alone one as poor as Pytheas, could possibly have completed the journeys that he claims.[68] For anyone seeking to do the job of exploration properly, a state-sponsored fleet is clearly a necessary prerequisite.[69] When *Histories* 3. 38. 2 observes that the region of northern Europe between the Don and the Narbo is destined to remain unknown until the curiosity of future investigators (*polypragmonountes*) drives them in that direction, it may be assumed that their work will best be done in the wake of a Roman conquering army.[70] This is, without doubt, a long way from the world of Odysseus.

---

[64] Polyb. 12. 25d. 1; 12. 25h. 1; Marincola (2007), 23–5.

[65] Polyb. 12. 28a. 2–4.

[66] For attempts to date these journeys, see Walbank (1957–79), i. 393–4. For the imperial context of these journeys, see van Paassen (1957), 307–8; Momigliano (1979), 66.

[67] For a sympathetic account of Pytheas' achievement, see Thomson (1948), 143–51.

[68] Polyb. 34. 5. 1–9; 34. 10. 6–7 attacks Pytheas. Note esp. 34. 5. 7 on Pytheas as ἰδιώτῃ ἀνθρώπῳ καὶ πένητι. For his motives in doing so, see Walbank (1962), 10–11. For disdain for the quality of evidence garnered by merchant voyagers, see also Polyb. 4. 39. 11; 4. 42. 7; 34. 10. 6–7; Caes. *B Gall*. 4. 20–1; Str. 2. 3. 4; 15. 1. 4: οὗτοι δ' ἰδιῶται καὶ οὐδὲν πρὸς ἱστορίαν τῶν τόπων χρήσιμοι; Tac. *Agr*. 24. 2; Nicolet (1991), 58, 67, 70.

[69] For a modern reflection of this theory, see Dion (1977), 175–81 arguing that Pytheas must have been a 'praemissus explorator' sent out by Alexander.

[70] Tandoi (1967), 50–1.

(4) ARRIAN ON ALEXANDER AND THE GYMNOSOPHISTS

It would be foolish to describe Polybius as anything as straightforward as a critic of Roman imperial expansion, but he himself had seen some of the worst of what that process brought and his *Histories* record the foreboding of the Greeks at the dark cloud rising across the Adriatic, the resentment felt at Roman meddling in the affairs of Asia Minor, and the shock of many Greeks at the resumption of hostilities against Carthage ahead of its final sack.[71] The effect is impressive in its polyphony. The dialogue generated between those passages that decry the *polypragmosyne* of imperial expansion and those others that celebrate the opportunities for scholarly *polypragmosyne* furnished by that same empire is necessarily complex.

The same process may also be seen in Arrian. Alexander, as we have seen, is given as much credit by Polybius as are the Romans for the increased opportunities for scholarly *polypragmosyne*, and later we will examine other witnesses to the same view. What, however, do the ancient biographies and histories of Alexander have to say about the impulses that first led him to enter into his expeditions? Here the key concept seems to be the longing or *pothos* that seizes him at different moments and sets him off on new journeys and new campaigns.[72] This Ehrenberg distinguishes from the 'indiscriminate restlessness' of *polypragmosyne* and therefore declines to map the individual psychology of Alexander onto the collective psychology of fifth-century Athens.[73]

Yet there remains one famous passage in which Alexander is accused of *polypragmosyne*, and it may be of value to revisit this and to connect it to other sections of Arrian's work. In book 7 of the *Anabasis*, Alexander encounters the gymnosophists of India, who respond to his arrival by beating their feet upon the ground.[74] When Alexander asks the meaning of this action, they reply that each man owns no more of the earth than that on which he stands and that Alexander himself is a restless meddler and a wretch who travels far

---

[71] Polyb. 5. 104. 10; 9. 37. 10; 18. 51. 1–2; 36. 9. 5–8.

[72] Arr. *Anab.* 1. 3. 5; 2. 3. 1; 3. 1. 5; 3. 3. 1; 4. 28. 4; 5. 2. 5; 7. 1. 1; 7. 16. 2. For this motif, cf. Curt. 4. 7. 8 'cupido . . . adeundi Iouem'; 9. 9. 1 'cupido uisendi Oceanum'.

[73] Ehrenberg (1947), 62–7.

[74] Arr. *Anab.* 7. 1. 5.

from his own land making trouble for himself and for others.[75] He should remember that his own death is near and that he will hold only as much earth as is needed to bury him.[76] Ehrenberg detects here the influence of Hellenistic philosophy, particularly Cynicism, and connects it to other fictions in which Alexander discourses with the gymnosophists and sets them questions to which they offer often surprising answers.[77] Yet there is more to say and it is worth underlining that what *polypragmosyne* means in this context is what we have already seen it to mean in many writers of the fifth and fourth century: the neglect of one's own affairs and the constant imposition of trouble on others as well as on oneself. It is further essential to note that Arrian introduces this meeting with the gymnosophists in the context of speculation on the full extent of Alexander's ambitions to travel onwards, be it by sailing south into the Arabian Gulf with a view to circumnavigating Africa, or to journey into the Black Sea, or potentially even to reach Britain.[78]

What matters here is that the *polypragmosyne* that the gymnosophists decry in Alexander, the readiness constantly to stir up trouble for others, is connected with the undertaking of ever more ambitious journeys of conquest and exploration. Hence the importance of two further passages from the same author's work on the geography and ethnography of India, the *Indica*. In the first of these, Arrian notes that nobody invaded India between Heracles and Alexander, not even Cyrus son of Cambyses, who attacked the Scythians and was in other respects the most restless or meddling of all the rulers of Asia.[79] Arrian adds that, because of their justice, no Indian had ever launched a military expedition outside his own country.[80] In this way the attitude of the Indians is the opposite of that attributed to Alexander by the sophists: where he leaves his own country out of *polypragmosyne*, it is their commitment to justice that induces them

[75] Arr. *Anab.* 7. 1. 6: πολυπράγμων καὶ ἀτάσθαλος ἀπὸ τῆς οἰκείας τοσαύτην γῆν ἐπεξέρχῃ πράγματα ἔχων τε καὶ παρέχων ἄλλοις.
[76] Arr. *Anab.* 7. 1. 6.
[77] Ehrenberg (1947), 62–3. For Alexander and the gymnosophists, see e.g. Plut. *Alex.* 64.
[78] Arr. *Anab.* 7. 1. 1–4.
[79] Arr. *Ind.* 9. 10: ἐπὶ Σκύθας ἐλάσαντα καὶ τἆλλα πολυπραγμονέστατον δὴ τῶν κατὰ τὴν Ἀσίαν βασιλέων γενόμενον.
[80] Arr. *Ind.* 9. 12: οὐ μὲν δὴ οὐδὲ Ἰνδῶν τινα ἔξω τῆς οἰκείης σταλῆναι ἐπὶ πολέμῳ διὰ δικαιότητα.

never to quit their own. This passage may now be compared with the closing chapter of the *Indica* and Arrian's reflections on what may be known of the world to the south of the Arabian Gulf. Arrian refers to the men sent out by Alexander to sail as far as they could to the right of the Persian Gulf, but adds that nobody has ever passed beyond the cape that Nearchus describes as appearing opposite Carmania. He comments that, were these regions able to be sailed or marched over, they would have been revealed as such by the *polypragmosyne* of Alexander.[81] Arrian needs no telling that the same *polypragmosyne* that is so rightly deplored in Alexander also facilitates the composition of works such as the *Indica*. The justice of the home-loving Indians is all very admirable but it is of little help to those who wish to map the world beyond.

(5) DIODORUS SICULUS AND IMPERIAL
POLYPRAGMOSYNE

It will be apparent that the concept of *polypragmosyne* is central to Polybius', and later to Arrian's, understanding of geographical knowledge, of empire, and of the expansion of both. The ensuing pages seek to trace the same ideas in a succession of geographers and historians of the Roman empire.

Of all the extant Greek historians, the closest to Polybius in the range of senses that he attributes to *polypragmosyne* is Diodorus Siculus. He applies the concept to personal involvement in politics;[82] to the individual's interference in what is not appropriate to him;[83] to prying inquiry by an individual;[84] to the statesman's bid to inform himself about a situation or individual;[85] to state supervision of morals;[86] and, when negated, to the failure to take an interest in what otherwise might be expected to be a matter of concern.[87] Most

---

[81] Arr. *Ind.* 43. 8–10: δοκέω δὲ ὡς εἴπερ πλωτά τε ἦν καὶ βαδιστὰ <τὰ> ταύτῃ, ὑπ᾽ Ἀλεξάνδρου ἂν τῆς πολυπραγμοσύνης ἐξελήλεγκτο πλωτά τε καὶ βαδιστὰ ἐόντα.

[82] Diod. Sic. 10. 7. 3; 13. 94. 2.

[83] Diod. Sic. 4. 44. 1; 11. 56. 7.

[84] Diod. Sic. 10. 8. 3.

[85] Diod. Sic. 9. 8. 1; 12. 19. 1.

[86] Diod. Sic. 2. 41. 3.

[87] Diod. Sic. 20. 41. 5; 20. 43. 6; 20. 54. 7; cf. 16. 5. 1.

significantly, the term features both in diplomatic debates where one party expresses amazement at the intervention of another in their proper sphere of influence,[88] and, as already noted, in accounts of scholarly research, be it the efforts of Herodotus to study the Nile or the hours spent by Ctesias of Cnidus reading through the archives of ancient Persia.[89]

Yet where Diodorus most closely parallels the patterns of thought established in Polybius is in his account of the Eastern embassy of Scipio Aemilianus, commonly dated to the years 140–139 BC.[90] Justin describes this repeatedly as a voyage of inspection and the formulation parallels one Roman way of thinking about the voyages of Odysseus.[91] A similar formulation is also present in both Strabo and Plutarch: to the former the tour of inspection concerns itself with peoples and cities; to the latter with cities and peoples and kings.[92] It is as if Scipio is composing his own pragmatic history. Should he need a hand, the Stoic Panaetius is along to help out.[93] This then is the context in which it may be appropriate to consider the extended account of the visit to Alexandria at Diodorus Siculus 33. 28b. 1–3. The purpose attributed by Diodorus to the Egyptian

---

[88] Diod. Sic. 15. 51. 4; 21. 1. 5; 23. 2. 1; 28. 12; 28. 15. 2–4.

[89] Diod. Sic. 1. 37. 3–4; 2. 32. 4. For these passages, see Sect. 2.

[90] Diodorus cites no source for this passage, but Theiler (1982) includes it as fr. 127 in his edition of Posidonius and attributes it to the latter's *Histories after Polybius*. The passage is excluded from the more cautious edition of Edelstein and Kidd (1972–88), but it is worth noting that Posidonius fr. 125a Theiler = Plut. *Mor.* 777A, fr. 125c Theiler = Ath. 273 A–B, and fr. 126 Theiler = Ath. 549 D–E explicitly cite Posidonius and Polybius for different aspects of the embassy, including the visit to Ptolemy Physcon. Malitz (1983), 249–51 follows Theiler's attribution. For discussion of the contribution of Posidonius to different aspects of geography, see Momigliano (1979), 67, 71–2 and Nicolet (1991), 64–6. Note esp. Nicolet (1991), 65 for Posidonius as 'an encyclopaedist—mathematician, physicist, philosopher, historian—and a man of his time interested in the development of Roman politics in the world'.

[91] Just. *Epit.* 38. 8. 8–11 describes the embassy and the contrasting moral figures cut by Ptolemy and Scipio. Note esp. the reference to the inspection of allied kingdoms: 'ad inspicienda sociorum regna ... Africanus, dum inspicit urbem, spectaculo Alexandrinis fuit'. For Scipio as an imperial Odysseus, consider Hor. *Epist.* 1. 2. 18–20 on Homer's hero as the 'utile ... exemplar' who 'urbis | et mores hominum inspexit'. Horace too is thinking about Hom. *Od.* 1. 1–3 but opts for Zenodotus' νόμον over the vulgate νόον in v. 3.

[92] Str. 14. 5. 2: ἐπισκεψόμενον τὰ ἔθνη καὶ τὰς πόλεις; Plut. *Mor.* 200E–F: πόλεων ἐθνεῶν βασιλέων ἐπίσκοπον.

[93] Cic. *Acad. Pr.* 2. 2. 5; Plut. *Mor.* 200F, 777A–C. The suggestion at Ath. 549D that the companion of Scipio was Posidonius appears erroneous.

embassy is the detailed inspection or survey of the entire kingdom.[94]
Ptolemy Physcon endeavours to seduce the party with feasts and
entertainments; the austere and frugal Romans concern themselves
not with such fripperies but rather with a detailed examination of all
that is truly significant,[95] and of what so rich a land and so numerous
a population has to offer in terms of security and growth of empire.[96]
Historians decry the suggestion that the closing reference to the
potential might of Egypt should it acquire leaders worthy of it implies
any Roman plan to annex or occupy.[97] But the ambassadors surely
concluded that, should just such a ruler emerge, this would consitute
a threat to Roman domination and require swift attention. For now
Egypt could struggle on under the corpulent Physcon,[98] just as the
pirates of Cilicia could be left to enfeeble the Seleucids and fill up the
slave market on Delos.[99] Here again, therefore, we see that detailed
examination of countries and kings which Polybius associates with
pragmatic history. This is scholarly *polypragmosyne* in the service of
empire. It may not lead directly to that other *polypragmosyne* which
is the direct intervention in the affairs of the land surveyed, but it is
vital preparatory work should the need or the aspiration subsequently arise.

(6) STRABO, PLINY, AND IMPERIAL GEOGRAPHY

The fundamental interdependence of scholarship and empire is
encapsulated in Polybius' assertion that the conquests of Alexander
and the Romans have opened up new fields for the *polypragmosyne*
of the learned.[100] He is neither the first nor the last ancient geographer to make such an admission. Writing in the third century BC,
the great scholar of Ptolemaic Alexandria, Eratosthenes, attributes
the recent expansion of geographical knowledge to the conquests

[94] Diod. Sic. 33. 28b. 1: κατασκεψόμενοι, 3: κατασκεψάμενοι.
[95] Diod. Sic. 33. 28b. 2: τὰ θέας ἄξια πρὸς ἀλήθειαν ἐπολυπραγμόνησαν ἀκριβῶς.
[96] Diod. Sic. 33. 28b. 2: ὡς εὖ διάκειται πρὸς ἡγεμονίας ἀσφάλειάν τε καὶ μέγεθος.
[97] Gruen (1984), ii. 715 and n. 207 citing H. Winkler (1933), 67–73.
[98] For the corruption of Alexandria under Ptolemy Physcon, see esp. the eyewit-
ness account of Polyb. 34. 14.
[99] Str. 14. 5. 2.   [100] Polyb. 3. 59. 3–4.

of Alexander.[101] The Augustan geographer Strabo goes one step further and acknowledges first Mithridates and his generals, then the Parthians.[102] Half a century later, Pliny the Elder asks why more was done to further learning in those days when the sea was infested by pirates than in the present, when peace is secure and the emperor devoted to the furtherance of letters.[103] Yet the same scholar also celebrates what Rome's advance has done for the expansion of medical science and his works make numerous references to recent advances in various fields of knowledge.[104]

Scholars need empire and empire needs scholars.[105] Such is the weight of the geographers' programmatic reflections on their task. How this may then be reflected in the more detailed exposition of lands and places has already been illustrated by reference to Polybius' voyages of exploration along the coast of North Africa in a borrowed Roman fleet and at the time of the Third Punic War. That passage is itself transmitted by Pliny the Elder and it is essential to look to his *Natural History* and before it to the *Geography* of Strabo in order to document the broader patterns that emerge.

It is hard to think of a Greek intellectual more devoted to Rome than Strabo. Throughout the seventeen books of the *Geography*, he appears unwilling to offer any direct criticism of the empire or of its impact on the conquered peoples. He acknowledges his personal friendship with Aelius Gallus and comments on what this gentleman's Arabian expedition revealed (and what it might have revealed but for the actions of the rascal Syllaeus).[106] Elsewhere he looks to the reports of Roman provincial governors and the historians of

---

[101] Eratosth. ap. Str. 1. 2. 1; 1. 3. 3.

[102] Str. 1. 2. 1: τὰ δὲ ἐπέκεινα μέχρι Μαιωτῶν καὶ τῆς εἰς Κόλχους τελευτώσης παραλίας Μιθριδάτης ὁ κληθεὶς Εὐπάτωρ ἐποίησε γνώριμα καὶ οἱ ἐκείνου στρατηγοί· οἱ δὲ Παρθυαῖοι τὰ περὶ τὴν Ὑρκανίαν καὶ τὴν Βακτριανὴν καὶ τοὺς ὑπὲρ τούτων Σκύθας γνωριμωτέρους ἡμῖν ἐποίησαν.

[103] Plin. *HN* 2. 117–18; 14. 1–7; Naas (2002), 408–16, and (2011), 68–9.

[104] For medicine, see Plin. *HN* 27. 1–3. Those studies that focus on Pliny's more histrionic laments for the current failure to expand knowledge ignore his references to recent acquisitions. See e.g. *HN* 9. 160; 17. 43, 116, 137, 162; 18. 172, 183, 209, 317; 22. 128; 23. 56; 25. 17, 59, 86, 87; 26. 38; 34. 2, 127; 37. 45–6.

[105] For the relationship between geography and empire and the passages discussed above, see Berger (1903), 327–32, 500–1; Fraser (1972), i. 520, 527, 535, 538; Murray (1972), 201–2; Dion (1977), 235–6; Gabba (1984); Conte (1994), 73–6; Clarke (1999), 66–76; Murphy (2004), 163–4; Woolf (2011), 78–9.

[106] Str. 2. 5. 12; 16. 4. 22, 24; 17. 1. 53.

Pompey's Eastern campaigns,[107] but also attributes the lack of accurate information on north-eastern Europe beyond the Elbe to Augustus' policy of restraint.[108] If the Romans have a fault, it is an
insufficient devotion to knowledge (φιλείδημον) and undue readiness
to parrot what the Greeks have already said about distant peoples.[109]

Rome, however, is far from being the geographer's only point of
reference. Alexander's Eastern campaigns are a crucial spur to geographical investigation,[110] and the extended account of India draws
repeatedly on the claims of those who travelled with him or held
commands under him.[111] Strabo's family is also deeply implicated in
the politics of the Pontic kingdom, and his initial acknowledgement
of what Mithridates did for geography is borne out by a number of
subsequent observations.[112] The same is true for the Parthian empire
and its historians,[113] though the loss of Strabo's *Histories* denies us a
more extensive account of their achievement.[114]

Pliny, meanwhile, devotes books 3–6 of his *Natural History* to an
exposition of the geography of the known world.[115] Each book takes
the reader on an extended journey, measuring the distances between
places, describing their most noteworthy features, and offering information on how they were discovered. The last feature has no
prominence in book 3, which covers the most familiar part of the
globe, from western Spain through southern Gaul, the Augustan
regions of Italy, and up to the northern Adriatic. Book 4, by contrast,
enters only recently charted terrain. Having journeyed down the
Adriatic and on around Greece, it takes the reader up into Thrace
and Scythia, then on into the islands of the Baltic, round the outer
Ocean and back to northern Spain. Here we hear of twenty-three
islands off southern Scandinavia discovered by Roman arms;[116] are
informed that Agrippa underestimated the dimensions of Germany

---

[107] Str. 2. 5. 33; 11. 3. 5; 11. 6. 4.
[108] Str. 7. 1. 4. For repeated acknowledgement of relative ignorance of this region,
see Str. 7. 2. 4; 7. 3. 1, 17.
[109] Str. 3. 4. 19.
[110] Str. 1. 2. 1; 1. 3. 3; 2. 1. 4–8; 11. 11. 6; 15. 2. 10; 15. 3. 6; 16. 1. 11.
[111] Str. 15. 1 *passim*.
[112] Str. 1. 2. 1; 11. 2. 13–14.
[113] Str. 1. 2. 1; 2. 5. 12 (cf. 15. 1. 3); 11. 6. 4; 11. 11. 6.
[114] Str. 11. 9. 3.
[115] For Plinian geography and empire, see also Cotta Ramosino (2001), 218–23;
Murphy (2004), 129–64; Ash (2011).
[116] Plin. *HN* 4. 97: 'Romanis armis cognitae'.

because Raetia was only just conquered and incompletely measured at the time of his death, and the country as a whole only later and then incompletely known;[117] and learn of how but thirty years back, that is to say in the reign of Claudius, Roman arms had brought knowledge of Britain as far as the forest of Caledonia.[118] Book 5 then travels along the coast of North Africa from west to east and finishes with a detailed account of Asia Minor. This is how it finds room for Polybius' voyages of exploration. It also records the 19 BC triumph of L. Cornelius Balbus over the Garamantes and the unjust Mauretanian policy of Gaius, the war that it provoked, and the expansion of knowledge that followed in its wake.[119] Finally, book 6 travels east from the Black Sea and describes lands as far afield as India and Ceylon. Much information is attributed to Nero's Eastern commander Corbulo,[120] and to those sent out by the emperor to explore Meroe,[121] and more detailed information on Ceylon is attributed to a delegation sent from the island after Annius Plocamus, a tax-farmer of the reign of Claudius, was blown off course and pitched up on its shore.[122] Other key information derives from Dionysius of Charax, a local scholar sent ahead by Augustus to prepare for the Eastern campaign of his adopted son Gaius,[123] though Pliny himself chooses instead to follow Roman arms (*Romana arma sequi*) and to draw on the memorandum composed for Gaius by King Juba.[124] Aelius Gallus is also cited in this context.[125] Yet the key figure in book 6 is necessarily Alexander the Great, and much else is attributed to the admirals he sent out to explore the Indian Ocean,[126] and to the

---

[117] Plin. *HN* 4. 98: 'nam Germania multis postea annis nec tota percognita est'.

[118] Plin. *HN* 4. 102: 'XXX prope iam annis notitiam eius Romanis armis non ultra uicinitatem silvae Calidoniae propagantibus'.

[119] Plin. *HN* 5. 11–14, 36–7; Murphy (2004), 160–1.

[120] Plin. *HN* 5. 83; 6. 23, 40.

[121] Plin. *HN* 6. 181–2, 184–6.

[122] Plin. *HN* 6. 84–5.

[123] For this otherwise unknown figure and his possible identity with the much better attested Isidorus of Charax, see Roller (2003), 217–19.

[124] Plin. *HN* 6. 141, 149, 156, 170, 175, 176, 177, 179. For Juba's role in the Arabian campaign and his work *On Arabia*, see Roller (2003), 212–43; note esp. 219 and 221 questioning Pliny's suggestion that the works of either Dionysius or Juba were actually written in advance of the campaign.

[125] Plin. *HN* 6. 160–1; Murphy (2004), 130.

[126] For citation of Alexander's admirals Nearchus and Onesicritus, see Plin. *HN* 2. 185; 6. 96, 107, 109, 124; 12. 34; 15. 68. For Timosthenes admiral of Ptolemy Philadelphus, see Plin. *HN* 5. 47, 129; 6. 15, 163, 183, 198.

various Greeks who followed him into India in his own time and during the reigns of his successors.[127] To understand the land dimensions of India Pliny will therefore step in the footsteps of Alexander and will cite the distances calculated by those who measured his journeys.[128] And where Alexander halts, there will be others to take up the task. For at 6. 49 Pliny notes that, though Alexander stopped at the banks of the river Iaxartes and at the altars established by Hercules and Dionysus, one Demodamas, general (*dux*) of kings Seleuchus and Antiochus, actually crossed the river and travelled on. Pliny therefore follows him (*sequimur*) most particularly in his account of this region. As soldiers follow a leader, so the geographer follows a source, an authority. He travels in the footsteps of empire.[129] When again Alexander stops at the banks of the Hypanis, Pliny simply turns to Seleucus Nicator as his guide.[130]

Nor is Pliny's geography restricted to books 3–6. Already in the more theoretical book 2 and throughout his account of man, of other land animals, of fish, birds, and insects (books 7–11); of flora, agriculture, and gardening (books 12–19); of the medicinal use of plants (books 20–7) and beasts (books 28–32); and of minerals, art history, and gems (books 33–7), he can be relied upon to offer new and striking information on the theme of conquest and exploration. In book 2, for instance, he draws attention to the contribution to knowledge of fleets such as those of Augustus, Alexander, Seleucus, and Antiochus.[131] In book 9 also, the fleets of Alexander and Ptolemy are cited as sources for various remarkable creatures of the sea.[132] Alexander's troops and his victories also receive due credit,[133] and in book 8 it is he who urges on Aristotle the acquisition of zoological learning.[134] Numerous Roman sources also resurface: Juba and his

---

[127] Plin. *HN* 2. 168; 6. 40, 51–2, 58–62. For Pliny's citation of later sources alongside those from the time of Alexander, but failure to explore the contradictions between the two, see Dihle (1980).

[128] Plin. *HN* 6. 61: 'uerum ut terrena demonstratio intellegatur, Alexandri Magni uestigiis insistemus. Diognetus et Baeton itinerum eius mensores scripsere...' For Baeton, see also Plin. *HN* 7. 11.

[129] Plin. *HN* 6. 49: 'transcendit eum amnem Demodamas, Seleuchi et Antiochi regum dux, quem maxime sequimur in his, arasque Apollini Didymaeo statuit'.

[130] Plin. *HN* 6. 63.

[131] Plin. *HN* 2. 167–8, 185.

[132] Plin. *HN* 9. 5–7. For more on the fleets of Alexander, see Plin. *HN* 13. 140–1; 16. 221; 32. 63; Ash (2011), 8–9.

[133] Plin. *HN* 10. 185; 12. 21, 24, 25, 34; 13. 50; Ash (2011), 9.

[134] Plin. *HN* 8. 43–5; cf. 10. 185.

memorandum for Gaius,[135] Nero's Meroe survey,[136] a variety of
legates and provincial administrators,[137] most notable among them
Licinius Mucianus whose service in Lycia proves rich in wondrous
claims.[138] When in book 16 Pliny reports on the miserable existence
of the Chauci of northern Germany, this is on the basis of his own
service under Corbulo in AD 47.[139] This then is a body of information
acquired through conquest, survey, and occupation.[140] It could not
exist without empire and it makes its own distinctive contribution to
the propagation and the defence of that empire, whether it be
through Baeton's Alexandrian itineraries or the imperial memoranda
and surveys produced for Augustus by Dionysius of Charax and Juba
or commissioned for Meroe by Nero. It is a mark of the interdependence of war and geography that Pliny should identify the Nile as
one entity that better reveals its secrets in time of peace.[141]

Strabo and Pliny know what they owe to empire and Pliny's
references to lands discovered by Roman arms and to scholars
following in the footsteps of generals are strikingly figured acknow-
ledgements of this debt. All this is important, but it is no less
important to acknowledge how far both men fall short of reprodu-
cing the tensions that I have found in Polybius, Arrian, and Diodorus
and to try to identify why this is the case.

The two great geographers of the Roman world are, in their
different ways, the intellectual descendants of Polybius. We have
already seen Pliny quote the Greek historian's record of his voyage
along the coast of Africa, and Polybius is among the most important

---

[135] Plin. *HN* 12. 39, 56, 60, 67, 80; 13. 34; 15. 99; 25. 14; 31. 18; 32. 10; 33. 118; 36.
163; 37. 24, 69, 73, 108, 114. Roller (2003), 227 notes that some claims attributed to
Juba may in fact derive from his *Libyka*. I am baffled by the claim of Woolf (2011), 72
that 'there is little sign that the senate or emperors saw synergies between geographical research and the wider interests of the Roman people'.
[136] Plin. *HN* 12. 19. See also Plin. *HN* 37. 45–6 for the Roman knight sent out
to acquire amber for Nero's gladiatorial games.
[137] Plin. *HN* 9. 80, 89–91 and 32. 15 for Trebius Niger; 10. 134 for Egnatius
Calvinus, prefect of the Alps; 15. 83, 91 for L. Vitellius in Syria; 19. 11 for Fulvius
Lupus in Egypt; 19. 35 for Lartius Licinius in Spain.
[138] Plin. *HN* 7. 36; 11. 167; 12. 9; 19. 12; 31. 16, 19; 36. 131, 134. For Mucianus, see
Ash (2007).
[139] Plin. *HN* 16. 2–4; Citroni Marchetti (1982), 137–8.
[140] Woolf (2011), 132 claims on the basis of the 'exhaustive survey' of Healy
(1999) 42–62 that the only examples in Pliny of reports from military expeditions
are those from Paulinus in Mauretania and Gaius in Arabia. This is manifestly wrong.
[141] Plin. *HN* 5. 51.

sources for the geographical portions of Pliny's work.[142] Strabo, meanwhile, refers to his own *Histories* and indicates that they consisted of four preliminary books, including an account of the deeds of Alexander, followed by others taking up from where Polybius left off.[143] He also tells us that his geographical work shares with them the aim of being of use to statesmen and the people as a whole,[144] and of contributing to ethical and political philosophy.[145] It will dwell on those things that are grand and distinguished and which contain that which is either pragmatic, memorable, or entertaining.[146] Those reading the *Geography* must necessarily decide for themselves the overall balance between the three categories here set out, but it cannot be denied that a key element in both Strabo's historical and his geographical work is the Polybian category of the pragmatic.[147]

For all this distinctly Polybian vocabulary and approach, one term is striking by its absence. For Strabo refers to *polypragmosyne* only once in the course of the seventeen books of the *Geography* and then with regard to Ionian Corycum and the meddling of those locals who listen out at the port for information concerning the planned routes of ships calling in, in order then to launch piratical assaults against them.[148] The phrase 'and the Corycian was listening' thus becomes

---

[142] See the various Latin fragments collected at Polyb. 34. 15–16.

[143] Str. 1. 1. 22; 2. 1. 9; 11. 9. 3. *FGrH* 91 T2 indicates that the work as a whole stretched to 47 books.

[144] Str. 1. 1. 22: πολιτικὸν καὶ δημωφελές; 1. 1. 23: πρὸς τοὺς αὐτοὺς ἄνδρας, καὶ μάλιστα τοὺς ἐν ταῖς ὑπεροχαῖς.

[145] Str. 1. 1. 23: χρήσιμα ... εἰς τὴν ἠθικὴν καὶ πολιτικὴν φιλοσοφίαν.

[146] Str. 1. 1. 23: ἐν δὲ τοῖς ἐνδόξοις καὶ μεγάλοις καὶ ἐν οἷς τὸ πραγματικὸν καὶ εὐμνημόνευτον καὶ ἡδὺ διατρίβειν. Engels (1999), 91–3 points to this passage and to the readiness to include material that is entertaining or memorable as well as pragmatic. Yet it seems exaggerated on this basis to deny the fundamentally pragmatic character of the *Geography* as the same scholar does at Engels (1999), 155 and (2010), 73. On this topic, see also Berger (1903), 495–8, 501, 534; Gabba (1984), 25.

[147] For pragmatic history and the πολιτικός, see Polyb. 9. 1. 4. For further statements of Strabo's pragmatic geography, cf. Str. 1. 1. 1: πρὸς τὰς πολιτικὰς καὶ τὰς ἡγεμονικὰς πράξεις; 1. 1. 16: ἐπὶ τὰς πράξεις ... τὰς ἡγεμονικάς; 1. 1. 18: περὶ τοὺς ἡγεμονικοὺς βίους καὶ τὰς χρείας; 1. 1. 23 for all minor matters excluded unless they can stir τὸν φιλειδήμονα καὶ τὸν πραγματικόν; 2. 5. 8: πρὸς ... τὰς ἡγεμονικὰς χρείας; 2. 5. 13: πρὸς τὰς χρείας τὰς πολιτικάς; 2. 5. 34 on the limited interest of climate and celestial bodies for τῶι πολιτικῶι. Note also Str. 1. 4. 8 contesting the claim of Eratosthenes that there is no practical use (πραγματικόν) in the study of boundaries and 13. 1. 54 on how the wreck of the textual tradition of Aristotle left the later Peripatetics unable to discuss matters of practical value (φιλοσοφεῖν πραγματικῶς).

[148] Str. 14. 1. 32.

proverbial for those yearning to learn about that which is not their business.[149] Elsewhere the *philopragmosyne* of Homer is exemplified by the fact that he is not ignorant of the ebb and flow of tides while the same concept is invoked in order to describe the priests of Egypt and their meticulous recording of patterns of rainfall.[150] It is but one of a variety of phrases that denote love of learning or possession of great knowledge.[151] *Periergia*, on the other hand, is associated with superfluous precision and detail and lacks any positive connotation.[152] Pliny, likewise, employs *curiosus* to indicate the zeal with which Mithridates and Orpheus researched herbal medicines,[153] the interests of the artist Myron,[154] and the recherché explanation of Greek religion offered by Apion,[155] but he also uses the term to refer to a detailed description,[156] or to indicate care or precision in craft and agriculture.[157] Where Pliny praises the same qualities in scholarly work, it is generally by use of *diligens*, *subtilis*, and their cognates.[158] When he wishes to express what it is about the natural world that inspires study, the key concept is wonder.[159] The crucial point is that none of these terms can straddle the worlds of scholarly investigation and of imperial expansion—and set the two in implicit relation with each other—as *polypragmosyne* surely can do in Greek.

---

[149] Str. 14. 1. 32: φιλοπευστοῦντας τὰ μὴ προσήκοντα.

[150] Str. 1. 1. 7; 17. 1. 5.

[151] Str. 1. 2. 29 attributes Homer's knowledge of the Nile to his τὸ φιλείδημον... καὶ... τὸ φιλέκδημον, while 3. 4. 19 regrets the Romans' want of τὸ φιλείδημον, hence undue reliance on Greek sources for Spain. Other key terms are 1. 2. 20: τὸ πολυμαθές, cf. 16. 2. 10: πολυμαθέστατος; 14. 1. 16: φιλομαθείας, cf. 14. 5. 13: φιλομαθοῦντες; 17. 1. 5: φιλιστορῶν; 9. 5. 17: πολυΐστωρ. The standard term for care in Strabo is ἐπιμέλεια and this is applied to scholarly work at 1. 2. 20 and 9. 3. 11.

[152] Str. 1. 2. 3; 2. 3. 2; 15. 1. 21.

[153] Plin. *HN* 25. 7, 12.

[154] Plin. *HN* 34. 58.

[155] Plin. *HN* 30. 99. My colleague Amin Benaissa compares this to Apion *FGrH* 616 T 10c = Africanus ap. Euseb. *Praep. evang.* 10.10.16, where Apion is described as περιεργότατος γραμματικῶν.

[156] Plin. *HN* 21. 179.

[157] Plin. *HN* 13. 75; 18. 19.

[158] See e.g. Plin. *HN* 5. 40; 6. 141; 19. 32; 25. 5; 30. 4; 31. 106; 32. 26 for *diligens* applied to the work of Eratosthenes and Polybius, Juba, Mithridates, Hermippus, Theophrastus, and Sextius. See also Plin. *HN* 18. 335; 26. 11 for *subtilis* applied to Aristotle and Herophilus.

[159] Note how Beagon (2011) refers in its title to Pliny's curiosity but illustrates this attitude through its use of *mirus* and its cognates.

What is missing from both Strabo and Pliny may be explained in terms of their general attitude to empire. For where Polybius gives voice to Greek critics of Roman expansion, Arrian's gymnosophists denounce the restless meddling that allows Alexander to push back the frontiers of knowledge, and where Diodorus can put charges of *polypragmosyne* in the mouths of critics of Roman imperial meddling while using the same word to describe the laudable investigations of the Roman embassy to Egypt, all such tensions fall away in the works of Strabo and Pliny. For Strabo has nothing to say against Rome and, as has been noted, his affection for empire extends even to Mithridates and to the Parthians. Pliny, meanwhile, can decry the vicious treatment of the Mauretanian royal family by Gaius and even sympathize with their ensuing revolt, but the fault lies with one vicious ruler and not with the empire as a whole.[160] The good Claudius is entirely justified in sending Suetonius Paulinus to crush the revolt. The extension of geographical knowledge as far as the Atlas mountains and beyond is but a beneficial side-effect of this process.[161] The Romans may even have found specimens of the euphorbea, the local plant celebrated by the learned Juba and later given a starring role in Pliny's celebration of the medicinal benefits of empire.[162]

(7) IMPERIAL GEOGRAPHY AND THE PERSONALITY OF THE EMPEROR

The ancient geographical survey is the synthesis of all that has been discovered about the known world in the centuries up to the time of the writer. So much is evident from the sources cited by Pliny for books 3–6 of the *Natural History*, which run from Hecataeus of Miletus in the sixth century BC to entirely contemporary figures

---

[160] For Gaius' misdeeds in Mauretania, see Plin. *HN* 5. 2, 11. For Pliny's demonization of Gaius, cf. Plin. *HN* 7. 45 where he and Nero are coupled as 'faces generis humani'.

[161] Plin. *HN* 5. 14–15; Ash (2011), 7–8.

[162] For Juba and the euphorbea, see Plin. *HN* 5. 16; 25. 77–9; 27. 1–3. For Juba's extraordinary learning, see Juba *FGrH* 275 T2a = Plut. *Caes.* 55. 2: τοῖς πολυμαθεστάτοις ἐναρίθμιος ... συγγραφεῦσιν; T10 = Plut. *Sert.* 9. 10: τοῦ πάντων ἱστορικωτάτου βασιλέων; T12a = Ath. 83B: ἄνδρα πολυμαθέστατον; T12b = Plin. *HN* 5. 16: 'studiorum claritate memorabilior etiam quam regno'.

such as Mucianus and Corbulo. The primary axis of investigation is spatial and the moment at which any particular region entered the world of knowledge a secondary concern. This is not to imply that either Strabo or Pliny is indifferent to how and when the boundaries of geographical knowledge were advanced—the earlier sections of this study offer ample evidence to the contrary—but their material is displayed in the form of a journey and the impetus is always to move forward along the prescribed route and to take in the next province, the next land.[163]

What holds for the works of Strabo and Pliny is perhaps even more true of a work of the intervening decades: the *Chorographia* of Pomponius Mela.[164] The start and end point of the three books of this survey is identical: the promontory of Ampelusia, where the Atlantic coast of Africa meets the southern shore of the Mediterranean.[165] All that intervenes is a journey along the southern and eastern coast of the Mediterranean, through the Hellespont and around the Black Sea, then back out along the northern coast of the Mediterranean until it joins the Atlantic. Mela then travels northwards through the outer seas and round to the land of the Sarmatians, the Caspian Sea, and on to India. His work concludes with a circumnavigation of the Arabian gulf and of the seas south along the coast of Africa and north up the other side. In all this Mela adheres almost exclusively to the spatial axis and even contrives to give an account of India that omits any mention of Alexander the Great.[166] Twice, however, he does observe that uncertainty long endured over specific issues until a moment of discovery. In the case of the southward shore of Africa, that moment is identified as the voyages of exploration of Hanno the Carthaginian and of Eudoxus of Alexandria.[167] For the revelation of what lies beyond the Caspian Sea, Mela quotes Cornelius Nepos on the gift to Q.

[163] For the geographical text figured as a journey, see e.g. Str. 7. 5. 1: τοῖς περιοδευθεῖσι τόποις; 8. 3. 11: ἐπειδὰν τὴν ἐξῆς χώραν περιοδεύσωμεν; 8. 6. 4: ἀναλαβόντες δ' ἐφοδεύσωμεν πάλιν τὰ κατὰ τὴν Ἀργείαν.

[164] The key passage for the dating of the *Chorographia* is Pompon. 3. 49. Frick (1880), p. v takes this as referring to Gaius' planned invasion of Britain and dates the work to AD 40–1. For convincing arguments in favour of a later date of AD 43–4 and the reign of Claudius, see Parroni (1984), 16–22.

[165] Pompon. 1. 24; 3. 107.

[166] Pompon. 3. 61–71.

[167] Pompon. 3. 90 = Cornelius Nepos, *Exempla* fr. 6 Peter; Pompon. 3. 93.

Metellus Celer, proconsul of Gaul, from the king of the Boti of Indian mariners who had been swept off course and driven north and west to the shore of Germany.[168] When, moreover, he does reflect on the prospects for the future expansion of knowledge, it is with respect to his own historical moment: the character of Britain and those it begets will soon be the subject of more certain information because the greatest of emperors, victor over peoples not so much undefeated in the past as just unknown, is now in the process of opening up a country previously closed.[169] A work so largely indifferent to the history of knowledge cannot finally resist the excitement of its own moment and of living under an emperor ready to extend the boundaries of the known.

Pomponius Mela locates himself in time precisely at the moment that the emperor promises to transform the spatial plane that is the writer's overwhelming concern. The Roman historians, by contrast, are far from indifferent to the world of knowledge opened up by force of arms, but what they reveal most strikingly are the factors that make one reign an age of advance and exploration, another at best one of consolidation and at worst of decline. This point may be illustrated with regard to a number of authors and we will see much where the decisive factor is the emperor's own thirst for knowledge and curiosity. It is, however, appropriate to start from a central passage of Tacitus and its excavation of the impact on historical narrative of a ruler apparently indifferent to conquest or advance.

A father indicted by his son, accusations of sedition against the aged and infirm, a historian put on trial for daring to praise the assassins of Julius Caesar: such is the woeful catalogue interrupted at *Annals* 4. 32–3 as the historian laments the absence from his work of all that made the pages of his predecessors so stirring and so grand, yet goes on to observe that the close investigation of even such vicious and demeaning events can contain much to instruct the reader. This is indeed one of the most famous portions of the *Annals*, and the complex relationship between the terms here deployed and

----

[168] Pompon. 3. 45 = Cornelius Nepos, *Exempla* fr. 7 Peter. For analysis of this episode, see Bengtson (1954–5).

[169] Pompon. 3. 49: 'Britannia qualis sit qualesque progeneret mox certiora et magis explorata dicentur. quippe tamdiu clausam aperit ecce principum maximus, nec indomitarum modo ante se uerum ignotarum quoque gentium uictor, propriarum rerum fidem ut bello adfectauit, ita triumpho declaraturus portat'.

the narrative of the rest of book 4 has been much studied.[170] Yet one key formula merits closer attention and will offer a suitable point of departure for the themes to be addressed in this section.

The key passage is the historian's explanation of the absence from this work of the huge wars, the sacked cities, and the kings put to flight and taken prisoner which it was the lot of his predecessors to recount.[171] For Tacitus observes that the inglorious and confined character of his study is dictated by the times which he describes: peace secure or scarcely shaken, the affairs of the city wretched, the emperor unconcerned to extend the boundaries of the empire.[172] As the state consumes itself from within, there is neither any threat from without, nor any impulse from the emperor himself to carry the fight to peoples previously unknown or at least untouched.[173] It is therefore down to the character of Tiberius that there will be none of what 4. 33 goes on to describe as the typical features of previous imperial histories: ethnographic disquisitions, vicissitudes of battle, the glorious deaths of generals.[174] And the adjective which best describes that character is *incuriosus*. Tiberius therefore, inasmuch as he is unconcerned to expand the boundaries of the empire, deprives the historian of his reign of the opportunity to describe for the reader new worlds hitherto unknown to them as Julius Caesar

---

[170] Most useful for the purposes of this argument have been Giua (1985); Woodman (1998), 128–41.

[171] Tac. *Ann.* 4. 32. 1: 'ingentia … bella, expugnationes urbium, fusos captosque reges'.

[172] Tac. *Ann.* 4. 32. 2: 'immota quippe aut modice lacessita pax, maestae urbis res et princeps proferendi imperi incuriosus'.

[173] For Tacitus' phrasing, cf. Tac. *Ann.* 1. 3. 6 stating that the only war ongoing at the death of Augustus was that against the Germans 'abolendae magis infamiae ob amissum cum Quinctilio Varo exercitum quam cupidine proferendi imperii aut dignum ob praemium', and 1. 11. 4 for the 'consilium coercendi intra terminos imperii'; Carneades ap. Cic. *Rep.* 3. 24; Verg. *Aen.* 6. 794–5 on Augustus who 'super et Garamantas et Indos | proferet imperium'; Ov. *Met.* 5. 371–2 and Venus' exhortation to Cupid to make Dis fall in love and thus extend her realm into the world below: 'Tartara quid cessant? cur non matrisque tuumque | imperium profers?'; *Mon. Anc.* 30: 'protuli fines Illyrici ad ripam fluminis Danuui'; Anon. *Con. Liv.* 20 on Drusus who 'protulit in terras imperium novas'; *ILS* 212. 37–40 and Claudius' pride in the occupation of Britain: 'iam si narrem bella, a quibus | coeperint maiores nostri, et quo processerimus, uereor ne nimio | insolentior esse uidear et quaesisse iactationem gloriae pro | lati imperii ultra oceanum'. See also Johnson (1996), 128.

[174] Tac. *Ann.* 4. 33. 3: 'situs gentium, uarietates proeliorum, clari ducum exitus'. For such material offered to Q. Cicero by Julius Caesar's invasion of Britain see Cic. *Q Fr.* 2. 14. 2; 2. 16. 4; Tandoi (1967), 15.

had done in his ethnographic account of the Germans in the *De Bello Gallico* or before him Posidonius had done for the Celts.[175] The indifference of the ruler frustrates the curiosity of the historian and leaves him no opportunity to sate that of his reader. There are no worlds left to map save those already known, and the ethnography of Capri which Tacitus goes on to furnish is significant by its very insignificance.[176]

To the late Latin glossaries, *incuriosus* equates to the Greek *apragmon* and *incuriositas* to *apragmosyne*.[177] Yet the abstract noun is an even later formulation than is *curiositas* itself and the adjective relates primarily to the ideas of neglect or indifference associated with the much earlier term *incuria*. Though *incuriosus* might most obviously be taken as antonym to *curiosus*, what it most commonly negates is that adjective's secondary sense of 'careful' and only more rarely its more common sense of 'curious'. *Incuriosus* is also a distinctively Tacitean term: it features once in Sallust,[178] and the adverb *incuriose* once again in the same writer and three times in Livy,[179] but it is otherwise unattested prior to Pliny the Younger,[180] nor does any other Latin writer come close to the eighteen occasions on which Tacitus deploys it in his work.[181] In the majority of these instances, Tacitus clearly implies culpable neglect of responsibility.[182] In other instances, however, what is implied is indifference to a particular category or absence of any positive initiative.[183] What therefore does Tacitus imply when he describes the emperor as *princeps proferendi imperi incuriosus*? There is, it should be noted, no suggestion here

---

[175] For Posidonius on the Celts, see Momigliano (1979), 67–69, 72; Nicolet (1991), 65. For Caesar's ethnographic excursuses and their dependence on, among others, Posidonius, see Momigliano (1979), 72; Nicolet (1991), 67.

[176] Woodman (1998), 138 and 140.

[177] *CGL* ii. 242.

[178] Sall. *Hist.* 4. 36M.

[179] Sall. *Hist.* 2. 42M; Livy 8. 38. 2; 29. 3. 8; 29. 32. 2.

[180] Plin. Ep. 8. 20. 1. For my reasons for excluding Sen. *Ep.* 95. 50, see Ch. 2 Sect. 3.

[181] Tac. *Ann.* 2. 88; 4. 23, 32, 45; 6. 17; 14. 38; 15. 31; *Hist.* 1. 13, 34, 49, 79; 2. 17, 88; 3. 6, 56; 4. 28; 5. 22; *Agr.* 1. 1. Tacitus also uses the noun *incuria* at *Ann.* 1. 50; 3. 31; 4. 16, 36, 48; 12. 57; 16. 4; *Hist.* 4. 78; *Agr.* 20. 1. *Curiosus* is entirely absent from his work.

[182] Tac. *Ann.* 4. 45; 6. 17; 14. 38; *Hist.* 1. 79; 2. 88; 3. 6, 56; 4. 28; 5. 22.

[183] Tac. *Hist.* 1. 13: 'Otho pueritiam incuriose, adulescentiam petulanter egerat'; 1. 34: 'credula fama inter gaudentis et incuriosos'; 1. 49 on Galba 'famae nec incuriosus nec uenditator'; 2. 17: 'sed longa pax ad omne seruitium fregerat facilis occupantibus et melioribus incuriosos'; *Ann.* 4. 23: 'Ptolemaeo Iubae filio incurioso'.

that Tiberian *incuria* leads to neglect of established borders and puts the empire at risk. If he is neglectful of any established obligation, it must be one requiring each and every emperor to push the empire forward. Florus would surely see things this way, for he blames Rome's failure to expand her territories in the one hundred years from the reign of Augustus on the inertia of the Caesars.[184] Yet Tiberius himself could as easily claim that he did no more than to hold true to the counsel of the dying Augustus.[185] What he lacks, it seems, is the impetus, the motive force, to drive the empire forward, and this makes all the more pointed the causal link drawn between his character and the brake he puts on the positive drive of the historian to investigate and of the reader in turn to learn.

If the Tacitean Tiberius is the embodiment of indifference to the expansion of empire and of knowledge, other parts of the same writer's work reveal the contrary impulse and document what results from it. I refer in particular to Tacitus' two works on the northern provinces of the Roman empire—the *Germania* and the *Agricola*—both of which feature prominently the same motif. From its first chapter, the *Germania* refers to those peoples and chieftains of Germany whom war has opened up and lately exposed to knowledge,[186] though later chapters will confess that no more has been discovered of the northern Pillars of Hercules since Ocean barred the way to Germanicus,[187] and that the Elbe, once the planned outpost of empire, is now merely heard of.[188] In the *Agricola*, meanwhile,

---

[184] Flor. *praef.* 8: 'a Caesare Augusto in saeculum nostrum haud multo minus anni ducenti, quibus inertia Caesarum quasi consenuit atque decoxit, nisi quod sub Traiano principe mouit lacertos et praeter spem omnium senectus imperii quasi reddita iuuentute reuirescit.'

[185] Tac. *Ann.* 1. 11. 4; *Agr.* 13. 2; Cass. Dio 53. 10. 4–5; 54. 9. 1; 56. 33. 5–6; 56. 41. 7 asserting a strictly defensive policy. For discussion of this alleged policy, see Lana (1980), 24; Nicolet (1991), 29 n. 1; Laederich (2001), 28–30 with ample bibliography.

[186] Tac. *Germ.* 1. 1: 'nuper cognitis quibusdam gentibus ac regibus, quos bellum aperuit'. See further Tandoi (1967), 24.

[187] Tac. *Germ.* 34. 2: 'nec defuit audentia Druso Germanico, sed obstitit Oceanus in se simul atque in Herculem inquiri. mox nemo temptauit, sanctiusque ac reuerentius uisum de actis deorum credere quam scire'. The reference is to the brother of Tiberius, also named Drusus Germanicus at Tac. *Hist.* 5. 19. 2, and of whom Suet. *Claud.* 1. 2 states that he 'Oceanum septemtrionalem primus Romanorum ducum nauigauit'. For further voyages recorded for AD 5, see *Mon. Anc.* 26. 4; Plin. *HN* 2. 167.

[188] Tac. *Germ.* 41. 2: 'in Hermunduris Albis oritur, flumen inclutum et nomen olim; nunc tantum auditur'.

Tacitus' revered father-in-law is the man who discovers and con-
quers the hitherto unknown Orkneys,[189] whose third expeditionary
force opens up new peoples,[190] who can claim that Rome now holds
Britain not in chatter and rumour but with camps and arms, and who
can summarize his achievement with the statement that the island
has been found and subdued.[191] Where the indifference of Tiberius
to the expansion of the empire could be blamed for the absence from
the *Annals* of new ethnographic material (*situs gentium*), now the
campaigns of Agricola make it possible for his son-in-law to provide
the first authoritative ethnography (*situm populosque*) of Britain.[192]

It is worth noting the degree to which Tacitus associates the
exploration of Britain and the northern Ocean with two figures in
particular: Drusus Germanicus and Cn. Iulius Agricola. The former
died on campaign in Germany in 9 BC. He left a son, who not only
made war against the same German tribes but also followed his father
into the northern Ocean.[193] To Tiberius, however, such vigour appears to have been more of a threat than a source of pride: *Annals* 2.
22. 1 and 2. 26. 6 show Germanicus all too aware of the *inuidia* that
haunted the rest of his career.[194] Much the same story is told of
Agricola. Tacitus closes his biography with a poignant account of the
former governor's final years, the refusal of any further command,
and the growing recognition that the emperor fundamentally dis-
trusted a man whose achievements looked set to put his own ficti-
tious triumphs in the shade.[195] Once again, therefore, we see the
special contribution of history: to reveal what it is about a given
period or regime that fosters either the growth, the decline, or just the
miserable stagnation of knowledge.

[189] Tac. *Agr.* 10. 4: 'incognitas ad id tempus insulas, quas Orcadas uocant, inuenit
domuitque'.
[190] Tac. *Agr.* 22. 1: 'nouas gentes aperuit'.
[191] Tac. *Agr.* 33. 3: 'finem Britanniae non fama nec rumore sed castris et armis
tenemus: inuenta Britannia et subacta'. For a consistently insightful discussion of the
motif of knowledge as conquest in the *Agricola*, see Clarke (2001), esp. 95 and 100–2.
See also Tandoi (1964), 144–5.
[192] Tac. *Agr.* 10. 1. Cf. Clarke (2001), 108.
[193] For this voyage, see Tac. *Ann.* 2. 23; Albinovanus Pedo fr. Courtney = Sen. *Suas.*
1. 15. Hence the appeal of Freinsheim's emendation 'Druso <et> Germanico' or
perhaps 'Druso <aut> Germanico' at Tac. *Germ.* 34. 2.
[194] For Drusus Germanicus and his son set up as antitypes to 'Tiberio *incuriosus*
di conquiste', see Tandoi (1967), 33, 59–60.
[195] Tac. *Agr.* 39–43.

(8) THE EMPEROR AS EXPLORER AND
POLYPRAGMON

In signal contrast to the indifference of Tiberius stands the political
and intellectual *polypragmosyne* attributed to other wearers of the
purple. This is particularly prominent in the works of Cassius Dio,
who offers a wide range of references to *polypragmosyne*, and whose
enthusiasm for the work of Thucydides, most notably for his
speeches, and the implications for how he thinks about the Roman
empire are the subject of the final section of this chapter. For now let
me point to three episodes from the later portions of his work. In the
first, Vespasian establishes his credentials as a quietist by declining to
invade the Parthians on the grounds that it is not right to intervene in
the affairs of others.[196] Trajan, by contrast, takes as his model the
campaigns of Alexander, reaches Ocean, sends a boat off to India,
and takes a keen interest in (ἐπολυπραγμόνει) the affairs of its people.
He even proclaims in a report to the senate that he has travelled
further than Alexander though in truth he is unable to preserve that
which Alexander subdued.[197] Yet it is perhaps the AD 200 Egyptian
campaign of Septimius Severus which best embodies the drive for
knowledge and the drive for power. Septimius travels up the Nile in a
bid to reach Ethiopia, is held back by illness, but still devotes himself
to studying everything, even that which is thoroughly hidden, and is
the type to leave absolutely nothing unexplored.[198]

In Dio, as in Diodorus, it is Egypt where the pursuit of power and
the pursuit of knowledge run together most absolutely, and this too is
true of my final example. For in the tenth book of the *Pharsalia*,
Caesar, entertained by Cleopatra at a banquet of unparalleled splendour, fixes his attention on the aged sage Acoreus. And now the man
who has convulsed the Roman state in his headlong pursuit of power,

---

[196] Cass. Dio 65. 15. 3: οὐ προσήκει αὐτῶι τὰ ἀλλότρια πολυπραγμονεῖν.

[197] Cass. Dio 68. 29. 1.

[198] Cass. Dio 76. 13. 2: καὶ ἐπολυπραγμόνησε πάντα καὶ τὰ πάνυ κεκρυμμένα· ἦν
γὰρ οἷος μηδὲν μήτε ἀνθρώπινον μήτε θεῖον ἀδιερεύνητον καταλιπεῖν. For this
account of the πολυπράγμων and his pursuit of learning, cf. Philo *Mig.* 216: τὸ
φιλομαθὲς ζητητικὸν καὶ περίεργον ἐστι φύσει, πανταχῆι βαδίζον ἀόκνως καὶ
πανταχόσε διακῦπτον καὶ μηδὲν ἀδιερεύνητον τῶν ὄντων μήτε σωμάτων μήτε
πραγμάτων ἀπολιπεῖν δικαιοῦν. Joly (1961), 39 n. 24 is right to question the consist-
ency of Philo's critique of curiosity, for Philo *Congr.* 125 and *Aet.* 134 use very similar
phrasing in celebration of the lover of learning.

who has just been presented with the head of Pompey, confesses indeed that, so great is his love for the truth, such his fascination with the origins of the Nile, had he but the sure hope of achieving this goal, he would abandon the civil war.[199] The pursuit of knowledge and the pursuit of power are expressions of the same psychological impulse.[200]

(9) CAESAR AT VESONTIO—CASSIUS DIO AND THUCYDIDES

The enthusiasm of Cassius Dio for Thucydides is well known.[201] This is particularly visible in the speeches he attributes to his characters, and what results is the tendency of various figures from Roman history to think about their situation in terms that recall the political debates of fifth-century Athens. This is already visible in Dio's account of the reign of Ancus Marcius, where the king realizes that simply to avoid injustice is no guarantee of peace, and that quietism without action cannot bring salvation.[202] The formulation is drawn straight from the speech of Thucydides' Pericles in which he exhorts the Athenians not to lose heart in the face of plague and of successive campaigns against their land.[203] When, however, Ancus Marcius realizes that the joy of quietism is likely to be destroyed by those who pursue it to excess, the obvious point of reference is the speech of Alcibiades urging Athens to undertake the Sicilian Expedition.[204]

---

[199] Luc. 10. 188–92: 'sed, cum tanto meo uiuat sub pectore uirtus, | tantus amor ueri, nihil est quod noscere malim | quam fluuii causas per saecula tanta latentis | ignotumque caput: spes sit mihi certa uidendi | Niliacos fontes, bellum ciuile relinquam'. Berti (2000) ad loc. rightly compares these lines to Sen. *Q Nat.* 6. 8. 3 on Nero's sponsorship of investigations of the source of the Nile and description of the emperor as 'ut aliarum uirtutum ita *ueritatis* in primis *amantissimus*'. For the myth of Alexander commissioning Aristotle to conduct a similar mission, see Str. 17. 1. 5.

[200] On this point, see also Murphy (2004), 143–4.

[201] Litsch (1893); Kyhnitzsch (1894); Gabba (1955); Millar (1964), 42, 177; Zecchini (1978), 33–4.

[202] Cass. Dio fr. 8: οὐδέ ἐστι τὸ ἄπραγμον ἄνευ τοῦ δραστηρίου σωτήριον. For context, see Zonar. 7. 7.

[203] Thuc. 2. 63. 3: τὸ γὰρ ἄπραγμον οὐ σώιζεται μὴ μετὰ τοῦ δραστηρίου τεταγμένον.

[204] Cass. Dio fr. 8: τὸ τερπνὸν τῆς ἀπραγμοσύνης τάχιστα καὶ ῥᾶιστα τοῖς πέρα τοῦ καιροῦ σπουδάζουσιν αὐτὴν ἀπολλύμενον; Thuc. 6. 18. 6: πόλιν μὴ ἀπράγμονα τάχιστ' ἄν μοι δοκεῖν ἀπραγμοσύνης μεταβολῆι διαφθαρῆναι.

The upshot of these reflections is that Ancus takes all that he can from the Latins with their consent and without injustice, but where they are unwilling he simply launches a campaign and takes these things anyway.

The *locus classicus* for Dio's interpretation of Roman imperialism in the light of Athenian *polypragmosyne* is the speech of Caesar at Vesontio at 38. 36–46, especially that portion of the speech stretching to section 40.[205] The year is 58 BC and Caesar is seeking an excuse to make war against Rome's former ally Ariovistus.[206] His men, however, express disquiet and argue that the war is none of their business, has not been decreed, and is the product of Caesar's personal ambition.[207] The reference to what is or is not one's business has already been noted in Vespasian's refusal to make war on the Parthians and is a key marker of debates about *polypragmosyne* from the fifth century onwards. It is therefore also a keynote of Caesar's speech defending the proposed campaign which he addresses to his subalterns.[208] Whereas, he argues, a private citizen may find that the best course for him is that of least resistance, for a people it is fitting ($\pi\rho o\sigma\acute{\eta}\kappa\epsilon\iota$) to choose and to do what is best.[209] Even in our private affairs, the best guarantee of good standing is to be active ($\delta\rho a\sigma\tau\eta\rho\acute{\iota}ous$), but the safest man can seem to be the one who lives the quietest life.[210] A city, by contrast, and especially an imperial city, will be undone should it follow such a course.[211] Much here repeats the Thucydidean reflections of Ancus Marcius; the specific concern for what possession of an empire obliges a city to do echoes the thoughts of Pericles and Alcibiades but also those of Cleon in the Mytilenean debate.[212]

---

[205] Gabba (1955), 302–3 notes the imperfect suture between Cass. Dio 38. 36–40 and 41–6.

[206] For Ariovistus registered as an ally of Rome in Caesar's consulship, see Cass. Dio 38. 34. 3.

[207] Cass. Dio 38. 35. 2: καὶ ἐθρύλουν ὅτι πόλεμον οὔτε προσήκοντα οὔτε ἐψηφισμένον διὰ τὴν ἰδίαν τοῦ Καίσαρος φιλοτιμίαν ἀναιροῖντο.

[208] See esp. Cass. Dio 38. 37. 1, where Caesar picks up on the specific terms of the complaint, but note also 38. 36. 1; 38. 37. 2, 3; 38. 40. 2, 3.

[209] Cass. Dio 38. 36. 1.

[210] Cass. Dio 38. 36. 12: ἀνὴρ μὲν ὅστις ἀπραγμονέστατός ἐστι, καὶ ἀσφαλέστατος εἶναι δοκεῖ.

[211] Cass. Dio 38. 36. 2: πόλις δέ, ἄλλως τε καὶ ἀρχὴν ἔχουσα, τάχιστ' ἂν ὑπὸ τοῦ τοιούτου καταλυθείη.

[212] Thuc. 2. 63. 1–2; 3. 37. 2; 6. 17. 7; 6. 18. 1.

Caesar goes on to outline the message that his officers should address to their men. They are to be reminded of how their ancestors actually built the empire, how they strove for constant growth and regarded inactivity as a short cut to disaster.[213] The appeal to paternal example is another point of contact with the speech of Alcibiades,[214] while Caesar's reference to not shunning wars recalls what Pericles says of not shunning toil.[215] No less Thucydidean is the grim warning against senescence through inactivity.[216] Likewise the emphasis on quite how many people are conspiring against Rome.[217] The doctrine of preventive aggression works as well for Caesar against Ariovistus as it did for Alcibiades against Syracuse.[218] If we did not already know that this was a discourse in favour of imperial *polypragmosyne*, Caesar even reflects on what deters a man from meddling with that which does not belong to him.[219]

An all-too easy first response is to dismiss this speech as but a sterile literary exercise crying out for the mockery of a Lucian.[220] A more productive alternative might be to consider how and to what effect Dio maps this moment in Rome's advance onto the experience of Athens at the outset of the Peloponnesian War and when contemplating the Sicilian Expedition. Centuries before, Carneades had borrowed some of the Thucydidean Cleon's more amoral formulations as he urged the Romans to disregard considerations of justice when thinking about their empire.[221] Now, in the aftermath of the reign of Marcus Aurelius, the fresh outbreak of conflict with Parthia, and the AD 167 invasion of Transpadane Italy by the Quadi and

---

[213] Cass. Dio 38. 37. 3 – 38. 38. 1; 38. 39. 1.

[214] Thuc. 6. 17. 7; 6. 18. 6.

[215] Cass. Dio 38. 37. 3: οὐδὲ τοὺς πολέμους φεύγοντες; Thuc. 2. 63. 1: μὴ φεύγειν τοὺς πόνους. For exhortation to πόνος in the speech of Caesar, see Cass. Dio 38. 39. 2.

[216] Cass. Dio 38. 38. 1: κατατριφθείη καὶ καταγηράσειεν; Thuc. 6. 18. 6: τρίψεσθαι … ἐγγηράσεσθαι.

[217] Cass. Dio 38. 40. 1–2: ἐπιβουλεύσει … ἐπιβουλεύεσθαι; Thuc. 3. 37. 2: ἐπιβουλεύοντας; 3. 40. 1, 5; Gabba (1955), 306.

[218] Cass. Dio 38. 40. 2: προκαταλαμβάνεσθαι; Thuc. 6. 18. 2: προκαταλαμβάνει. For this theory of Roman imperial strategy, see Gabba (1955), 303.

[219] Cass. Dio 38. 40. 3: πολυπραγμονεῖν τὰ μὴ προσήκοντα. The sentence as a whole is suitably convoluted (and Thucydidean) in its structure.

[220] Luci. *Hist. conscr.* 15, 18, 26 mocks the sub-Thucydidean speeches inserted by contemporary historians of the Parthian Wars.

[221] Carneades ap. Cic. *Rep.* 3. 21 = Lactant. *Inst.* 5. 16. 4 echoes Cleon at Thuc. 3. 40. 4; Capelle (1932), 86–9.

Marcomanni, the doctrine of preventive aggression once advanced by Alcibiades and now put in the mouth of Caesar may have seemed ever more relevant.[222] Alcibiades, as we have seen, also warns his fellow Athenians of the senescence of empire and Dio's Caesar takes up the theme. This too has some meaning for the Rome of the second century. Reference has already been made to the work of Florus and to his complaint that Rome's failure to expand her borders in the century since the reign of Augustus is to be blamed on the inertia of the Caesars. It should now be noted that this claim comes in a passage that considers the stages of Roman history in terms of the life cycle of a human being and treats the centuries after Augustus as a decline into old age.[223] Only now under Trajan and to the surprise of all does Rome move her arms and enjoy the restoration of youth.[224] This is the same Trajan whose ambitious imperial policy and investigation of India Dio himself describes in terms of *poly-pragmosyne*. If Trajan had not finally delivered the rejuvenation he once promised, Dio may have wondered what could be hoped for from Septimius Severus instead.

In short, the same fear stalks Trajan's Rome that once stalked the Athens of Pericles and Alcibiades, and this fear Cassius Dio retrojects both to the early Rome of Ancus Marcius and to the time of Caesar and the Gallic Wars: that a nation that has grown strong through activity and expansion risks decline into mediocrity should it opt instead for indolence and quietism. We know in advance that Caesar at Vesontio will lead his men forward to victory and that the Gallic Wars will not be his nation's Sicily. How much longer Rome's luck will last is rather harder for Cassius Dio to tell. There is something potentially sobering for Romans of the third century AD in thinking of themselves as Athenians of almost eight hundred years before.

(10) CONCLUSION

Homer's Odysseus is a totemic figure within the history of ancient curiosity. The great hero who visits the cities of many men and gets

---

[222] Gabba (1955), 310–11 makes this case.

[223] Flor. *praef.* 8 'quasi consenuit'. For this motif in Roman historiography, cf. Sen. ap. Lactant. *Div. inst.* 7. 15. 14; Bessone (2008).

[224] Flor. *praef.* 8: 'sub Traiano principe mouit lacertos et praeter spem omnium senectus imperii quasi reddita iuuentute reuirescit'.

to know their minds is an inspiration to those scholars who travel in his wake and particularly to the great geographer-historians Herodotus and Polybius. Nor are they alone. In the *Metamorphoses* of Apuleius, the one consolation enjoyed by Lucius for his transformation into an ass is that, ignored by all bystanders, he is able to observe their words and deeds, give free rein to his innate *curiositas*, and thus emulate that wisest of men who obtained the greatest wisdom through visiting cities and discovering the minds of their peoples.[225] The Euhemeristic scholar Palaephatus likewise divides the audiences for myth into those devoid of wisdom and knowledge, who simply believe what they are told, and those sage and curious who remain insistent in their scepticism.[226] Placing himself somewhere between the two—but surely closer to the latter—Palaephatus insists that some genuine phenomenon must lie behind each myth but one that has been distorted in the telling. In order to get to the bottom of each case, he has therefore travelled to many a land and interrogated the elders that he met,[227] and what he now writes is the product of autopsy and investigation.[228] He too is an Odysseus even if his version of Aeolus, Scylla, and the Sirens is a long way from that of *Odyssey* 9–12.

Yet there is a crucial element of discontinuity in how the sons of Odysseus conduct their investigations. The travels of Herodotus do not serve the interests of any single polity nor are they sponsored by one. Polybius, by contrast, disparages the claims to truth of a privateer navigator such as Pytheas and looks to the resources of the Roman state in order to map the coast of North Africa or visit the Celts and the Ligurians. As Polybius himself acknowledges, from the time of Alexander, empire is the great engine driving the growth in geographical knowledge, be it that of Macedon or Rome or, as Strabo adds, of the Mithridatic kingdom and of Parthia. Historians

---

[225] Apul. *Met.* 9. 13: 'multarum civitatium obitu et uariorum populorum cognitu summas adeptum uirtutes'. Note Lucius' confession that the sort of knowledge he gained left him some way short of the wisdon of Ulysses: 'nam et ipse gratas gratias asino meo memini, quod me suo celatum tegmine uariisque fortunis exercitatum, *etsi minus prudentem, multiscium* reddidit.'

[226] Palaephat. *praef.*: ἀνομίλητοι σοφίας καὶ ἐπιστήμης ... πυκνότεροι τὴν φύσιν καὶ πολυπράγματοι.

[227] Palaephat. *praef.*: ἐπελθὼν δὲ καὶ πλείστας χώρας ἐπυνθανόμην τῶν πρεσβυτέρων ὡς ἀκούοιεν περὶ ἑκάστου αὐτῶν.

[228] Palaephat. *praef.*: καὶ τὰ χωρία αὐτὸς εἶδον ὡς ἔστιν ἕκαστον ἔχον, καὶ γέγραφα ταῦτα οὐχ οἷα ἦν λεγόμενα, ἀλλ' αὐτὸς ἐπελθὼν καὶ ἱστορήσας.

still talk of the intervention of one state in the affairs of another as *polypragmosyne*, but the same writers also recognize that the *polypragmosyne* of the individual scholar is dependent on, and serves, the activities of whichever expansionist and interventionist power covers his back.

In fifth-century Athens, imperial *polypragmosyne* is an expression of collective psychology. In the Rome of the Caesars, the key factor is the personality of the individual emperor. Should expansion stall and geographical knowledge witness no advance, this is due to the *incuriositas* of a Tiberius or the *inertia* of the Caesars as a whole. Should a Trajan or a Septimius Severus again renew the nation's imperial mission, this is apt to be described in terms of their personal *polypragmosyne*. In the case of both Dio's Severus and Lucan's Caesar, it is also clear that the impulse to conquer is intimately linked with the impulse to know, and that such characters are quite able to switch between the two and to take equal satisfaction from the gratification of either.

This chapter begins with Thucydides and the Athenians' openness to *apodemia* and it ends with the profoundly Thucydidean speech put by Dio into the mouth of Caesar at Vesontio. Here we find ourselves back in the thought-world of fifth-century Athens, celebrating growth through activity, and confronting the fear that the nation content just to guard what it has already won risks decline into mediocrity and old age. Yet what matters is that this is more than just the mentality of Athenian imperial *polypragmosyne*. It is also—and no less—the mentality of a Florus and of all those who saw it as a necessary proof of Rome's enduring vitality that she should push back the boundaries of empire and win new lands. The warning that the Thucydidean Alcibiades offers to Athens has lost none of its eloquence for the Rome of the second and third centuries AD.

4

Polypragmosyne and the Divine

(1) INTRODUCTION

In a speech transmitted in the *Florilegium* of Stobaeus and now incorporated in the *Corpus Hermeticum*, Momos, the ancient embodiment of censure, takes issue with Hermes over the creation of man.[1] This is a creature curious of eye and talkative of tongue who will seek to hear even those things that are not proper to him.[2] He will boldly witness the fair mysteries of Nature.[3] He will direct his intelligence to the very limits of the earth.[4] Human beings will dig up the roots of plants and study the character of juices and will investigate the nature of stones.[5] They will cut open the bodies of animals, even of their fellow humans, in order to discover the origin of their own being.[6] They will study what nature exists within holy shrines,[7] and will look aloft and seek to study the movement of the world above.[8] They will even array themselves in inquisitive presumption to

---

[1] Stob. *Flor.* 1. 49. 44. The transmitted text of the passage as a whole is problematic in many places. This is made clear by Scott (1924), i. 480–5. For his commentary on the speech of Momos, see Scott (1924), iii. 535–43. The rather neater text of Festugière and Nock (1954), iv. 14–16 presupposes much of the work already done by Scott. My attention was drawn to this passage by Mette (1956), 232–4.

[2] Stob. *Flor.* 1. 49. 44: περίεργον ὀφθαλμοῖς καὶ λάλον γλώσσῃ, ἀκουστικὸν μέλλοντα εἶναι καὶ τῶν αὐτῷ μὴ προσηκόντων.

[3] Stob. *Flor.* 1. 49. 44: τὸν ὁρᾶν μέλλοντα τολμηρῶς τῆς φύσεως τὰ καλὰ μυστήρια.

[4] Stob. *Flor.* 1. 49. 44: μέχρι τῶν περάτων γῆς τὰς ἑαυτοῦ μελλήσοντα πέμπειν ἐπινοίας.

[5] Stob. *Flor.* 1. 49. 44: ῥίζας φυτῶν ἀνασκάψουσιν ἄνθρωποι καὶ ποιότητα ἐξετάσουσι χυλῶν, λίθων φύσεις ἐπισκοπήσουσι.

[6] Stob. *Flor.* 1. 49. 44: διὰ μέσου ἀνατεμοῦσι τῶν ζώων τὰ ἄλογα οὐ μόνον, ἀλλὰ καὶ ἑαυτούς, ὡς ἐγένοντο ἐξετάζειν θέλοντες.

[7] Stob. *Flor.* 1. 49. 44: τίς ἐνδοτέρω τῶν ἱερῶν ἀδύτων φύσις ὑπάρχει.

[8] Stob. *Flor.* 1. 49. 44: τὰ μέχρις ἄνω διώξουσι, παρατηρῆσαι βουλόμενοι τίς οὐρανοῦ καθέστηκε κίνησις.

make for the heavens and will direct their souls at the very elements themselves.[9] Some check must be offered to these ambitions.

The indignation of Momos offers an apt point of entry into many of the issues to be discussed in this chapter. From its earliest manifestations, the language of *polypragmosyne* is applied to man's restless desire to know. It is characteristically employed by those seeking to hold another back from unwelcome investigation of their affairs. The comic *polypragmon* may regard nothing human as strange to him, but those with whom he meddles would sooner he simply minded his own business. In the ensuing pages the same conflicts are played out on a higher level. Which are the proper boundaries of man's knowledge of religion and the divine? Which modes of investigation are so much not our business that to pursue them is to succumb to an impious or even fatal curiosity? This is a major issue and one on which one of the key witnesses to ancient ideas of curiosity—the *Metamorphoses* of Apuleius—may be said to turn. This will therefore be one focus of attention in the ensuing pages. Yet the same themes are also developed to striking effect in the works of writers such as Philo and Pliny, while close attention to Seneca will reveal how the terms employed in order to set limits to human knowledge can be turned against their inventors and made to assert the propriety of our pursuit of understanding.

(2) IMPIOUS AND FATAL CURIOSITY

There are few better places to start an account of this issue than Plato's *Apology*. Here Socrates describes what he calls the first accusations against him, that is to say those commonly circulating views that had prejudiced many Athenians against him even before he was formally indicted. He first summarizes these as being that he is a clever man who studies the heavens and everything in the world below and makes the weaker argument the stronger.[10] Shortly afterwards he offers a second version of the same accusations. Now the claim is that he acts unjustly and meddles by investigating those things below

---

[9] Stob. *Flor.* 1. 49. 44: μέχρις οὐρανοῦ περίεργον ὁπλισθήσονται τόλμαν... ἐκτενοῦσιν ἐπὶ καὶ τὰ στοιχεῖα τὰς ψυχὰς αὐτῶν.

[10] Pl. *Ap.* 18b–c: ὡς ἔστιν τις Σωκράτης σοφὸς ἀνήρ, τά τε μετέωρα φροντιστὴς καὶ τὰ ὑπὸ γῆς πάντα ἀνεζητηκὼς καὶ τὸν ἥττω λόγον κρείττω ποιῶν.

the earth and in the heavens, that he makes the weaker argument the stronger, and teaches others the same things.[11] Socrates denies that there is any truth to these views but recognizes that they may expose him to charges of denying the existence of the gods.[12] Xenophon combats just such a view when he attributes to Socrates the conviction that one should follow the established religious customs of the state since those that do otherwise are meddlesome and vain.[13]

The type of prejudice that the Socrates of the *Apology* must confront is made clearer by a passage from the seventh book of Plato's *Laws*.[14] Here the speakers consider the rights and wrongs of astronomy and the Athenian begins by summarizing the conventionally held view, that one should neither investigate the god most great and the heavens or interfere by seeking causes, since this is impious.[15] The use of the verb 'we say' (φαμεν) is potentially misleading in this context and Cicero's *De Natura Deorum* well illustrates what can go wrong.[16] Yet what the Athenian goes on to argue is that the study of the planets is indeed pious because it rescues them from misrepresentation and reveals the true regularity of their movement. Even more clearly, then, than in the *Apology*, the view that the study of the heavens is a form of meddling, far from being the philosopher's own view, is a popular misconception that he seeks to undermine.

The popular view that mortals should not seek to transcend the due limits of their knowledge is encoded in a series of stories describing what happens when curiosity leads to the violation of sacred prohibitions.[17] Pausanias, for instance, tells of what happened when Herse and Aglauros ignored the instructions of Athena not to meddle with

[11] Pl. *Ap.* 19b: Σωκράτης ἀδικεῖ καὶ περιεργάζεται ζητῶν τά τε ὑπὸ γῆς καὶ οὐράνια καὶ τὸν ἥττω λόγον κρείττω ποιῶν καὶ ἄλλους ταὐτὰ ταῦτα διδάσκων.
[12] Pl. *Ap.* 18c.
[13] Xen. *Mem.* 1. 3. 1: περιέργους καὶ ματαίους.
[14] Pl. *Leg.* 820e–822d.
[15] Pl. *Leg.* 821a: τὸν μέγιστον θεὸν καὶ ὅλον τὸν κόσμον φαμεν οὔτε ζητεῖν δεῖν οὔτε πολυπραγμονεῖν τὰς αἰτίας ἐρευνῶντας· οὐ γὰρ οὐδ' ὅσιον εἶναι.
[16] Cic. *Nat. D.* 1. 30 has Velleius attribute the view to Plato himself.
[17] Plut. *Mor.* 522F identifies one of the characteristic faults of *polypragmones* as being that they become viewers of sacred things that it is not right for them to see (ἱερῶν ἃ μὴ θέμις ὁρᾶν γίνονται θεαταί). This impulse and its consequences is familiar from Eur. *Bacch.* 912, where Pentheus is addressed as σὲ τὸν πρόθυμον ὄνθ' ἃ μὴ χρεὼν ὁρᾶν shortly before the fatal journey to Cithaeron to spy on the Bacchants. For what happened to Aeschylus, when he fastened in undue detail (περιεργότερον) on the mysteries of Demeter in various of his plays, see Aesch. test. 93b = Anon. in Arist. *Eth. Nic.* 1111a8 ed. Heylbut, *Commentaria in Aristotelem Graeca*, 23 vols. (Berlin, 1882–1909), xx. 145. 23.

what was inside and opened the box containing Erichthonios. The princesses threw themselves off the Acropolis and died.[18] The same writer also tells of the audacious curiosity that led an uninitiated man to enter the shrine of Isis. When he emerged he told what he had seen and promptly died.[19] Aelian ascribes a similar fate to the *polypragmon* who conceived a passionate desire to look on the sacred serpent of Metelis in Egypt and then told others what he had seen.[20] He also employs the language of appetite as he tells of the uninitiated man who thirsted to see the mysteries of Demeter and Persephone and fattened his greedy and unruly eye with an evil feast.[21] This too is defined as ill-fated curiosity and results in the sinner's demise.[22] Philo makes much the same claim with regard to the tabernacle of the Jews.[23]

The same writers who tell of what happens to those who push their curiosity beyond the proper bounds also decline to tackle topics that will lead them into impiety. A good warning of what may happen if they do not do so is offered by the *Epistle of Aristeas*. This is a narrative composed at some point in the second or first centuries BC and purports to be the account sent by Aristeas, a leading figure at the court of Ptolemy II, to his brother Philocrates of the process by which seventy-two learned Jews were brought from Jerusalem to Alexandria in order to translate the Pentateuch into Greek.[24] Aristeas presents both himself and his brother as figures of *periergia* and *philomatheia* and does so in such a way as to suggest that the one

---

[18] Paus. 1. 18. 2: ἐς τὴν παρακαταθήκην μὴ πολυπραγμονεῖν. See also Apollod. *Bibl.* 3. 14. 6: αἱ δὲ ἀδελφαὶ τῆς Πανδρόσου ἀνοίγουσιν τὴν κίστην ὑπὸ περιεργίας καὶ θεῶνται τῶι βρέφει παρεσπειραμένον δράκοντα. For the story of Pandora's box told in similar terms, see Babr. *Fab.* 58, where it is opened by man lacking self-control and yearning to know what is in it (εἰδέναι σπεύδων τί ποτ᾽ ἦν ἐν αὐτῷ).

[19] Paus. 10. 32. 17: πολυπραγμοσύνης τε καὶ τόλμης; Merkelbach (1962), 25–6.

[20] Ael. *NA* 11. 17.

[21] Ael. fr. 46a D–F: ἀνὴρ λίχνον ὄμμα καὶ ἀσελγὲς πιαίνων κακῆι ἑστιάσει τὰ τῆς Φερακράτης ὄργια ἐδίψωσε θεάσασθαι ἀτέλεστος ὤν.

[22] Ael. fr. 46b D–F: πολυπραγμοσύνης δυστυχοῦς. Contrast the sense of πολυπραγμονεῖν at Ael. fr. 55b D–F, where the god urges his devotees not to concern themselves because he has the issue under consideration. The story told is clearly that narrated at Xen. *Hell.* 6. 4. 29–32, in which Iason of Pherae conceives a passionate desire for the gifts dedicated at the temple of Apollo at Delphi and suffers a violent end as a result.

[23] Philo, *Ebr.* 135 refers to the death penalty for anyone touching or looking on the tabernacle out of curiosity of the eyes (διὰ περιεργίαν ὀφθαλμῶν). For more on such narratives, see Magnien (1950), 29–32.

[24] For an introduction to this text and the various scholarly disputes around it, see Gruen (1998), 206–22.

is synonymous with the other.[25] It is this characteristic that leads
Aristeas to participate in the embassy to Eleazer,[26] but he and
Philocrates know that curiosity must be reined in by piety and
must be directed at that which can benefit the mortal mind.[27] All
this stands in stark contrast to the Greek historian Theopompus, who
succumbs to madness on account of his desire to investigate the laws
of the Jews and bring them to the attention of the world at large.
Only when a dream assures him that this impious *periergia* is the
root of his troubles does he desist and then return to sanity.[28] The
same sufferings are also experienced by the tragedian Theodectes,
who inserts passages from the Scriptures into his works and succumbs to blindness as a result.[29] Where Theopompus and Theodectes take it upon themselves to make use of what is not theirs,
Ptolemy II engages in elaborate diplomatic overtures and waits for
the consent of Eleazer before his translation is made.[30]

For a good example of prudence in matters relating to the divine,
we may turn to Pausanias, who, though no stranger to the neutral or
even positive evaluation of scholarly *polypragmosyne*,[31] disavows
such an approach to the cult of Lycaian Zeus in Arcadia and reasserts
the very piety that some of those he describes have forgotten.[32]
Similar qualms must underlie Aelian's reluctance to examine the
depths of the sea or the chasm of Pluto in India.[33] Dionysius of

---

[25] Epist. Arist. 1, 3, 7, 128, 171, 322. For synonymity, note Epist. Arist. 128 and 171,
which opens the account of Eleazer's explanation of the laws of Jews with reference to
the *periergia* of Philocrates and closes it with reference to his *philomatheia*.

[26] Epist. Arist. 3: τὴν προαίρεσιν ἔχοντες ἡμεῖς πρὸς τὸ περιέργως τὰ θεῖα κατανοεῖν.

[27] Epist. Arist. 1–2, 7, 322.

[28] Epist. Arist. 315: δι' ὀνείρου δὲ σημανθέντος, ὅτι τὰ θεῖα βούλεται περιεργασάμενος
εἰς κοινοὺς ἀνθρώπους ἐκφέρειν, ἀποσχόμενος δὲ οὕτως ἀποκαταστῆναι. The passage
quoted at Theopomp. FGrH 115 T11 as Epist. Arist. 313–15 is in fact Joseph AJ 12.
111–12. For a further Jewish example, see Joseph AJ 10. 210. Gruen (1998), 216 suggests
that Theopompus' mistake was to quote carelessly from the Scriptures, but this must be
based on a misunderstanding of Aristeas' Greek.

[29] Epist. Arist. 316.

[30] Note also Epist. Arist. 317 for the care with which Ptolemy preserves the
translation after it has been made.

[31] Paus. 1. 28. 7; 5. 20. 2; 6. 19. 9; 8. 41. 10; 9. 20. 3; 9. 30. 3, 12.

[32] Paus. 8. 38. 7: ἐπὶ τούτου τοῦ βωμοῦ τῶι Λυκαίωι Διὶ θύουσιν ἐν ἀπορρήτωι·
πολυπραγμονῆσαι δὲ οὔ μοι τὰ ἐς τὴν θυσίαν ἡδὺ ἦν, ἐχέτω δὲ ὡς ἔχει καὶ ὡς ἔσχεν ἐξ
ἀρχῆς.

[33] Ael. NA 9. 35; 16. 16. In both cases the investigation disavowed would in fact be
physically impossible, but it is important that 9. 35 should observe that the depths of
the sea are the realm of marine divinities (θεοὶ δὲ θαλάττιοι καὶ ἐνάλιοι δαίμονες
εἰλήχασι τὸν χῶρον καὶ μέντοι καὶ ὁ τῆς ὑγρᾶς οὐσίας δεσπότης), while 16. 16 should

Halicarnassus in turn refuses to ask meddling questions (*polyprag-monein*) about the sacred objects hidden in the temple of Vesta nor does he think that anyone else should do so who wishes to maintain piety towards the gods.[34] Cicero too must be thinking in very similar terms in the *De Domo* when he asks the college of pontiffs what is so arrogant as to try to give them lessons in religious practice, what so stupid as to tell them what one has found in their books, and what so meddling (*curiosum*) as to wish to know those things concerning which the ancestors desired only the priests to be informed.[35] Later in the same speech the orator states that he does not investigate the augural books, has no meddlesome curiosity to investigate their law, and is content to know only as much as the rest of the populace have discovered from their frequent responses in public meetings.[36] Similar protestations of ignorance are offered with regard to the pontifical law; should Cicero have such knowledge, he would pretend not to, lest he seem an irritant to others and a meddler to the pontiffs themselves.[37] In another speech with a strong religious theme, the *De Haruspicum Responsis*, Cicero assaults Clodius in terms familiar from what has already been seen in the accounts of impious *polypragmosyne* offered by Pausanias and Aelian. For the impious penetration of the all-female rites of the Bona Dea is a

emphasize how little men know of the chasm of Pluto (ἀπόρρητοι σύριγγες καὶ ὁδοὶ κρυπταὶ καὶ διαδρομαὶ ἀνθρώποις <μὲν> ἀθέατοι).

[34] Dion. Hal. *Ant. Rom.* 2. 66. 6.
[35] Cic. *Dom.* 33; Bös (1995), 48–9.
[36] Cic. *Dom.* 39: 'non sum in exquirendo iure augurum curiosus'.
[37] Cic. *Dom.* 121: 'non dissimulo me nescire ea quae, etiam si scirem, dissim-ularem, ne aliis molestus, uobis etiam curiosus uiderer'. The issue here is the validity or otherwise of the dedication of Clodius' Temple of Liberty. Only one pontiff—L. Pinarius Natta—was present and he the brother of Clodius' wife, but the argument turns on the specific doorpost he held as he delivered the formula of dedication. Did it belong to the Temple of Liberty or to the 'ambulatio' Cicero suggests that Clodius' seeks to build? Cicero goes on to lecture the pontiffs on the pontifical law, but note 138 for the assertion that he has done so only on the basis of what information is accessible to all. What they hold inside, may stay there: 'ac si, pontifices, neque is cui licuit, neque id quod fas fuit dedicauit, quid me attinet iam illud tertium quod proposueram docere, non iis institutis ac uerbis quibus caerimonias postulant ded-icasse? dixi a principio nihil me de scientia uestra, nihil de sacris, nihil de abscondito pontificum iure dicturum. quae sunt adhuc a me de iure dedicandi disputata, non sunt quaesita ex occulto aliquo genere litterarum, sed sumpta de medio, ex rebus palam per magistratus actis ad conlegiumque delatis, ex senatus consulto, ex lege. illa interiora iam uestra sunt, quid dici, quid praeiri, quid tangi, quid teneri ius fuerit.'

violation not only by but also of the eye and one that renders Clodius
unfit to serve as a priest.[38] In a key passage on this episode, Cicero
therefore asks whether any sacrifice is so hidden as that which excludes
not just meddling (*curiosos*) but even wandering (*errantis*) eyes; to
stumble in would be put down to innocent error (*imprudentia*), actually to seek such knowledge is something considerably worse (*impro-
bitas*).[39] He himself is happy to disavow any too-clever questioning of
religious tradition and to defer to the wisdom of the ancestors.[40]

(3) APULEIUS ON THE PERILS AND PLEASURES
OF CURIOSITY

Eyes which actually seek to see what they have no right to see as
against eyes that inadvertently come on the same revelation: this is a
distinction with which few students of Ovid can fail to be familiar.
For the *Tristia* protest that the poet's exile is in part due to the fact
that he saw by accident (*imprudenti*) something which he should
never have seen,[41] and that what he pays for is but a fatal mistake
(*error*).[42] What results is an uncomfortable identity between the poet
and the Actaeon of his own *Metamorphoses*;[43] and that which leads
to Actaeon's destruction is never more than a youthful error.[44]
Striking therefore to turn to Apuleius, *Metamorphoses* 2. 4, and to
note that the last detail in the long description of the statue of Diana
in the atrium of Byrrhena is Actaeon staking out the goddess
(*in fonte loturam Dianam opperiens*), the curious gaze (*curioso
optutu*) which Actaeon directs at her, and his final transformation
into a stag. This then is no youthful innocent and in his lack of

---

[38] Cic. *Har. resp.* 8, 26, 33, 57. For more on the same theme, see Cic. *Dom.* 105. For
the requirement in Greek and Roman religion that a priest be fully sound of body, see
Pl. *Leg.* 759c; Anaxandr. fr. 40 K-A; Dion. Hal. *Ant. Rom.* 2. 21. 3; Cic. *Att.* 2. 9. 2; Sen.
Controv. 4. 2; Plin. *HN* 7. 104–5; Plut. *Mor.* 281C–D; Gell. *NA* 1. 12. 3; Cass. Dio 54.
24; Garland (1995), 64–5, 191; Vlahogiannis (1998), 19; Wilgaux (2009).

[39] Cic. *Har. resp.* 37; Bös (1995), 50.

[40] Cic. *Har. resp.* 37.

[41] Ov. *Tr.* 2. 103–4.

[42] Ov. *Tr.* 2. 109.

[43] Ov. *Tr.* 2. 105–6; *Met.* 3. 138–252.

[44] Ov. *Met.* 3. 142: 'quod enim scelus error habebat?'; 3. 175: 'per nemus ignotum
non certis passibus errans'.

innocence he is a necessary warning to a hero, Lucius, whose curiosity for knowledge of every sort will lead to his own metamorphosis into an ass.[45]

The *Metamorphoses* of Apuleius are a key text for anyone interested in the ancient understanding of curiosity.[46] The theme is also prominent in the much briefer *Onos* of Lucian—and must therefore have featured strongly in the longer Greek narrative that stands behind both these works—but Apuleius offers a vastly more sophisticated handling of the topic.[47] The Actaeon paradigm is itself important as a warning against the dangers of curiosity, and the narrators of both the *Onos* and the *Metamorphoses* represent themselves as first falling into danger through curiosity, then finally learning the lesson of their experiences. Yet Apuleius develops this outer structure to truly striking effect; categories are first separated, then conflated; and what appears to be the acquisition of wisdom is made to appear little more than the transference of an uncured psychological drive.

The Lucius of the *Onos* travels to Thessaly and conceives a powerful desire to witness some of the magical and bizarre activity for which that land is famous.[48] This is expressed in terms of *eros* and *epithymia* and the object of the desire is essentially visual.[49] When he sees the wife of his host transform herself into a bird, his alleged reason for wishing to emulate her is the desire to learn by experience

---

[45] For the symbolic importance of the Apuleian Actaeon, see Wlosok (1969), 73–4 = (1999), 146–8; Sandy (1972), 179; J. J. Winkler (1985), 168. For other ancient versions in which Actaeon deliberately gazes at Diana, see Hyg. *Fab.* 180; Nonnus, *Dion.* 5. 299–314, esp. 305: θηητὴρ δ᾽ ἀκόρητος ἀθηήτοιο θεαίνης, and 5. 477–81, esp. 477: Ἀρτέμιδος ... ἀθηήτοιο, 480: τολμηροῖς βλεφάροισιν.

[46] Mette (1956); Lancel (1961); Rüdiger (1963); Schlam (1968); Wlosok (1969) = (1999); Moreschini (1972); Sandy (1972); Griffiths (1975), 248–50; Penwill (1975); Scobie (1975), 80-2; Walsh (1988); Callari (1989); DeFilippo (1990); Schlam (1992); Bös (1995), 58–84; Hijmans jr. (1995); Kirichenko (2008).

[47] For the relationship between the three texts, see Mette (1956), 228–32; Rüdiger (1963), 61–4; Walsh (1988), 74–5; Mason (1994).

[48] For magic and fatal curiosity in this period, see also Cass. Dio 69. 11. 2–3, who suggests that Hadrian's favourite Antinous died in a magic rite and says of Hadrian that τά τε γὰρ ἄλλα περιεργότατος ... ἐγένετο, καὶ μαντείαις μαγγανείαις τε παντοδαπαῖς ἐχρῆτο. For the same claim, see Suda α 527. Note also Hdn. 4. 12. 3 attributing a similar character to Caracalla: περιεργότατος γὰρ ὢν οὐ μόνον τὰ ἀνθρώπων πάντα εἰδέναι ἤθελεν, ἀλλὰ καὶ τὰ θεῖά τε καὶ δαιμόνια πολυπραγμονεῖν. For curiosity regarding magic and penetration of forbidden realms of knowledge, see Wlosok (1969), 72–3, 81 = (1999), 145–6, 151–2.

[49] Luci. *On.* 4: ἐπεθύμουν δὲ σφόδρα μείνας ἐνταῦθα ἐξευρεῖν τινα τῶν μαγεύειν ἐπισταμένων γυναικῶν καὶ θεάσασθαί τι παράδοξον ... τῶι ἔρωτι τῆς ταύτης θέας δοὺς ἐμαυτόν, 5: σὺ ὁ φάσκων ἐπιθυμεῖν ταύτης τῆς παραδόξου θέας, 11: πάλαι γὰρ τῆς παραδόξου ταύτης θέας ἐπιθυμῶ, 12: πολυχρονίου ἐπιθυμίας.

whether once transformed he will retain the soul of a man, but there is precious little else to suggest that this is a man in pursuit of any higher revelation.[50] When instead he is turned into a donkey and realizes that he is in danger from wolves or other wild beasts, he puts a different construction on what he has done and laments his untimely curiosity.[51] When later he and his gardener master take refuge from the soldier whom the latter has assaulted, it is the same indiscriminate curiosity that leads Lucius to stick his head out of an upper window and expose himself to recapture.[52] Restored at last to human form and offering sacrifice to the gods who saved him, Lucius describes himself as one rescued not from a dog's arse but from the curiosity of a donkey.[53] A lesson has been learned.

To many—not least to those of a religious disposition—it can come as something of a relief to learn that curiosity is a very bad thing.[54] It endows the hero's experiences with an uncomplicated moral meaning and calms any anxiety that one might actually have enjoyed reading about them. Stolen, burdened and beaten, made to serve a gang of high-camp charlatans, and finally turned into a freak-show attraction, Lucius may feel that this is all too high a price to pay for the chance to glean gossip unobserved and the gratifying increase in the dimensions of his member.[55] This basic pattern holds true for Apuleius no less than for Lucian, and in both cases the hero's spiritual journey from curiosity to its rejection is quite easy to plot. Apuleius may even be said to outdo Lucian in his statement of the moral of the story, for the primary narrative of Lucius' error and enlightenment is enriched by a succession of secondary tales and images that make much the same point. This is the case not just for the image of Actaeon staking out Diana but also for the merchant Aristomenes' tale at 1. 5–19 of his encounter with the witches of Thessaly and the crone's extended story of Cupid and Psyche at 4. 27–6. 24.[56] Lucius and the reader are exposed to one statement after another of the same essential moral, but something remains to

---

[50] Luci. *On.* 13; Kirichenko (2008), 347.

[51] Luci. *On.* 15: ὢ τῆς ἀκαίρου ταύτης περιεργίας.

[52] Luci. *On.* 45: πάντα περίεργος.

[53] Luci. *On.* 56: ἐξ ὄνου περιεργίας.

[54] Callari (1989) appears immune to the pleasures of this text. See also Lancel (1961), 45–6; Schlam (1968), 124–5. For a critique of such approaches, see Moreschini (1972), 518–20.

[55] Apul. *Met.* 3. 24; 9. 12–13. For penis size, note also Luci. *On.* 56.

[56] Sandy (1972), 180; Moreschini (1978), 36–7.

suggest that the *Metamorphoses* is more than the sum of any wisdom it can impart.

Lucius, as we first meet him, is travelling to Thessaly on business. This is the case in both the *Onos* and the *Metamorphoses* and in both texts the hero-narrator identifies himself as enjoying philosophical associations suggestive of some capacity for higher wisdom. Whereas in Lucian the connection is with the sophist Dekrianos, in Apuleius Lucius can boast of connections on his mother's side with the great Plutarch and his Stoic nephew Sextus.[57] Yet not even this tie to the author of the *Peri Polypragmosynes* can save Lucius from his own curiosity.[58] For the man himself this may be regarded as a misfortune; for the narrative as whole it is a blessing. For curiosity is the motor driving the *Metamorphoses* forward and without it there would be no story.[59] Apuleius has, moreover, brought this factor into play even earlier than does Lucian. For whereas in the *Onos* the travelling companions of Lucius serve only to warn him against his prospective host, the miser Hipparchus, and his household, in Apuleius they have a much more fundamental role. Joining these two as they rest on the roadside, Lucius hears the one offer an incredulous response to a tale told by the other. A man, as he tells us, habitually thirsty for the unusual,[60] he intervenes to ask the storyteller to share the tale with one who is 'not curious, just the sort to want to know everything or at least as much as possible'.[61] This is an interesting distinction, but one of dubious validity. For, as was noted in the second chapter of this study, Menander's *periergos* Karion, and with him Cicero the self-styled *curiosus*, confess that that there is nothing sweeter for one of their disposition than to know everything.[62] In the *De Finibus* Cicero also identifies the indiscriminate desire to know everything as the mark of the *curiosus*.[63] In denying his curiosity Lucius finds an indirect way to admit to it.

[57] Luci. *On.* 2; Apul. *Met.* 1. 2; 2. 3. For Lucius' studies in Athens, see also Apul. *Met.* 1. 24.

[58] DeFilippo (1990) makes particularly effective use of this connection to Plutarch. See also Walsh (1988), 75.

[59] Lancel (1961), 26; Moreschini (1972), 523–4 and (1978), 34; Callari (1989), 162.

[60] Apul. *Met.* 1. 2: 'sititor alioquin nouitatis'. For curiosity and the pursuit of novelty, see Plut. *Mor.* 519A–B, 522D; Luci. *Ver. hist.* 1. 5.

[61] Apul. *Met.* 1. 2: 'non quidem curiosum, sed qui uelim scire uel cuncta uel certe plurima'.

[62] Cic. *Att.* 4. 11. 2 misquoting Men. *Epit.* fr. 2b Arnott: οὐδέν ἐστι γὰρ | γλυκύτερον ἢ πάντ' εἰδέναι. For discussion, see Ch. 2 Sect. 4.

[63] Cic. *Fin.* 5. 49: 'atque omnia quidem scire, cuiuscumque modi sint, cupere curiosorum . . . est putandum'. For discussion, see Ch. 5 Sect. 5.

The story that the merchant Aristomenes goes on to tell is one that
might properly warn against any curiosity regarding the witches of
Thessaly.[64] He does little more than show kindness to the suffering
Socrates, but nevertheless the witch Meroe singles Aristomenes out
for punishment for his past loquacity and present meddling.[65] Aristomenes sees his companion's horrific end and flees in terror into
exile.[66] Yet the tale does nothing to deter Lucius from any interest in
magic. On the contrary, when Lucius wakes after his first night in
Thessaly, the story is clearly playing on his mind as he sets out to
learn more about this home of the magic arts:

> ut primum nocte discussa sol nouus diem fecit et somno simul emersus
> et lectulo, *anxius alioquin et nimis cupidus cognoscendi quae rara mir-*
> *aque sunt*, reputansque me media Thessaliae loca tenere, qua artis
> magicae natiua cantamina totius orbis consono ore celebrentur, fabu-
> lamque illam optimi comitis Aristomenis de situ ciuitatis huius exortam,
> *suspensus alioquin* et uoto simul et studio, *curiose* singula quaerebam.

> As soon as the new sun had driven off night and created day, emerging
> at once from my sleep and my bed, anxious in any case and overeager
> to learn of things rare and wondrous, and reflecting that I was in the
> middle of Thessaly, where the native songs of the magic art are
> celebrated by the unanimous voice of the whole globe, and that that
> story of my excellent companion Aristomenes had taken as its starting
> point the site of this city, on tenterhooks in any case with hope and
> eagerness, I began meticulously to ask about everything.[67]

I quote this passage in full because it is peculiarly illustrative of the
psychology of curiosity as it is presented in Apuleius. Of immediate
interest is the reference back to the tale of Aristomenes, but there is
much more here to note. In particular it is important to observe the
repeated use of the adverb *alioquin* to qualify Lucius' claim to have
been anxious (*anxius*) or on tenterhooks (*suspensus*). The same term
has already been employed at 1. 2 to qualify his self-description as a
thirster after novelty and there I translated it as 'habitual'. The point
in each instance is that Lucius describes an underlying state of mind
or disposition. This will become a leitmotiv of the work as a whole
as Lucius twice describes himself as habitually curious (*curiosus*

[64] Apul. *Met.* 1. 5–19.
[65] Apul. *Met.* 1. 12: 'faxo eum sero, immo statim, immo uero iam nunc, ut et
praecedentis dicacitatis et instantis curiositatis paeniteat'.
[66] Apul. *Met.* 1. 19.
[67] Apul. *Met.* 2. 1.

alioquin)[68] or at other times curious (*alias curiosus*).[69] Other adjectives coupled with the *curiositas* of Lucius to suggest that this is an innate disposition are *familiaris*,[70] *ingenita*,[71] and *genuina*.[72] The language of anxiety or other heightened emotional states is also frequent in evocations of his curiosity. At 2. 2 he picks up on his eager search for any evidence of Thessalian magic and describes himself as overwhelmed, even dumbstruck, with a torturing desire.[73] Nor does metamorphosis into a donkey do anything to calm this character: at 9. 12 he refers to himself as overwhelmed by innate curiosity and thoroughly anxious,[74] and at 9. 42 blames his self-exposure by peering out of the window on the fact that he was habitually curious and bestowed with the forward nature of a restless man.[75] All of this will be important when later we consider Lucius' account of his own initiation and how he imagines the mental state of the reader.

Lucius sets out on his investigations and these he conducts *curiose*. It will be noted that I have translated this as 'meticulously'. This is not to say that Lucius acts other than in a spirit of curiosity, but rather to emphasize the unusual density of terms employed by Apuleius to describe careful, painstaking, even obsessive activity and to suggest that these are expressions of the same impulse that elsewhere manifests itself as curiosity.[76] It can scarcely be an accident that, even before Lucius intervenes in the conversation on the road to Thessaly, we see him carefully (*curiose*) rubbing the sweat off the brow of his horse.[77] The same term recurs throughout the work and is often coupled with terms such as scrupulously (*scrupulose*) or

[68] Apul. *Met.* 2. 6; 9. 42.
[69] Apul. *Met.* 7. 13.
[70] Apul. *Met.* 3. 14; 9. 12.
[71] Apul. *Met.* 9. 13.
[72] Apul. *Met.* 9. 15. For all these phrases indicating innate curiosity, see Lancel (1961), 27; Rüdiger (1963), 65; Wlosok (1969), 71 = (1999), 145; Walsh (1988), 76; Callari (1989), 166; DeFilippo (1990), 475; Bös (1995), 62 n. 15. For a similar motif in the Greek novel, cf. Char. *Call.* 8. 1. 15 and 8. 4. 4 on Chaireas' innate jealousy.
[73] Apul. *Met.* 2. 2: 'attonitus, immo uero cruciabili desiderio stupidus'.
[74] Apul. *Met.* 9. 12: 'familiari curiositate attonitus et satis anxius'.
[75] Apul. *Met.* 9. 42: 'curiosus alioquin et inquieti procacitate praeditum'.
[76] Bös (1995), 60.
[77] Apul. *Met.* 1. 2. Schlam (1992), 48 observes that the adverb preserves 'the positive value of the base, *cura*' better than does the adjective. For similar views, see also Bös (1995), 79; Keulen (2007), 102. There is some truth in this, but it would be foolish therefore to regard the two as belonging to wholly separate semantic fields.

sedulously (*sedulo*).[78] Elsewhere actions are performed with care (*cura*) or with precision (*accurate*), the latter term frequently intensified by use of the comparative or the superlative.[79] No less common are the group of terms connected to ideas of diligence (*diligens, diligenter, diligentia*),[80] while characters also act painstakingly (*operose*)[81] or zealously (*studiose*).[82] All these terms may be said to belong to the category of care, but it is worth noting how Apuleius allows ideas of care and curiosity to bleed into each other. At 1. 18, for instance, Aristomenes meticulously and sedulously inspects the throat of Socrates for signs of the wound he has recently received,[83] while at 2. 29 Lucius reacts with curiosity at his first sighting of a priest of Isis.[84]

As Lucius describes the further stages of his hunt for all things magical, he emphasizes two factors already familiar from the *Onos*: desire and the yearning for revelation. He travels around the city tortured by longing and, even when he fails to finds any trace of the object of his desire, still he carries on.[85] For all that Byrrhena warns him against the witch Pamphile, he positively itches (*gestirem*) to become her pupil whatever the cost.[86] The same verb of urgent desire recurs in book 3 as Lucius seeks to discover the hidden cause of his troubles, and in both cases it is connected to his innate curiosity.[87] His greatest desire, meanwhile, is revealed to Photis as being the chance to learn of magic by direct observation.[88]

The connection between curiosity and the desire to see what is forbidden is one that we have already identified as typical of

---

[78] Apul. *Met.* 1. 18: 'curiose sedulo'; 5. 8: 'scrupulose curioseque'; 6. 1, 21; 7. 1; 8. 17; 9. 1, 20. For *sedulus* and *sedulo*, see also 6. 2: 'sollicite seduloque curantem'; 8. 18; 9. 41; 10. 1; 11. 19, 21, 22. For *scrupulosus* and *scrupulose*, see 3. 3.

[79] Apul. *Met.* 1. 26; 3. 5, 27; 4. 17; 8. 14, 31; 10. 34; 11. 14.

[80] Apul. *Met.* 3. 3, 15; 6. 28, 30; 9. 17, 30; 10. 14, 17, 28.

[81] Apul. *Met.* 1. 7.

[82] Apul. *Met.* 10. 14.

[83] Apul. *Met.* 1. 18: 'at ego curiose sedulo arbitrabar iugulum comitis, qua parte gladium delapsum uideram'.

[84] Apul. *Met.* 2. 29: 'immitto me turbae socium et … cuncta curiosis oculis arbitrabar'. For *arbitrari*, see also Apul. *Met.* 6. 19 but note that this is the product of emendation.

[85] Apul. *Met.* 2. 2: 'sic attonitus, immo uero cruciabili desiderio stupidus, nullo quidem initio uel omnino uestigio cupidinis meae reperto, cuncta circumibam tamen'.

[86] Apul. *Met.* 2. 6.

[87] Apul. *Met.* 2. 6: 'curiosus alioquin … gestirem'; cf. 3. 14: 'familiaris curiositatis admonitus factique causam delitescentem nudari gestiens'.

[88] Apul. *Met.* 3. 19: 'quod summis uotis expostulo … sum namque coram magiae noscendae ardentissimus cupitor'.

narratives of religious *polypragmosyne*.[89] It is also central to what follows in the *Metamorphoses*, most obviously in the disastrous temptation of Psyche.[90] Here the heroine is repeatedly instructed by her husband not to look on his form.[91] She obeys this command until led astray by her envious sisters. There follows a detailed description of the sleeping Cupid, one which the reader sees through the eyes of the heroine.[92] When therefore this is treated as a symptom of Psyche's curiosity, the reader may find something of his own response in her.[93] He will not, however, share her unhappy fate. Psyche, moreover, appears unable to learn from experience. Permitted at last to leave the underworld, but unable to resist the temptation to look inside the jar she carries with her, she falls victim to a rash curiosity.[94] Her husband's chiding emphasizes the repetition of the original error.[95] The similarity to Pausanias' tale of Herse, Aglauros, and the box of Erichthonios will be noted, but the motif is one that goes back to the sailors of Odysseus and their misplaced interest in the bag of the winds. The motif of the return from the world below also suggests Orpheus and Eurydice or Lot and his wife.[96] This is the realm of folk tale.[97]

The closing books of the *Metamorphoses* nicely illustrate both the pleasures and the perils of curiosity. On the one hand, the sole comfort he finds in his life in the mill is the opportunity to watch unobserved and take note of the ways of men.[98] He may not acquire

[89] For the *Metamorphoses* as a religious text, see esp. Merkelbach (1962), 1–90.

[90] For the origin of curiosity in the eye, see Rüdiger (1963), 65–6; Bös (1995), 60, 71. For Psyche's story as a mirror for that of Lucius, see Merkelbach (1962), 1–2; Moreschini (1978), 36–7.

[91] Apul. *Met.* 5. 6: 'sed identidem monuit ac saepe terruit, ne quando sororum pernicioso consilio suasa de forma mariti quaerat neue se sacrilega curiositate de tanto fortunarum suggestu pessum deiciat nec suum postea contingat amplexum.' For this warning repeated, see Apul. *Met.* 5. 11.

[92] Apul. *Met.* 5. 22.

[93] Apul. *Met.* 5. 23: 'quae dum insatiabili animo Psyche, satis et curiosa, rimatur atque pertractat et mariti sui miratur arma'.

[94] Apul. *Met.* 6. 20: 'mentem capitur temeraria curiositate'; Merkelbach (1962), 47–8 with comparison to the mystic 'cista'.

[95] Apul. *Met.* 6. 21: 'rursum perieras, misella, simili curiositate'.

[96] Merkelbach (1962), 22 dubs such stories 'Verbotsmythen'.

[97] Note how Merkelbach (1962), 21–2 and 35 introduces comparisons with the tales of Little Red Riding-Hood and Cinderella. See also Rüdiger (1963), 64. This is not to say that the story is not also a profound reflection of mystery religion or a middle-Platonic allegory. For the latter aspect, see Moreschini (1978), 36–7; Kenney (1990), 19–22; S. J. Harrison (2000), 252–9 with ample bibliography.

[98] Apul. *Met.* 9. 13; cf. 9. 22.

the wisdom of a Ulysses, but a plentiful supply of salacious anecdotes is not necessarily something to be spurned.[99] Against this must be counted the instinctive curiosity that, as has already been noted, exposes Lucius and his master to capture by the soldiers, but further pleasure can be seen in book 10 as he refreshes his curious eyes with the spectacle of the games, at which he is later destined to perform, and the meddlesome wind plays with the silks of the actress taking the role of Venus.[100] The very visual and powerfully erotic language employed to evoke the latter scene will make many readers as grateful as is Lucius for the meddling of the wind.[101]

The very games that so gratify the hero's curious eyes also bring the great crisis of his life as a donkey. Overcome with modesty at the prospect of appearing in a live inter-species sex show, and anxious lest he should be attacked by a wild beast while in the throes of passion, Lucius makes a run for the exit. This, however, is spring and he therefore has reason to hope that he may soon find the very roses that Photis had once assured him would restore him to his former self.[102] In the *Onos*, those roses are indeed supplied by the flower-bearer at the games.[103] We may therefore wonder whether anything more than this is required by the logic of the *Metamorphoses*.[104] In this novel, however, the flight from the games is but a prelude to Lucius' dream vision of the goddess Isis, who offers roses but only in exchange for the promise of his lifelong devotion.[105] The roses are duly consumed and Lucius restored to his prior form, but his soul now belongs to the goddess.[106] This is the necessary context for his final reflections on the problem of curiosity.

[99] Kirichenko (2008), 357.

[100] Apul. *Met.* 10. 29: 'curiosos oculos patente porta spectaculi prospectu gratissimo reficiens'; 10. 31: 'quam quidem laciniam curiosolus uentus satis amanter nunc lasciuiens reflabat, ut dimota pateret flos aetatulae, nunc luxurians aspirabat, ut adhaerens *pressule* membrorum uoluptatem graphice liniaret.' See also Bös (1995), 76–7.

[101] At the same time the wind at Apul. *Met.* 10. 31 must also recall Ariston of Chios as quoted at Plut. *Mor.* 516F = *SVF* i. 401: καίτοι καὶ 'τῶν ἀνέμων μάλιστα δυσχεραίνομεν' ὡς Ἀρίστων φησίν 'ὅσοι τὰς περιβολὰς ἀναστέλλουσιν ἡμῶν·' ὁ δὲ πολυπράγμων οὐ τὰ ἱμάτια τῶν πέλας οὐδὲ τοὺς χιτῶνας, ἀλλὰ τοὺς τοίχους ἀπαμφιέννυσι, τὰς θύρας ἀναπετάννυσι, καὶ 'διὰ παρθενικῆς ἁπαλόχροος' ὡς πνεῦμα διαδύεται καὶ διέρπει, βακχεῖα καὶ χοροὺς καὶ παννυχίδας ἐξετάζων καὶ συκοφαντῶν.

[102] Apul. *Met.* 3. 25; 10. 29.

[103] Luci. *On.* 54.

[104] J. J. Winkler (1985), 213–14; van Mal-Maeder (1997), 101.

[105] Apul. *Met.* 11. 6; Kirichenko (2008), 358.

[106] Apul. *Met.* 11. 12–13.

For many readers the crucial final verdict on curiosity is that offered to the restored Lucius by the priest of Isis:

'multis et uariis exanclatis laboribus magnisque Fortunae tempestatibus et maximis actus procellis ad portum Quietis et aram Misericordiae tandem, Luci, uenisti. nec tibi natales ac ne dignitas quidem, uel ipsa, qua flores, usquam doctrina profuit, sed lubrico uirentis aetatulae ad seruiles delapsus uoluptates *curiositatis inprosperae sinistrum praemium* reportasti.'

'Having endured many and various travails and having been driven by the great storms of Fortune and the greatest winds, you have come at last, Lucius, to the harbour of Rest and the altar of Pity. Nor did your family heritage, not even your high standing or that learning in which you flourish do you anywhere any good, but at that slippery point of verdant youth, you fell to servile pleasures and gained the unhappy reward for your ill-fated curiosity.'[107]

The fact that these words are delivered by a priest of Isis has also been made the centre of a brilliant study by DeFilippo, which draws heavily on Plutarch's *De Iside et Osiride* and the association of the donkey with Seth, enemy of Isis, and makes important connections with Plutarchan middle-Platonism.[108] Yet the ardent embrace of Isiac religion is also susceptible to a more sceptical interpretation and one that would suggest that Lucius has maybe not been cured of his old instincts but rather has found an alternative target to which to direct them.[109]

What, it may be asked, was the attraction of magic and what now is the attraction of Isiac religion? Whether by meddlesome peeping or due initiation, it appears to be the opportunity to gain access to secrets from which the ordinary world is excluded. It is therefore significant that both in book 3 and in book 11 Lucius is a man in pursuit of arcane secrets (*arcana secreta*).[110] This fundamental similarity is further highlighted if we compare the scene of Pamphile's witchcraft and the incomprehensibly lettered metal plates (*ignorabiliter laminis litteratis*) that she brings forth.[111] How different are these

[107] Apul. *Met.* 11. 15.
[108] DeFilippo (1990), note esp. 485–6 citing Plut. *Mor.* 352B for true Isiac attendants as 'those who carry in their souls, as in a box, the sacred *logos* about the gods which is pure of all superstition and meddlesomeness (*periergia*)'.
[109] Sceptical readings of Lucius' experiences in book 11 were opened up by the seminal J. J. Winkler (1985), 203–27. For more emphatic assertions of this position, see van Mal-Maeder (1997); S. J. Harrison (2000), 238–52.
[110] Apul. *Met.* 3. 15; 11. 21; Schlam (1968); 121–2; Sandy (1972), 182; V. Schmidt (1982), 271.
[111] Apul. *Met.* 3. 17.

from the books marked by incomprehensible letters (*libros litteris
ignorabilibus praenotatos*) brought forth by the priest of Isis at the
novel's close?[112] When Photis is about to reveal her mistress's magic
arts, she first shuts the door lest her words slip out and, by this
profanation, she commit a great crime.[113] The purpose of their
unintelligible script is likewise to protect the sacred books of Isis
from the curiosity of the profane.[114] Lucius is now in a position both
to know secrets and to withhold knowledge from others. The reader
may be eager for revelation, but he will only be told as much as can
be passed on to the profane without need of expiation.[115] To do more
would only expose the hearer to punishment for his rash curiosity
and the speaker likewise for his impious loquacity.[116] There is something a trifle smug in this formula.

The connections between magical and mystic initiation are
scarcely exhausted by the evidence cited above. Nor have scholars
failed to pick up on this.[117] That Lucius himself sees the interrelation
between the experiences is indicated by the way that, at 3. 15, just as
she is about to expose him to the world of magic, Photis observes that
he has already been initiated into several mystery cults.[118] Attention
has also been drawn to the prayer formula first employed at *Metamorphoses* 2. 6 and significantly varied by the priest at 11. 29,[119] and
to how both Pamphile at 3. 15 and Isis at 11. 25 are claimed to

---

[112] Apul. *Met.* 11. 22.

[113] Apul. *Met.* 3. 15: 'ne sermonis elapsi profana petulantia committam grande
flagitium'.

[114] Apul. *Met.* 11. 22: 'a curiositate profanorum lectione munita'.

[115] Apul. *Met.* 11. 23: 'quod solum potest sine piaculo ad profanorum intelligentias
referri, referam'; V. Schmidt (1982), 269–70.

[116] Apul. *Met.* 11. 23: 'sed parem noxam contraherent et aures et lingua, ista
impiae loquacitatis, illae temerariae curiositatis'. For rash curiosity, cf. Apul. *Met.* 6.
20; Schlam (1968) with interesting discussion. For loquacity as the constant companion of curiosity, see also Apul. *Met.* 1. 12: 'praecedentis dicacitatis et instantis
curiositatis', Apul. *Met.* 5. 28: 'uerbosa et satis curiosa', and compare the material
collected in Ch. 2 Sect. 9.

[117] The crucial contributions are Wlosok (1969), 78–9 = (1999), 151–3; Alpers
(1980); V. Schmidt (1982).

[118] The overlap with what Apuleius says of himself at *Apol.* 55. 8 is striking. See
V. Schmidt (1982), 270; Hunink (1997) ad loc.; S. J. Harrison (2000), 243. For the
pursuit of initiation in all available cults and the pursuit of learning, see also Diog.
Laert. 8. 2; Iambl. *VP* 14 and 19 for the activities of the young Pythagoras in Sidon
and Egypt.

[119] Apul. *Met.* 2. 6: 'quod bonum felix et faustum itaque, licet salutare non erit',
cf. Apul. *Met.* 11. 29: 'quod felix itaque ac faustum salutareque tibi sit'; Wlosok
(1969), 78 = (1999), 151; V. Schmidt (1982), 270.

enjoy mastery over the elements.[120] No less important is the degree
to which, at *Metamorphoses* 2. 7 and 11. 5, both the maid Photis and
Isis take on the appearance of the Paphian Venus. This is further
underlined by the description of their hair.[121] The question that
therefore arises is how this pattern is to be interpreted. Is Photis
the morally defective antitype of Isis and integration into the cult
of the goddess proof of the hero's progress?[122] Or does Lucius' relationship first with magic, then with the mysteries, indicate an ongoing
susceptibility to a particular mode of experience?[123] In the pages that
follow I hope to show that Apuleius subtly suggests continuity over
change and to demonstrate how this can be made sense of in terms of
contemporary thought. This has no direct bearing on the specific
question of whether Lucius the devotee of Isis and Osiris has found
true wisdom or yet another route to folly, but it does indicate an interest
in personality types and how they can lead us to act for good or ill.

I begin with the text itself and what it indicates about those
disposed to curiosity. Essential here is my observation that curious
behaviour in the *Metamorphoses* can shade into something that is
careful, meticulous, or painstaking. One key adjective was *sedulus*
and it is therefore important that Isis demands of her new devotee a
sedulous devotion and that Lucius subsequently makes sedulous
inquiries about the religious life, is prompted by a dream to even
more anxious devotion to sedulous worship, and, though impatient
for initiation, practises a sedulous worship with a quiet mind and an
admirable taciturnity.[124] In his pursuit of knowledge of magic, Lucius
also demonstrated a heightened state of anxiety. It is therefore
important to note not only the use of the comparative adverb
sollicitius already quoted, but also the manner in which the priest
moderates Lucius' yearning for initiation, curbs his insistency
(*instantiam*), and soothes a mind that is habitually anxious.[125]
When the demand for a third initiation comes, Lucius is troubled

---

[120] Apul. *Met.* 3. 15: 'erae meae miranda secreta, quibus obaudiunt manes, turbantur
sidera, coguntur numina, seruiunt elementa', cf. Apul. *Met.* 11. 25: 'tibi respondent
sidera...gaudent numina, seruiunt elementa'; Wlosok (1969), 79 = (1999), 152;
V. Schmidt (1982), 72–5.

[121] Alpers (1980), 199–202; V. Schmidt (1982), 277.

[122] Alpers (1980); V. Schmidt (1982).

[123] Bös (1995), 65, 79; S. J. Harrison (2000), 249 n. 174.

[124] Apul. *Met.* 11. 6: 'sedulis obsequiis'; 19: 'sedulo'; 21: 'sollicitius sedulum colendi
frequentabam ministerium'; 22: 'sedulum...culturae sacrorum ministerium'.

[125] Apul. *Met.* 11. 21: 'alioquin anxium mihi permulcebat animum'.

by no trifling care and in a state of great mental suspense.[126] Until
one last dream arrives, he is tossing about in thought and stirred to
the point of madness.[127] Lucius even attributes to his reader the same
emotions that he himself experiences and imagines the state of
eagerness and anxiety in which the reader must be asking about the
next stages of the initiation.[128] This may indeed be how we react to
his story, but here Lucius does no more than turn the audience into
the mirror image of his own neuroses. The same obsessive personality is still on view; only the object of the obsession has changed.

It is one thing to identify the key traits displayed by Lucius and
quite another to ask what tools are available with which to analyse
them. One answer to this question has been that offered by DeFilippo, who considers Apuleian *curiositas* in terms of the Platonic
division of the soul and the association of *polypragmosyne* with the
epithymetic personality.[129] There is much here that works extremely
well but the full symbolic reading proposed is one that requires us to
interpret the final book as a break with the past and Lucius as a man
made new. An alternative schema may therefore usefully be introduced and it is one suggested at *Metamorphoses* 11. 22 by the claim
that Lucius and the priest Mithras are linked by a shared astrological
pattern.[130] For the second century AD was one of the great periods of
ancient astrological science and the works of both Claudius Ptolemaeus and Vettius Valens devote much attention to the particular
personality types identified with specific planetary and astral influ-
ences.[131] In his note on this passage of book 11, Griffiths argues that
what is here implied is that Lucius and Mithras were born in the
same month, that is under the same sign of the zodiac.[132] What that
month might be he does not, however, suggest. Yet, if we turn to the
astrologers, one pattern immediately emerges: curious people or
periergoi are consistently identified with the influence of Hermes.[133]

---

[126] Apul. *Met.* 11. 29: 'nec leui cura sollicitus, sed oppido suspensus animi'.

[127] Apul. *Met.* 11. 29: 'cogitationis aestu fluctuantem ad instar insaniae percitum'. For
what Lucius has to feel anxious about in this context, see J. J. Winkler (1985), 221–3.

[128] Apul. *Met.* 11. 23: 'quaeras forsitan satis anxie, studiose lector, quid deinde
dictum, quid factum'. For the reader constructed as curious, see Bös (1995), 78–9.

[129] DeFilippo (1990).

[130] Apul. *Met.* 11. 22: 'diuino quodam stellarum consortio... mihi coniunctum'.

[131] Wlosok (1969), 76 n. 4 = (1999), 149 n. 32 points to the possible relevance of
Vettius Valens to Apuleius. I hope that I have developed this suggestion effectively.

[132] Griffiths (1975), 283.

[133] Ptol. *Apotel.* 3. 14. 18; Vett. Val. ed. Pingree pp. 7. 24; 10. 7; 37. 4; 40. 4, 10; 42.
10; 44. 2; 48. 25; 66. 32; 184. 15; 372. 3; 413. 1.

Vettius Valens, in his initial account of the planet, associates Hermes with those of an intellectual and inquisitive disposition and specifies those inclined to study the heavens.[134] Claudius Ptolemaeus offers a list of good and bad attributes associated with the influence of Hermes: the good include qualities intellectual and scholarly as well as a propensity to mystery cults; the bad take in the unjust desire to enhance one's possessions.[135] In all other instances, what is described are either zodiacal signs said to belong to the house of Hermes or where the influence of Hermes is combined with that of other planets.[136] When the influence is that of Ares or Kronos, this can result in morally disreputable traits.[137] More commonly the influence is benign and those described as *periergoi* are men in love with learning (*philomatheis*) or full of knowledge (*polyistores*).[138] Yet what is most significant for this investigation is the repeated juxta-position of phrases referring to those born under the influence as 'curious, initiates in secret cults'.[139] In one instance this is coupled with their description as people with knowledge of things of which one may not speak.[140] The implication of this pattern for Lucius should therefore be clear: any reading informed by astrology will regard curiosity and the drive for initiation as expressions of the same planetary influence. Griffiths himself does not offer any hypothesis for the month or star sign under which Lucius and Mithras were born, but the text would suggest that they are both

[134] Vett. Val. ed. Pingree pp. 4. 5–5. 2.

[135] Ptol. *Apotel.* 3. 14. 36.

[136] The signs of the zodiac in the house of Hermes are Virgo and Gemini. For the propensity to natural philosophy of those born under these signs, see also Manil. 4. 158–9, 190–7. T. Barton (1994), 112 on Mercury comments that 'The planet . . . was thought to make people good at mathematics, natural philosophy and using words'.

[137] Vett. Val. ed. Pingree, pp. 41. 31–42. 11; 48. 23–9; 371. 31–372. 3, esp. 372. 3: βαθυπόνηροι δὲ καὶ περίεργοι ἔσονται. See also Heph. *Apotel.* ed. Pingree, vol. 1, p. 149. 6. In ancient astrology Zeus and Aphrodite fall into the category of benefics, Ares and Kronos that of malefics. Hermes, by contrast, can tend to good or evil depending on which other planets exert their influence. This is coherent with the capacity of *periergia* to find both good and bad expression depending on its target. For this doctrine, see T. Barton (1994), 96–102. It should also be noted that Ptol. *Apotel.* 3. 14. 14 and 31 and Vett. Val. ed. Pingree, p. 14. 21 find no redeeming feature in *polypragmones* and associate them with the influence of Ares or of Kronos.

[138] Vett. Val. ed. Pingree, pp. 37. 1–5; 44. 2; 184. 15; Ptol. *Apotel.* 3. 14. 18: περιέργους, φιλοπεύστας.

[139] Vett. Val. ed. Pingree, pp. 7. 24; 10. 7; 37. 4; 48. 25 = 413. 1–2: περίεργοι, ἀποκρυφῶν μύσται.

[140] Vett. Val. ed. Pingree, p. 48. 25 = 413. 1–2: ἀπορρήτων πραγμάτων συνίστορας.

men of Hermes, of Mercury. If, moreover, it is deemed unusual that a
priest of Isis should actually bear the name of a quite different
Eastern divinity, it may be worth observing that the god Mithras
was occasionally identified in antiquity with Hermes.[141]

It should now be evident that the *Metamorphoses* offers rather
more than just an account of how one man learns the perils of
curiosity. The self-aware reader will indeed be glad that Lucius
dabbled in magic and therefore set himself off on the chain of
adventures that make the novel as entertaining as it is. Yet for Lucius
himself there can be little doubt that the consequences of his initial
curiosity are in large part unhappy and that he would have done
better never to have involved himself in the Thessalian arts. The
lesson is there to be learned and it is one that is underlined by sundry
other representations of the consequences of curiosity, be they the
tale of Aristomenes, the Actaeon ecphrasis, or the parable of Cupid
and Psyche. The crucial problem, and therefore that on which I have
chosen to concentrate, is how that lesson of the consequences of
curiosity is communicated to Lucius and what impact this has on his
subsequent behaviour. For it is apparent from the *Onos* that nothing
in his Greek model compelled Apuleius to make Isis the source of his
hero's rescue or her priest the bearer of the novel's 'message'. Nor
does Lucius himself express any discomfort with that message or
with its implications for his subsequent life. Those who seek to prove
that he remains a fool have therefore had to appeal to the hidden
author manipulating his voice.[142] My contribution falls deliberately
short of offering any final judgement on the resolution of the novel.
Yet it does suggest a significant reinterpretation of the apparent
opposition between magic and Isiac religion and argues that the
curiosity that once caused Lucius so much trouble is now redirected
at an alternative object of devotion. What makes Apuleius' work so
important for this study as a whole is, not so much the moral lessons
that stand out so clearly even at first reading, but rather his striking
insights into curiosity as a mental state and the degree to which this
understanding is informed by, or overlaps with, both Platonic psychology and the wisdom of the astrologers. From Lucius' first actions to
his last, Vettius Valens would have little difficulty in identifying the
powerful influence of Hermes.

---

[141] Reitzenstein (1927), 228; Vermaseren (1963), 113; Griffiths (1975), 282.
[142] van Mal-Maeder (1997), 105–6.

(4) *POLYPRAGMOSYNE* AND THE HEAVENS

This chapter took as its point of departure two passages from Plato in which investigation of the heavens or the cosmos is represented as an essentially meddlesome activity.[143] In both instances what is forsworn is any examination of the realm traditionally assigned to the gods, and the language employed is coherent with the definition of *polypragmosyne* to be inferred from the *Republic*, that is behaviour which is unjust because it interferes with something proper to another and not to the agent. The heavens are the world of the gods and any attempt to reveal their secrets an unwarranted invasion of that realm. And what is true of science and cosmology is sure to apply even more exactly to magic and to its ambition not just to understand the supernatural but also to control it.

It is therefore significant that, before he ever enters Thessaly and the world of magic, the Apuleian Lucius has already formed an admiration for the Chaldaean astrologer Diophanes.[144] The implication is that magic and astrology are cognate modes, both devoted to the pursuit of illicit knowledge, and that both will attract the *curiosus*.[145] And one author who has something to say in this respect must be Philo of Alexandria. An important example of how Philo introduces Greek categories into the exegesis of the Old Testament is offered by the *De Fuga*, where the burning bush is taken to symbolize those religious mysteries which it would be *polypragmon* (and *philopragmon* and *periergon*) to wish to penetrate.[146] Yet even more common in Philo as a symbol of the disavowal of such investigation is the journey of Terah and Abraham from Chaldaea to Haran.[147] Philo himself often expresses a considerable degree of respect for Chaldaean science, and in this he is not out of step with ancient Stoicism.[148] Moses, like Abraham, is exposed to the Chaldaeans in

<hr>

[143] Pl. *Ap.* 19b; *Leg.* 821a; Burkert (1985), 273 and n. 56.

[144] Apul. *Met.* 2. 12–14; Bös (1995), 66.

[145] For Magi and Chaldaeans among the barbarian fathers of philosophy, see Diog. Laert. 1. 1: γεγενῆσθαι γὰρ παρὰ μὲν Πέρσαις Μάγους, παρὰ δὲ Βαβυλωνίοις ἢ Ἀσσυρίοις Χαλδαίους.

[146] Philo *Fug.* 161–3; cf. Joseph *AJ* 2. 267.

[147] For Abraham the Chaldaean and his eventual rejection of their science, see also Joseph *AJ* 1. 154–68.

[148] Bréhier (1925), 164–70 is extremely helpful on this matter. See also the discussion of Sen. *Q Nat.* 2. 32. 6–8 in Inwood (2005), 196. For further citation of Chaldaean views, see Sen. *Q Nat.* 7. 4. 1; 7. 28. 1.

his youth;[149] but all that they finally can offer is that which can be perceived, while the true sage will advance to that which can be understood.[150] It is this advance which the journey to Haran will symbolize.[151] Elsewhere, however, what the Chaldaeans stand for is something rather more disreputable, and it is here that the language of *polypragmosyne* will come into prominence.[152] For now astrology becomes an invasion of the divine realm;[153] its practitioners are instructed to come down from the heavens;[154] and the onward journey to Haran is one which puts such meddling in the past.[155]

Philo stigmatizes Chaldaean science as an unwarranted meddling in the world above, and does so in terms that recall the language and the intellectual categories of Plato. He is far from alone in this reference back to Plato. One striking parallel is offered by Pausanias, whose description of Atlas' investigations into the things below the earth and in the heavens strikingly recalls the terms of the indictment of Socrates.[156] In Latin writings, meanwhile, what matters most is the fundamental distinction between meddling and minding one's own business. Those who deprecate mortal investigations of the heavens and beyond do so by suggesting that this is a sphere that does not belong to us. Those who celebrate scientific curiosity emphasize that there is no region of the skies in which we do not belong.

Pliny the Elder is in many ways the greatest embodiment of the ancient curiosity.[157] The obsessive devotion to study is underlined in

---

[149] Philo *Mos.* 1. 23; Bréhier (1925), 167.

[150] Bréhier (1925), 168.

[151] For discussion, see Blumenberg (1983), 284–6.

[152] For this second current in Philo's writing on astrology, see Bréhier (1925), 169.

[153] Philo *Mig.* 184.

[154] Philo *Mig.* 185: κατάβητε οὖν ἀπ᾽ οὐρανοῦ.

[155] Philo *Mig.* 187 treats such pursuits as a form of meddling: μεταναστάντες οὖν ἀπὸ τῆς κατ᾽ οὐρανὸν περιεργίας ἑαυτούς, ὅπερ εἶπον, οἰκήσατε, τὴν μὲν Χαλδαίων γῆν, δόξαν, καταλιπόντες, μετοικισάμενοι δὲ εἰς Χαρράν, τὸ τῆς αἰσθήσεως χωρίον, ὃ δὴ σωματικός ἐστιν οἶκος διανοίας. See also Philo *Som.* 1. 54: τί δὲ πολυπραγμονεῖς ἃ μή σε δεῖ, τὰ μετέωρα; τί δὲ τὴν ἐν τοῖς μαθήμασιν εὑρεσιλογίαν ἄχρις οὐρανοῦ τείνεις;

[156] Paus. 9. 20. 3: Ἄτλαντα καθήμενον πολυπραγμονεῖν τά τε ὑπὸ γῆς φασι καὶ τὰ οὐράνια; The only departure from Pl. *Ap.* 19b is the attribution of a direct object to the verb πολυπραγμονεῖν. For Atlas as scientist, see also Diod. Sic. 3. 60: τὰ περὶ τὴν ἀστρολογιαν ἐξακριβῶσαι, 4. 27: περιττότερον... αὐτὸν τὰ κατὰ τὴν ἀστρολοίαν ἐκπεπονηκότα; Diog. Laert. 1. 1; Schol. Ap. Rhod. *Argon.* 4. 264; Schol. Lycoph. *Alex.* 879; Vitruv. 6. 7. 6: 'cursum solis et lunae siderumque omnium uersationum rationes uigore animi sollertiaque curauit hominibus tradenda'; Plin. *HN* 2. 31; Serv. at Verg. *Aen.* 1. 741.

[157] Dihle (1980), 135; Conte (1994), 68; Beagon (2011).

the preface to the *Natural History*, in which he proclaims that the following thirty-six books contains twenty thousand matters worthy of care (*dignarum cura*) drawn forth from two thousand volumes, many of which have been neglected by scholars on account of the inaccessibility of their subject matter (*secretum materiae*).[158] Yet one subject is explicitly shunned by Pliny and that is the investigation of any regions beyond the boundaries of the universe (*mundus*).[159] It is, he states, madness to step beyond, to try to take the measure of anything without knowing what is one's own, or to imagine that the mortal mind can see what the universe itself cannot hold.[160] There is in this a step backwards from the Lucretian celebration of Epicurus and his ability to burst through the walls of the universe and travel the realms beyond.[161] Instead of the heroic rejection of those forces holding man down, Pliny bases the limits of his project on what the mortal mind can hold and what man can properly take to be his business.[162] There will be no place in his study for purely theoretical accounts of worlds and stars too many to count or suns and moons as great in number.[163]

So far the emphasis of this survey has been on how the language of *polypragmosyne* is employed in order to set limits on mortal investigation of the heavens. There are considerable differences in terms of what each author seeks to proscribe (Chaldaean astrology is a long way from the theoretical physics shunned by Pliny), but one constant is the attempt to measure precisely what it is man's business to study. In turning now to the scientific writings of Seneca the Younger, I hope to demonstrate the continuity of such language but also its redeployment in order to offer a much more inclusive account of what truly belongs to man.[164]

Seneca's writings demonstrate more than one understanding of what it means to be *curiosus*. At *Epistle* 56. 12, what is at issue is that

---

[158] Plin. *HN* 1 pref. 17.

[159] Plin. *HN* 2. 1–4; Labhardt (1960), 214–15.

[160] Plin. *HN* 2. 4: 'furor est, profecto furor, egredi ex eo et, tanquam interna eius cuncta plane iam nota sint, ita scrutari extera, quasi uero mensuram ullius rei possit agere qui sui nesciat, aut mens hominis possit uidere quae mundus ipse non capiat'.

[161] Lucr. 1. 62–79.

[162] Plin. *HN* 2. 1: 'huius extera indagare nec interest hominum nec capit humanae coniectura mentis'.

[163] Plin. *HN* 2. 3.

[164] For *curiosus* in Seneca, see also Dionigi (1983), 233–4; Tasinato (1994), 52–5; Berno (2003), 315–16 and n. 75.

passionate disposition so clearly exemplified by the Lucius of the
Metamorphoses: he who is aroused at hearing a voice or some chance
sound has in him some fretfulness and rooted fear which makes him
curiosus.[165] This Seneca compares to Aeneas' description of his own
anxieties as he escapes Troy.[166] The solution he proposes is to train
oneself to indifference as he himself has done by taking lodgings
above the constant racket of a bathhouse.[167] Another passage that
relates perhaps even more closely to Apuleius is that at *De Brevitate
Vitae* 12. 5 in which Seneca describes how the *occupati* obsess over
the details of a dinner party:

> conuiuia mehercules horum non posuerim inter uacantia tempora,
> cum uideam quam *solliciti* argentum ordinent, quam *diligenter* exole-
> torum suorum tunicas succingant, quam *suspensi* sint quomodo aper a
> coco exeat, qua celeritate signo dato glabri ad ministeria discurrant,
> quanta arte scindantur aues in frusta non enormia, quam *curiose*
> infelices pueruli ebriorum sputa detergeant.

> By Hercules, I cannot count their parties as free time, when I see how
> *nervously* they order the silver, how *diligently* they gird up the tunics of
> their rent boys, in what a state of *suspense* they are over how the boar
> comes forth from the cook or with what speed, when the signal is given,
> the lady-boys run to their tasks, with what art the birds are carved into
> even portions, how *carefully* the wretched little boys wipe off the spit of
> the drunks.

This is the world of neurotic anxiety, where *otium* shades into
negotium and *apragmosyne* into *polypragmosyne*.[168] The specific
adverb *curiose* relates to the care to be taken by the slave-boys over
their personal responsibilities, but what matters to the master is that
each member of the household should bring to his particular pointless occupation the same obsessive precision that the master brings to
the exercise as a whole.[169] The final lesson of the work is that life is
not brief if it is used well, but that too many people fritter away what

---

[165] Sen. *Ep.* 56. 12: 'habet intus aliquid sollicitudinis et habet aliquid concepti
pauoris quod illum curiosum facit'.
[166] Gummere's Loeb edition renders 'curiosum' as 'a prey to care', and this
seems appropriate in the context.
[167] Sen. *Ep.* 56. 5. For being *curiosus* as a source of further distress, see Sen. *Ira*
3. 11. 1.
[168] Note esp. Sen. *Brev.* 13. 1: 'non sunt otiosi quorum uoluptates multum negotii
habent'.
[169] Bös (1995), 51.

time they have on public careers or private hobbies that leave them no time for the higher pursuits of philosophical *otium*.[170] The man caught up in the demands of the patron–client relationship is urged to make his morning call on the great philosophers, who will never shut him out or be away from home;[171] Paulinus the *praefectus annonae* is exhorted to leave behind the meticulous supervision of the grain supply and to engage with the great problems of ethical and natural philosophy.[172]

In *Epistle* 108, Seneca represents his addressee Lucilius as burning with the desire to learn.[173] There is something here of the epithymetic character seen in the Lucius of both Lucian and Apuleius. Yet in this instance Seneca is actually minded to feed his pupil's appetite and, at the close of the letter, he puts off until another that which Lucilius had demanded, so that he may not come weary to a thorny topic and one that should be heard with ears erect and curious.[174] This therefore must be a more positive construction of curiosity and what makes the difference is the simple fact that it is now directed at an appropriate object.[175]

The rehabilitation of mortal curiosity is essential to two further works of Seneca: the *De Otio* and the *Quaestiones Naturales*. In the former that rehabilitation is achieved precisely through the process of redirection of energies already outlined in the *De Brevitate Vitae*. In both works Seneca argues for what some might see as a form of philosophical quietism, but which he represents as a higher public service, this time directed at the universal city to which all men of every generation belong.[176] Where other philosophies debate the rival merits of the active and the contemplative lives, Seneca contends that Nature has created us for both.[177] The desire to learn that

---

[170] Sen. *Brev.* 1. 3–4.

[171] Sen. *Brev.* 14. 3–15. 2.

[172] Sen. *Brev.* 19. 1–2.

[173] Sen. *Ep.* 108. 1: 'ista cupiditas discendi, qua flagrare te uideo'.

[174] Sen. *Ep.* 108. 39: 'ne ad rem spinosam et auribus erectis curiosisque audiendam lassus accedas'. For similar employment of *curiosus* in Neronian writers, see Petron. *Sat.* 46. 6; Asc. *Mil.* 3.

[175] Bös (1995), 52.

[176] Sen. *Ot.* 4.

[177] Sen. *Ot.* 5. 1: 'solemus dicere summum bonum esse secundum naturam uiuere; natura nos ad utrumque genuit, et contemplationi rerum et actioni'; cf. Sen. *Ot.* 5. 8: 'ergo secundum naturam uiuo si totum me illi dedi, si illius admirator cultorque sum. natura autem utrumque facere me uoluit, et agere et contemplationi uacare: utrumque facio, quoniam ne contemplatio quidem sine actione est'. Dionigi (1983), 88

Epistle 108. 1 attributes to Lucilius in particular now becomes the universal wish to discover things unknown.[178] The issue is what is to be learned. For this desire can manifest itself in voyages to distant places, in the gathering of the people for a show, in the pursuit of secrets, in the perusal of volumes of ancient history, and in the study of the customs of foreign peoples.[179] Yet when *De Otio* 5. 3 refers again to Nature and suggests that she has given us a curious spirit (*curiosum nobis natura ingenium dedit*), this is coupled with the suggestion that what she really wishes us to make the object of our curiosity is precisely Nature herself.[180] Man has been placed at the midpoint of the cosmos so that he may best study all around him, and he has been given a sublime head atop a flexible neck the better to follow the stars from their rising in the east to their fall in the west.[181] Nor is this just a matter of observation, for scientific research will move from the realm of the visible to that of the intelligible, and will come to discern the laws of nature which govern all these processes.[182] When Seneca claims that our contemplation bursts through the battlements of heaven, there is an obvious echo of the martial tones of Lucretius and his account of the triumph of the mind of Epicurus.[183] Yet the deployment in this passage of so antagonistic a motif jars precisely because the dominant claim is that to study nature is to live according to nature and that man has been made to achieve precisely such an end.[184]

The language of curiosity deployed in this passage coheres closely with that of Seneca's own major contribution to scientific thought, the *Natural Questions*. The subject of what is transmitted as book 7

points to a parallel in Arist. fr. 61 Rose = Cic. *Fin.* 2. 40: 'hominem ad duas res, ut ait Aristoteles, ad intellegendum et agendum esse natum'.

[178] Sen. *Ot.* 5. 1: 'si se unusquisque consuluerit quantam cupidinem habeat ignota noscendi'.

[179] Sen. *Ot.* 5. 2: 'nauigant quidam et labores peregrinationis longissimae una mercede perpetiuntur, cognoscendi aliquid abditum remotumque. haec res ad spectacula populos contrahit, haec cogit praeclusa rimari, secretiora exquirere, antiquitates euoluere, mores barbararum audire gentium.'

[180] For useful comment and supplementary references, see Williams (2003) ad loc.

[181] For liberation from trivial concerns and the freedom to pursue truly sublime scientific issues, see also Sen. *Brev.* 19. 1.

[182] For the same writer's celebration of science that passes beyond the visible to the intelligible, see also Sen. *Q Nat.* 6. 5. 2–3; 7. 30. 3–4; *Helv.* 20. 2; Beagon (2011), 78.

[183] Sen. *Ot.* 5. 6: 'cogitatio nostra caeli munimenta perrumpit'; Lucr. 1. 62–79, esp. 69–71: 'sed eo magis acrem | irritat animi uirtutem, effringere ut arta | naturae primus portarum claustra cupiret'. Dionigi (1983), 91 compares Epicurus fr. 364 Us.

[184] For Sen. *Ot.* 5. 3–5, see now Beagon (2011), 72–3.

of this work is the study of comets.[185] Seneca notes that there is much still to be known about this phenomenon and reflects on the gradual development of scientific knowledge: we know much which previous generations did not know, and our descendants will be amazed at quite how much still escaped our understanding.[186] And if much uncertainty still surrounds comets, this is not because nature determinedly excludes man from investigation: the comet, in fact, obliges us to be curious (*curiosos nos esse cogunt*).[187] This claim may now be considered in relation to the preface to book 1.[188] Here Seneca celebrates the study of nature and represents the mind as rising up into the grand, the enormous world which it studies, and learning to look down with scorn on the triviality of the world below. And where Philo could represent Chaldaean science as the invasion of a world to which man has no claim or Pliny disavow theoretical study of universes beyond our own as being no business of man,[189] Seneca claims that the mind returns to its place of origin, that the proof of its divinity is the delight that it takes in things divine, and that it is not among that which is proper to another but that which is proper to itself.[190] The language of propriety is telling and it underpins what follows. For Seneca now states that the curious spectator examines each individual phenomenon and investigates it; and why should he not engage in such investigation, for these things, he knows, are properly his concern.[191] This is a complex statement and one which cannot fully be understood without reference to Plato. The reader is required to remember that *curiosus* translates *polypragmon*, and then to allow it to translate two different senses of the same term at once. For *curiosus* here suggests both the *polypragmon* and his relentless pursuit of knowledge, be that the pointless and trivial or, as here, the grand and the noble, and the *polypragmon* as meddler in that which is not proper to him. Of these two forms of *polypragmosyne*, the

---

[185] For the likely as opposed to the transmitted ordering of the books of the *Natural Questions*, see Inwood (2005), 161–2.

[186] Sen. *Q Nat.* 7. 25. 3–5.

[187] Sen. *Q Nat.* 7. 25. 5.

[188] Inwood (2005), 161–2 and n. 18 admits that 'it would be satisfying' were the preface as transmitted also the actual preface to the work as a whole.

[189] Plin. *HN* 2. 1: 'nec interest hominum'.

[190] Sen. *Q Nat.* 1 *praef.* 12: 'in originem redit et hoc habet argumentum diuinitatis suae quod illum diuina delectant, nec ut alienis, sed ut suis interest'.

[191] Sen. *Q Nat.* 1 *praef.* 12: 'curiosus spectator excutit singula et quaerit. quidni quaerat? scit illa ad se pertinere'; Walsh (1988), 80.

former stands and is understood in an entirely positive light, while the latter is evoked but only in such a way as deliberately to deny its applicability in this context. Some may regard different branches of science as a form of trespass on the proper confines of the gods, but the Stoic knows that the entire cosmos is the dwelling place of gods and men and that the commonality (*koinonia*) of the two derives from the fact that both are instinct with the spark of reason (*logos*).[192] Understood this way, there is no corner of the universe to which the human mind may not properly ascend.

(5) CONCLUSION

The character of this work is fundamentally lexical. An inevitable consequence is that it may seem to trace a narrow path through some very broad fields. Two points may here be made. First, whole books could be written—and indeed have been written—on the dynamics of initiation and profanation, on the relationship between magic and religion, and on the piety or otherwise of cosmology. My own contribution has been to consider what role one family of words takes within such discourses. Second, the very words studied are limited in the range of texts in which they can appear. In particular, simple constraints of metre prevent the Latin hexameter poets from making the specific term *curiosus* work as hard as it does in the *De Otio* and the *Natural Questions*. This, however, does not prevent them from addressing the same issues by somewhat different means. Mention has been made in passing of the agonistic metaphors of Lucretius as he describes how Epicurus breaks through the defensive walls of the universe, travels beyond in mental flight, and returns with the spoils of true knowledge.[193] The same poet also counters his reader's fear that such investigation is an act of impiety on a par with the Giants' assault on Olympus.[194] Less familiar but no less noteworthy is the way in which Manilius moves between images of the magical drawing down of heaven, or of its conquest and capture, and the Stoic assertion that man is part of everything and that Nature

---

[192] *SVF* ii. 528; Inwood (2005), 158–9.
[193] Lucr. 1. 62–79. See Sect. 4.
[194] Lucr. 5. 117–19; cf. Arist. [*Mund.*] 391a10–11.

willingly bestows her secrets on him.[195] For the distinction between
perception and understanding and the celebration of man's ability to
see with the eyes of the mind, we may look not just to Lucretius and
Manilius but also to the Pythagoras of book 15 of Ovid's *Metamorphoses.*[196] *Cura* if not *curiositas* is a recurrent motif in poetic representations of scientific investigation.[197]

   To look first at specific terms and only then to consider the issues
that they help frame cannot but impose restrictions on the scope of a
study. Yet it also makes possible a more precise focus. What therefore
emerges with some clarity from these pages is the enduring vitality of
the early Greek contrast between curiosity and minding one's own
business even as the key terms—*polypragmosyne* and *periergia*—are
themselves rehabilitated and applied in a neutral or even positive
sense to the life of investigation and research. The mental energy
man must bring to theoretical physics may seem less admirable when
his theorems cast into question the traditional religious account of
the cosmos; experimental science is an uncomfortable category when
its investigations look worryingly like magic. This may be the time to
stand back and mind our own business, not pry into what properly
belongs to the gods.

   When in turn we examine how Cicero, Seneca, and Apuleius apply
the term *curiosus*, we see a literary culture that has learned to write in
one language but think in another. It may properly be felt that the
heightened emotional states these writers intermittently associate
with *curiosus* reflect the Varronian etymology of the term and its
association with the burning of the heart. This is certainly relevant
to the account of curiosity as a psychological state implicit in the
Metamorphoses. Yet even here there is as much or more to be learned
from the Platonic account of *polypragmosyne* and the epithymetic

---

[195] For drawing down, see Manil. 1. 3–4; 2. 129. For conquest and capture, see
Manil. 1. 95: 'uicit', 97: 'cepit'; 4. 392: 'mundoque potiri', 884: 'capto potimur mundo',
906: 'uictor'. For the underworld disturbed, see Manil. 1. 93; cf. 2. 46–8. For the ascent
to heaven, see Manil. 1. 96–8; 4. 390. For Jupiter disarmed, see Manil. 1. 104–5. For
Nature's indulgence of investigation and man as part of Nature, see Manil. 1. 11–12,
25–33, 40–50; 2. 105–27, 143–4; 4. 874–5, 884–97, 915–22. The problem is helpfully
discussed by Tandoi (1964), 162–4; Volk (2001).

[196] Manil. 4. 869–81; Ov. *Met.* 15. 60–72, esp. 62–4: 'isque licet caeli regione
remotus | mente deos adiit et quae natura negabat | uisibus humanis, oculis ea
pectoris hausit'. The echo of Lucr. 1. 64: 'caeli regionibus' is surely no accident. For
another natural philosopher in Ovid, see Numa at *Met.* 15. 4–7.

[197] Ov. *Met.* 15. 7; Manil. 1. 54; 2. 256, 433; 3. 43; 4. 502; Luc. 1. 638; 6. 429; 9. 621
with Wick (2004) ad loc.

soul or the personality types of Claudius Ptolemaeus and Vettius Valens. Elsewhere, be it in Cicero's association of the *curiosus* with religious prying, Apuleius' account of the drive for magical initiation, or Seneca's defence of scientific curiosity, the Latin writers are contributing to conversations characteristically conducted in Greek. What they have to say is no less striking or significant for that, but any informed account of why that is so must work between languages and cultures with at least some of the dexterity that they display. I hope to have offered some suggestions as to how this may be done.

5

Polypragmosyne, Periergia, and the Language of Criticism

(1) INTRODUCTION

The issues to be addressed in this chapter may best be introduced by reference to an epigram of the little-known Greek writer Antiphanes:

γραμματικῶν περίεργα γένη, ῥιζωρύχα μούσης
ἀλλοτρίης, ἀτυχεῖς σῆτες ἀκανθοβάται,
τῶν μεγάλων κηλῖδες, ἐπ᾽ Ἠρίννῃ δὲ κομῶντες,
πικροὶ καὶ ξηροὶ Καλλιμάχου πρόκυνες,
ποιητῶν λῶβαι, παισὶ σκότος ἀρχομένοισιν,
ἔρροιτ᾽, εὐφώνων λαθροδάκναι κόριες.

Idly curious race of grammarians, ye who dig up by the roots the poetry of others; unhappy bookworms that walk on thorns, defilers of the great, proud of your Erinna, bitter and dry dogs set on by Callimachus, bane of poets, darkness to little beginners, away with you, bugs that secretly bite the eloquent.[1]

It will be apparent that our poet has little time for those scholars who devote themselves to the criticism and elucidation of the poets; for they snipe at those truly distinguished and rejoice in the deliberate obscurities of others.[2] Their taste is for Erinna and Callimachus and,

---

[1] Antiphanes, *Anth. Pal.* 11. 322 = Callim. T 71 Pfeiffer. Ten epigrams of Antiphanes appear in the *Garland of Philip.* This work is dated by Gow and Page (1968), vol. i, pp. xlv–xlix to the reign of Gaius and the poets collected in it to the period between the early 1st century BC and AD 40.

[2] For σκότος in v. 5, one may compare Arist. *Mus.* 392b20; Cic. *Fin.* 2. 15; Str. 14. 1. 25; Clem. Al. *Strom.* 5. 8. 50, where his riddling language earns Heraclitus the title ὁ σκοτεινός. Hence Lucr. 1. 639: 'clarus ob obscuram linguam'. Yet even more relevant in this context must be Euphorion test. 10 van Groningen = Cic. *Div.*

while it remains unclear what exactly draws them to the former,[3] the latter is the Hellenistic poet-scholar par excellence, a figure acclaimed in antiquity for his exceptional learning,[4] but also at the centre of a group of poets who could be accused of writing only for the entertainment of the grammarians.[5] Further epigrams by Antipater and Philip decry the 'whelps of Zenodotus, soldiers of Callimachus',[6] the 'thorn-gathering bookworms descended from Aristarchus',[7] the 'Super-Callimachuses',[8] their contorted expressions,[9] futile mythological investigations,[10] and obscure diction.[11] Though Antiphanes himself cites no one school of poetry as the virtuous alternative to that of the Alexandrians, Antipater offers a libation to 'Archilochus and manly Homer' while Philip opts for the white path of verse over darkling obscurity.[12] This is clearly coherent with Antiphanes' preference for an unforced clarity of expression and thought.

2. 132: 'quid? poeta nemo, nemo physicus obscurus? illi vero. nimis etiam obscurus Euphorion. at non Homerus. uter melior?' For stylistic *periergia* and obscurity linked, see also Dion. Hal. *Dem.* 35 attributing to Aeschines the accusation that the great orator's faults include καὶ περιεργίαν καὶ τὸ σκοτεινὸν δὴ τοῦτο.

[3] Erinna was a poet of the mid-4th century BC whose 'Ηλακάτη or *Distaff* ran to 300 hexameters. Tributes are paid to her at *Anth. Pal.* 7. 11–13 and 9. 190. Gow and Page (1968), ii. 114 discussing *Anth. Pal.* 11. 322. 3 find little obvious obscurity in what remains of her work. Plin. *HN* 34. 57 records Erinna as indicating in her verses that one Myron had made a monument for a cicada, but this appears to be a garbled recollection of Anyte, *Anth Pal.* 7. 190 on Myro. See Gow and Page (1965), ii. 101.

[4] For learning as a feature of Callimachus' work, note Str. 9. 5. 17 calling him 'as greatly learned as anyone else' (πολυίστωρ, εἴ τις ἄλλος) and Achilles, *Life of Aratus* I p. 76, 6 Maass = Callim. T 79 Pfeiffer using the same adjective (Καλλιμάχου πολυΐστορος ἀνδρὸς καὶ ἀξιοπίστου). See also Suda s.v. Καλλίμαχος who describes him as 'most diligent' (ἐπιμελέστατος).

[5] Clem. Al. *Strom.* 5. 8. 50 = Callim. T 26 Pfeiffer: Εὐφορίων γὰρ ὁ ποιητὴς καὶ τὰ Καλλιμάχου Αἴτια καὶ ἡ Λυκόφρονος Ἀλεξάνδρα καὶ τὰ τοιούτοις παραπλήσια γυμνάσιον εἰς ἐξήγησιν γραμματικῶν ἔκκειται παισίν. For a similar grouping of poets, see Luci. *Hist. conscr.* 57 on the elaborate descriptive mode of Parthenius, Euphorion, and Callimachus.

[6] Philip 60. 2–3 G-P = *Anth. Pal.* 11. 321. 2–3.

[7] Philip 61. 2 G-P = *Anth. Pal.* 11. 347. 2.

[8] Philip 61. 6 G-P = *Anth. Pal.* 11. 347. 6.

[9] Philip 60. 5 G-P = *Anth Pal.* 11. 321. 5: συνδέσμων λυγρῶν θηρήτορες; Antipater 20 G-P = *Anth. Pal.* 11. 20. 3: ἐπέων κόσμον λελυγισμένον ἀσκήσαντες. For λυγισμός used to describe contorted expression, see also Ar. *Ran.* 775 with Dover (1993) ad loc.

[10] Philip 60. 5–6 G-P = *Anth. Pal.* 11. 321. 5–6: οἷς... | εὖαδε...ζητεῖν εἰ κύνας εἶχε Κύκλωψ; Philip 61. 3–4 G-P = *Anth. Pal.* 11. 347. 3–4: ποῖ γὰρ ἐμοὶ ζητεῖν τίνας ἔδραμεν Ἥλιος οἴμους | καὶ τίνος ἦν Πρωτεὺς καὶ τίς ὁ Πυγμαλίων;

[11] Antipater 20. 1 G-P = *Anth. Pal.* 11. 20. 1.

[12] Antipater 20. 5–6 G-P = *Anth. Pal.* 11. 20. 5–6; Philip 61. 5–6 G-P = *Anth. Pal.* 11. 347. 5–6.

The above remarks offer some context for the description of the race of the grammarians as *periergos*. This cannot be any sort of compliment and it may be assumed that any poet who writes in the same spirit as they read is to be dismissed in very similar terms. In the pages that follow, my principal aim is to consider what exactly it means to describe a writer as *periergos, polypragmon*, or even *curiosus*. Yet I shall also endeavour to look beyond the negative construction of such terms and to trace the key features of an aesthetic that positively pursues complexity of style and obscurity of subject matter. This, as will be seen, is also an aesthetic that resists the grand narrative and revels in the peculiar and the incidental. We will find it in prose as well as verse and not least in the compilations of the paradoxographers.

(2) *PERIERGOS, CURIOSUS,* AND LITERARY STYLE

A recurrent doctrine of Aristotle's biology is that nature does nothing *periergon*.[13] This is a judgement founded in scientific observation but pregnant with moral evaluation: the superfluous is also unnatural and therefore bad. This may be related to the tendency of a a wide range of Greek writings from Isocrates onwards to employ the terms *periergos* and *periergia* with regard to refinement or over-refinement in dress,[14] haircare,[15] perfume,[16] food,[17] drink,[18] art,[19] medical treatment,[20] and sundry other categories.[21] The same ideas can also, if

---

[13] Arist. *Gen. an.* 739b19–20, 744a36–8; *Part. an.* 661b23–5, 691b4, 694a15, 695b19.

[14] Ar. fr. 337 K-A; Isoc. 1. 27; Arist. *Pol.* 1267b25; Plut. *Mor.* 693B–C; Epict. *Diss.* 3. 1. 1, 39; Ael. *VH* 3. 19; 12. 1. For similar language in Latin, cf. Gell. *NA* 1. 5. 2: 'Demosthenen traditum est uestitu ceteroque cultu corporis nitido uenustoque *nimisque accurato* fuisse.'

[15] Arist. *Pol.* 1267b25; Plut. *Mor.* 406F; Epict. *Diss.* 3. 1. 1, 39; Luci. *Nigr.* 13; Suda ε 87, κ 2009, 2010, 2014.

[16] Plut. *Mor.* 713C–D.

[17] Archestratus fr. 57.7 Olson-Sens; Philo *Leg. All.* 3. 143–4; *Plant.* 159; *Ebr.* 211, 215; *Mut.* 173; *Ios.* 93; *Mos.* 1. 208–9; *Spec. Leg.* 1. 174; 2. 21; 4. 113; *Quod Omn. Prob.* 156; Plut. *Mor.* 150C, 668F; Dio Chrys. *Or.* 32. 62; Luci. *Nigr.* 15, 33; Suda λ 140.

[18] Philo *Som.* 2. 155; Plut. *Mor.* 692B, 692C; Luci. *Tox.* 46.

[19] Plut. *Mor.* 64A.

[20] Plut. *Mor.* 67F, 208E, 663C; cf. Theophr. *Char.* 13. 9; Suda χ 90.

[21] Philo *Praem.* 99; *Vit. Cont.* 52; *In Flacc.* 148; Cass. Dio. 76. 14. 3–4.

rarely, be expressed by reference to *polypragmosyne*.[22] To Plutarch, cleanliness in a woman is to be distinguished from *periergia*: she should bathe and anoint herself and may apply shampoo, but cosmetics, perfumes, gold, and purple are a step too far; Hera in *Iliad* 14 does well to cleanse herself with ambrosia and with oil, but golden brooches, earrings, and the girdle of Aphrodite are excessive and unfitting in a wife.[23] The same writer represents the move from verse to prose as equivalent to that moment in human history when the *periergia* of golden topknots, soft garments, long hair, and buskins was replaced by simpler and more economical forms of dress.[24] To Philo, meanwhile, *periergia* is the stuff of dyers and perfumers, cooks and bakers, butlers and wine-waiters,[25] and the concept is frequently linked with the excessive expenditure of *polyteleia*.[26] The unadorned and virtuous alternative is that food falling from heaven that nourished the Jews in the wilderness.[27]

Those activities on which the moralist turns a censorious eye are also fertile in analogies for the criticism of style. Antiquity was accustomed at least as early as the *Gorgias* of Plato to think of rhetoric and cookery as analogous activities.[28] Haircare likewise supplies the Latin writers with many a metaphor for composition: that which is rough and unrefined can be dubbed *incomptus* while overly elaborate prose prompts talk of ringlets and curling tongs.[29] It

[22] Ael. *VH* 12. 1 describes Aspasia as free from all female extravagance (πολυπραγμοσύνης δὲ ἁπάσης γυναικείας καὶ περιεργίας ἀπήλλακτο); *VH* 13. 1 refers to the naturally golden hair of Atalanta (ξανθὴ δὲ ἦν αὐτῆς ἡ κόμη οὔ τί που πολυπραγμοσύνηι γυναικείαι καὶ βαφαῖς ἅμα καὶ φαρμάκοις, ἀλλ᾽ ἦν φύσεως ἔργον ἡ χροιά). For an equivalent usage in Latin, see Val. Max. 9. 1. 3: 'curiosiorem sui cultum' and compare Lucr. 5. 1431 on the 'curis...inanibus' exemplified by fashion.

[23] Plut. *Mor.* 693B–C; Schol. T Hom. *Il.* 14. 187: τὴν τῶν ἀλειμμάτων περιεργίαν is even more censorious; so too Ach. Tat. 2. 38. 2: τῶν ἀλειμμάτων ἡ πολυπράγμων μηχανή. See also Schol. bT Hom. *Il.* 14. 188 on Homer's warning in this passage that the type of pleasure offered by Hera does not come χωρὶς περιέργου τινὸς δυνάμεως.

[24] Plut. *Mor.* 406D–E.

[25] See n. 17.

[26] Philo *Op.* 164; *Spec. Leg.* 2. 21; *Praem.* 99. See also Plut. *Mor.* 270E, 285B–C, 406E, 730C.

[27] Philo *Mos.* 1. 208–9.

[28] Pl. *Grg.* 462d–465e; Bramble (1974), 41–59; Gowers (1993), 40–6.

[29] *OLD* s.v. *calamistrum, cincinnus* b, *incomptus* 2; Cic. *Brut.* 262; *Orat.* 78; *De orat.* 3. 100; Quint. *Inst.* 8 pr. 22; Suet. *Aug.* 86. 2; Tac. *Dial.* 26. 1. See also Wisse et al. (2008) at Cic. *De orat.* 3. 100 citing a Greek parallel at Dion. Hal. *Comp.* 25. 32: ὁ δὲ Πλάτων τοὺς ἑαυτοῦ διαλόγους κτενίζων καὶ βοστρυχίζων καὶ πάντα τρόπον ἀναπλέκων.

will therefore be no surprise to find *periergia* and *periergos* also used
in literary criticism to describe an unduly elaborate style. Dionysius
of Halicarnassus, for instance, notes Aeschines' complaint that the
diction of Demosthenes is *periergos*.[30] This, Dionysius explains,
implies language which displays superfluous labour and constitutes
a departure from conventional usage.[31] Elsewhere, a fragment of the
comic poet Timocles has one character protest at the over-elaborate
and riddling language used by another to designate a table when he
could simply have said 'table';[32] Isocrates employs the same term to
denote affectation in speech;[33] Diodorus uses it when describing the
style of Gorgias;[34] Plutarch applies it to the style of Simonides,
Demosthenes, and others;[35] and Dionysius himself habitually refers
to elaborate speech as *periergos*,[36] while using its antonym *aperiergos*
for the plain style of Lysias.[37] Longinus in turn employs the closely
related term *periergasia* to describe that excess schoolboy ambition
that ends in frigidity, and describes how those who reach for the
elaborate, artificial, and pleasant finish in affectation and bad taste.[38]

It is appropriate at this point to return to Dionysius' attempt to
render in modern terms what Aeschines means by the *periergia* of
Demosthenes. Of particular interest here is the concept of superfluous labour (*peritte ergasia*). Two points may here be made. The first
regards the adjective *perittos*, which has a rather wider semantic
range in Dionysius than does *periergos*, but which can express

[30] Dion. Hal. *Dem.* 56 with apparent reference to Aeschin. 3. 229.
[31] Dion. Hal. *Dem.* 56: δεχέσθω δέ τις τὴν περιεργίαν τῶν ὀνομάτων ὑπ' αὐτοῦ
<λεγομένην> λέγεσθαι νυνὶ περιττὴν ἐργασίαν καὶ ἐξηλλαγμένην τῶν ἐν ἔθει.
[32] Timocles fr. 13. 4–5 K-A = Ath. 455F–456A: περιέργως <γε>, νὴ τὸν οὐρανόν· |
ἐξὸν φράσαι τράπεζα συντόμως.
[33] Isoc. 10. 2.
[34] Diod. Sic. 12. 53. 4.
[35] Plut. *Mor.* 400C, 402C; 802E–F, cf. 1004D for over-elaboration in argument.
[36] Dion. Hal. *Lys.* 6, 14; *Isoc.* 2, 3, 11; *Isae.* 3, 7; *Dem.* 9, 26, 35, 55, 56; *Thuc.* 28, 40,
47, 48; *Pomp.* 5; *De imit.* 9. 3. 7.
[37] Dion. Hal. *Lys.* 9, 15. Note also *Lys.* 14 for Dionysius' bafflement at Theophrastus' imputation that Lysias adopts an overwrought vocabulary: καὶ θαυμάζειν ἄξιον,
τί δή ποτε παθὼν ὁ Θεόφραστος τῶν φορτικῶν καὶ περιέργων αὐτὸν οἴεται ζηλωτὴν
γενέσθαι λόγων καὶ τὸ ποιητικὸν διώκειν μᾶλλον ἢ τὸ ἀληθινόν. For the effectiveness
of unadorned description, cf. Schol. bT Hom. *Il.* 22. 61–5 on how Priam sets out the
horrors attending the sack of a city without epithets, hence ἀπεριέργως.
[38] [Longinus], *Subl.* 3. 4: τί ποτ' οὖν τὸ μειρακιῶδές ἐστιν; ἢ δῆλον ὡς σχολαστικὴ
νόησις, ὑπὸ περιεργασίας λήγουσα εἰς ψυχρότητα; ὀλισθαίνουσι δ' εἰς τοῦτο τὸ γένος
ὀρεγόμενοι μὲν τοῦ περιττοῦ καὶ πεποιημένου καὶ μάλιστα τοῦ ἡδέος, ἐξοκέλλοντες δὲ
εἰς τὸ ῥωπικὸν καὶ κακόζηλον.

many of the same key ideas.[39] This potential synonymity is perhaps clearest in the critique of Thucydides' narrative of civil strife on Corcyra, a passage which Dionysius regards as so overwhelmed by its own elaboration that it emerges as neither enjoyable nor useful.[40] In other passages the convoluted Thucydides is the *perittos* par excellence,[41] but Plato also can stumble when he aims at undue elaboration in style or innovation in diction (*perittologia*).[42] On the other side of the scale, the same paragraph which dubs Lysias *aperiergos* also calls him *aperittos*.[43] And just as an elaborately decorated cake or a richly embroidered dress offend those who would hold them to the essential function of nourishment or warmth, so all that is *perittos* in prose sets verbal ornament over necessary content and communication.[44] The same sense of what is elaborate or recherché in diction is also apparent in Longinus.[45]

The second point to be made with regard to Dionysius' definition of stylistic *periergia* concerns its reception in Latin. The most enlightening work in this context is the *Institutio Oratoria* of Quintilian, which twice refers directly to the Greek concept. In the first book, Quintilian cites a letter of Augustus in which the emperor censures C. Caesar for writing *calidum* instead of *caldum* and calls this tendency *periergon*.[46] Augustus concedes that *calidum* is technically correct Latin, just over-correct and therefore aggravating.[47] The same fault is later identified by Quintilian himself when he refers to those who understand the ways of language but who speak pedantically rather than in Latin,[48] and compares them to Theophrastus of Eresus identified as an outsider by an Athenian crone precisely because his

---

[39] See e.g. the analysis of Dionysius' use of both terms at van Wyk Cronjé (1986), 249–50. For the wider semantic range of περιττός, note in particular its use at Dion. Hal. *Lys.* 11; *Dem.* 35, 36; *Thuc.* 27, 37, 47 to describe excellence in a person or a text. For the two terms treated as synonyms, see Hsch. π. 1667–8.

[40] Dion. Hal. *Thuc.* 28 discussing Thuc. 3. 81. 2 – 82. 1: ὅσα μηδὲ τὰς πρώτας ἀρετὰς ἔχει καὶ κοινοτάτας, ἀλλ᾽ ἐκνενίκηται τῷ περιέργῳ καὶ περιττῷ μήτε ἡδέα εἶναι μήτε ὠφέλιμα.

[41] Dion. Hal. *Dem.* 1, 10, 15; *Thuc.* 50.

[42] Dion. Hal. *Dem.* 5, 6, 25; *Comp.* 18; Mazzucchi (1992), 150-1.

[43] Dion. Hal. *Lys.* 15.

[44] Dion. Hal. *Dem.* 32; *Thuc.* 23.

[45] [Longinus], *Subl.* 40. 2.

[46] Quint. *Inst.* 1. 6. 19.

[47] Quint. *Inst.* 1. 6. 19: 'non quia id non sit Latinum, sed quia odiosum sit'.

[48] Quint. *Inst.* 8. 1. 3: 'multos enim, quibus loquendi ratio non desit, inuenias quos curiose potius loqui dixeris quam Latine'.

Attic Greek was too perfect.[49] Here too *curiosus* translates *periergos* and refers to a fussy over-precision of speech.

The second passage in which Quintilian refers to *periergia* is at the end of a catalogue of ways of speaking that may seem to contribute to ornament in speech but actually run contrary to it; for the first element of virtue is the absence of vice, and an over-ornamental speech will be sure to meet with the disapproval of the listener.[50] Those words that contribute neither to understanding nor to ornament are therefore to be deemed at fault.[51] It is in this context that Quintilian refers to *periergia* and defines it as superfluous labour, which stands in relation to good composition as the pedant does to the careful man or superstition to religion.[52] The terms of the analogy cannot but bring to mind the connection already drawn between linguistic pedantry and *periergia*; but the specific association of *periergia* with superfluous labour must draw its inspiration from Dionysius' attempt to explain what it is in the style of Demosthenes to which Aeschines so strongly objects.[53] For *operositas* must translate the Greek *ergasia* while the use of *superuacuus* to render *perittos* is in turn reproduced by the late-antique bilingual glossaries.[54] In this passage, therefore, Quintilian must refer not only to hypercorrect grammar and orthography but also in general to that which is overwrought and fussy.[55]

Quintilian does not directly translate *periergos* as *curiosus*, but the manner in which he discusses the Greek concept suggests that this is his understanding. What though of *curiosus* as a term of literary criticism in other Latin authors? Here it is important to recall the point noted in the second chapter, that in much Latin usage *curiosus* is no more than a synonym for *diligens* and has the sense of 'careful'.[56] In literary criticism Valerius Maximus applies it admiringly to the detail and eloquence with which Livy describes the

[49] Quint. *Inst.* 8. 1. 3: 'quod nimium Attice loqueretur'.
[50] Quint. *Inst.* 8. 3. 41–2.
[51] Quint. *Inst.* 8. 3. 55: 'uerbum omne quod neque intellectum adiuuat neque ornatum uitiosum dici potest'.
[52] Quint. *Inst.* 8. 3. 55: 'est etiam quae periergia uocatur, [cum] supervacua, ut sic dixerim, operositas, ut a diligenti curiosus et religione superstitio distat'.
[53] See Sect. 2.
[54] *CGL* ii. 405.
[55] On this passage, see also Hauser (1954), 12 n. 44.
[56] See Ch. 2 Sect. 2.

serpent of the Bagrada,[57] and a similarly positive evaluation is also visible as the Petronian Eumolpus speaks of the 'painstaking felicity' of Horace's style.[58] In neither of these instances does the adjective suggest that superfluous effort in composition that Quintilian decries.

Yet one Latin writer does appear to anticipate Quintilian's understanding of the term. In book 6 of the *De Lingua Latina*, Varro defines *curiosus* as suggesting an excess of *cura*.[59] This in turn may help to elucidate a textually problematic passage of book 7 of the same work. Here the scholar considers various pasages from early Latin writers illustrative of the metaphorical use of the noun denoting a projecting rock or stone:

> ibidem (*fr. Plaut. 100*): 'scrattae, scrup[i]pedae, s<t>rittabillae, tantu-lae.' ab excreando scratiae sic<c>as significat. scruppedam Aurelius (*Funai. p. 91*) scribit ab scauripeda: Iuuentius comicus (*fr. 5 R.*) dicebat a uermiculo piloso, qui solet esse in fronde cum multis pedibus; Valerius (*fr. poet. R. p. 273 B.*) a pede ac scrupea. ex eo Acci positum †curiosa: itaque est in Melanippa (*430. 431 R*): 'reicis abste religionem, scrup[p]eam imponas.' strittabillas a strettillando; strittare ab eo qui sistit <a>egre.

> In the same place (*fr. Plaut. 100*): 'parched, stumble-footed, tottering, tiny'. Parched [*scratiae*] derives from coughing [*excreando*] and means dry. Aurelius (*Funai. p. 91*) writes that stumble-footed [*scruppeda*] derives from lame-footed [*scaripeda*]: Iuventius the comic writer (*fr. 5 R.*) said that it came from a shaggy caterpillar, which is accustomed to live in leaves and has many feet; Valerius (*fr. poet. R. p. 273 B.*) derives it from foot and projecting rock. Hence the †curious† usage of Accius: thus there is in the *Melanippe* (*430. 431 R*): 'you cast off religious qualms from yourself, may you impose a projecting rock on yourself'. The adjective tottering [*strittabilla*] comes from the verb to totter [*strettillando*]; to totter [*strittare*] comes from one who stands with difficulty [*sistit aegre*].[60]

The text printed is that of Goetz and Schoell and the editors' estimate of its intelligibility made evident by the decision to print a dagger between *positum* and *curiosa*. Yet the apparatus criticus offers two emendations—Scaliger's suggestion <*pro*> *curiosa* and Ribbeck's *curiose*—and there are good grounds for believing that the latter is indeed correct. For if we follow the course of Varro's analysis of the

---

[57] Val. Max. 1. 8. ext. 19: 'a T. Livio curiose pariter ac facunde relatae'.
[58] Petron. *Sat.* 118. 5: 'Horatii curiosa felicitas'.
[59] Varro, *Ling.* 6. 46; Ernout (1949), 7.
[60] Varro, *Ling.* 7. 65.

adjective *scruppeda*, what leads from the citation of the grammarian Valerius to the fragment of the Accian *Melanippe* is the identification of the noun *scrupea*.[61] And what is striking about the phrase 'you cast off religious qualms from yourself, may you impose a projecting rock on yourself' is the process whereby a character casts off something as abstract as religious qualms, only then to be urged to impose on himself something as concrete as a projecting rock a.k.a. a stumbling block. For this character to avoid heedless or unscrupulous action, what will be required is something over which his conscious may trip up.

Now this is indeed a curious mode of expression, but its interpretation must be governed by recognition of the rule stated at the outset of this study: in classical Latin usage the term *curiosus* never has the object-oriented sense implicit in the English phrase I have just employed.[62] Roman writers may describe strange objects or phenomena as *mirabilia*, but they never call them curios or curiosities. Inasmuch as the quality of being *curiosus* is always vested in the human subject, the adjective can therefore only describe how Accius went about his writing, not any innate quality in the eventual result. The surviving fragments of Varro offer too few uses of *curiosus* or *curiose* for it to be possible to decide on which side of the divide he falls. It can, however, be concluded that Ribbeck's *positum curiose* is the correct emendation of the text and that what is implied is that the particular metaphor employed by Accius demonstrates a style at best painstaking, at worst unduly elaborate.[63]

Before quitting the realm of style, one last question may be posed. The surviving evidence points to an essentially pejorative understanding of words such as *periergos* and *perittos*. In order to find a positive connotation to *curiosus*, I have distinguished its less coloured sense of 'careful' or 'painstaking' from the more flamboyant associations of the Greek adjectives to which it relates when the emphasis is on that which is 'unduly elaborate'. Yet it may be asked to what extent we are the prisoners of the ancient critics and of their more conservative canons

---

[61] Note that the conventional noun here is *scrupus* and that *OLD* s.v. *scrupeus* b treats 'scrupeam' as a feminine accusative singular adjective qualifying 'religionem'.

[62] See Introd., Sect. 2.

[63] Contrast Kent (1938) ad loc. who reads 'ex eo Acci positum curiose' as 'From this Accius has set it down in an interesting way'. The text adopted is surely correct but the translation employs an object-oriented sense of the adverb incompatible with contemporary usage.

of style. As we go on to consider issues of content, it will become clear that many a writer regarded description as *perittos, periergos,* or *curiosus* as a badge of pride. One of these was Gallus, the great intermediary between the neoterics of the 50s BC and the elegists of the age of Augustus.[64] How then might he react to being told that his style betrayed a certain *periergia*? How might a poet like Catullus? In poem 64 the insistent use of a spondaic fifth foot,[65] the learned allusions to places as obscure as Idrias and Itonus,[66] the Graecisms and other verbal effects,[67] all suggest a work that is not so much about what it tells as about how it does so. This is a poet who would just love to be called *periergos*. It is in these terms that I would also revert to a suggestion advanced in the second chapter of this study with regard to the *curiosi* of the strikingly elaborate poem 7. There is no doubt that the primary function of this word is to asociate those who would count the kisses of Catullus and Lesbia with the busybodies of the comic stage. The second function is to add point to their specific concern with counting; for Philo speaks of the *periergia* of mathematical precision and Augustine betrays a similar understanding. Yet where those the poet disparages may be dubbed *curiosi* in the senses that I have set out, he himself is almost inviting identification as a stylistic *periergos* or *curiosus* through the arch and learned figures of innumerability that give the poem its special character. This may strike some as a rather far-fetched suggestion. It is offered in a spirit of generosity and of hope.

(3) *POLYPRAGMOSYNE, PERIERGIA,* AND THE PROBLEM OF USELESS LEARNING

The same terms that are applied to how we write also feature prominently in arguments about what we write about and what we study. The previous chapter's investigation of ancient accounts of what man does and does not have the right to study identified one

---

[64] Parth. *Amat. narr.* praef. 2: τὸ περιττὸν...ὃ δὴ σὺ μετέρχῃ.

[65] See the comments of Fordyce (1961) at Catull. 64. 3 and 79–81 and compare Cic. Att. 7. 2. 1.

[66] Catull. 64. 228, 300; Kroll (1980), 183: 'In der Nennung der wenig bekannten Stadt spricht sich eine gewisse Gelehrsamkeit aus'.

[67] Catull. 64. 18: 'nutricum tenus' is a striking example.

such discourse. A second turns on what it is either useful or useless for us to learn. The importance here of the *polypragmon* is that he is a man in love with learning,[68] though too often that learning is but the chatter and gossip of one who haunts the marketplace and the port.[69] He is therefore a natural target for those censorious of that indiscriminate acquisition of knowledge often associated with the concept of *philomatheia* and becomes the subject of high-minded lectures on how to turn his innate curiosity to more appropriate ends. The ensuing pages survey a number of such contributions in both Greek and Latin, and the reader is to be warned that they can adopt a rather pious and sometimes hectoring tone. They will not hold the stage for ever, and in the final sections of this chapter we will turn instead to those authors who positively take pride in dismantling the grand narratives on which they draw and relish instead the accumulation of knowledge that draws its charm from its singular disregard for questions of utility.

(4) PLATO'S *LOVERS* AND THE PROBLEM OF *POLYMATHEIA*

'Great learning does not teach wisdom'.[70] In this one short phrase the philosopher Heraclitus introduces a theme that runs through ancient reflections on the true value of scholarship and education. Great learning (*polymathie*) in the Heraclitean sense equates to the possession of a huge reservoir of information, and what he implies is that we can go on acquiring ever more knowledge of this sort without ever deriving from it true understanding or wisdom. The same view is also attributed to the early atomist philosopher Democritus while his successor Anaxarchus offers advice on how best to deploy great learning.[71]

Yet it must be stated from the outset that the history of ancient philosophy is far from a ceaseless defining down of appropriate fields of study and that it is also essential to trace the countervailing

---

[68] Plut. *Mor.* 515D: ἡ πολυπραγμοσύνη φιλομάθειά τις ἐστιν ἀλλοτρίων κακῶν; 515F: τὸ φιλοπευθὲς τοῦτο καὶ φιλόπραγμον.

[69] Plut. *Mor.* 519A–C.

[70] Heraclitus B40 D-K = Ath. 610B; cf. B129 D-K = Diog. Laert. 8. 6: πολυμαθίη νόον ἔχειν οὐ διδάσκει.

[71] Democritus B64 D-K = Stob. *Flor.* 3. 4. 81 and B65 D-K; Anaxarchus B1 D-K = Clem. Al. *Strom.* 1. 36.

tendency that takes delight in bringing home new data of almost every sort. 'All men by nature reach out for knowledge' is Aristotle's famous assertion of our innate disposition to inquire,[72] and his own body of work is ample testament to the truth of the claim at least as far as he himself is concerned: ethics and politics sit alongside poetics and natural science just as they do in the works of his successor Theophrastus.[73] When Athenaeus dubs Aristotle 'the most learned' (ὁ πολυμαθέστατος), this is in no sense a criticism.[74]

A crucial contribution to the problem of *polymathie* is Plato's short dialogue *The Lovers*.[75] The setting is the school of the teacher Dionysius. When Socrates arrives, he finds two young men in earnest argument about an issue from the works of either Anaxagoras or Oenopides.[76] To the athlete lover of one of the boys, they are just chattering about the heavens and muttering philosophical drivel.[77] His rival, however, has rather greater pretensions to culture and it is therefore to him that Socrates turns in order to discover first whether philosophy is a fine thing and second what it is at all.[78] The issue of *polymathie* arises when the youth expresses his own understanding of philosophy by reference to Solon's verse 'I grow old constantly learning many things',[79] and then states that young and old should spend their lives seeking to learn as many things as possible.[80]

The second formulation offered by the youth exposes him to the charge of pursuing indiscriminate learning, and Socrates therefore

---

[72] Arist. *Metaph.* 982b12–21: πάντες ἄνθρωποι τοῦ εἰδέναι ὀρέγονται φύσει.

[73] For the extraordinary range of topics tackled by Theophrastus, see the catalogue of his works at Theophr. test. 1 Fortenbaugh = Diog. Laert. 5. 42–50. Note also test. 2 Fortenbaugh = Suda s.v. Θεόφραστος for the claim that he died of exhaustion brought on by ceaseless writing and test. 58 Fortenbaugh = Theophylactus Simocatta, *Quaestiones Naturales* 19 (p. 35. 1–8 Positano), where he is dubbed the 'sea of knowledge' (τὴν τῆς γνώσεως θάλατταν).

[74] Ath. 505B, 692B, 696A.

[75] Diog. Laert. 9. 37 reports the doubts of Thrasyllus as to whether this dialogue really is by Plato and these persist in modern scholarship. For discussion, see Souilhé (1962), 107–12. The issues addressed in the *Lovers* also feature at Pl. *Resp.* 475c–e, where Socrates and Gorgias consider whether an undiscriminating appetite for knowledge is proper in the philosopher.

[76] Pl. *Amat.* 132a–b.

[77] Pl. *Amat.* 132b: ἀδολεσχοῦσι μὲν οὖν οὗτοί γε περὶ τῶν μετεώρων καὶ φλυαροῦσι φιλοσοφοῦντες.

[78] Pl. *Amat.* 132c–133b.

[79] Solon fr. 18 West: γηράσκω δ' αἰεὶ πολλὰ διδασκόμενος.

[80] Pl. *Amat.* 133c: ἵν' ὡς πλεῖστα ἐν τῷ βίῳ μάθῃ.

asks whether he equates philosophy with *polymathie*.[81] This in turn allows him to draw the athlete back into the conversation because he is perfectly placed to correct his rival's initial suggestion that love of gym should be equated with maximizing bodily exercise. On the contrary, he argues, the athlete's aim is the best possible physical condition, and this will be the product of measured rather than indiscriminate exertion.[82] Socrates then suggests that the same is also true of the soul.[83]

What then is the aim of learning? Socrates' interlocutor suggests that it is to gain the greatest possible reputation for the love of wisdom and that this is to be acquired by seeming competent in all disciplines but particularly those that relate to mental as opposed to manual activity.[84] It is not, he adds, necessary to possess every different skill, just to seem able to follow the words and deeds of those most trained in each of these.[85] Socrates in turn suggests that the figure sketched out is analogous to the multi-event athlete who is rewarded for all-round competence while remaining second to the true experts in the individual disciplines.[86] The problem with this version of philosophy, as he then forces the young man to agree, is that, while good men should be useful, the city will find the philosopher useless compared to the true expert in any one craft, be it medicine, carpentry, or navigation.[87] The philosopher then must be a specialist in his own right and the concluding sections of the dialogue identify what he can bring to the city as being understanding of justice (*dikaiosyne*) and of temperance (*sophrosyne*).[88] All in turn agree that *polymathie* and the pursuit of technical knowledge fall some way short of philosophy.[89]

The Lovers is a brief work and it leaves plenty of gaps in which dissent may find a home. One such is that towards the close of the dialogue as Socrates moves on from the demonstration that philosophers, to be useful to the city, must do more than enjoy a competence in discussion of a wide variety of crafts:

---

[81] Pl. *Amat.* 133c, e.   [82] Pl. *Amat.* 134a–c.
[83] Pl. *Amat.* 134c–d.   [84] Pl. *Amat.* 135b–c.
[85] Pl. *Amat.* 135c–d.   [86] Pl. *Amat.* 135e–136b.
[87] Pl. *Amat.* 136b–d.   [88] Pl. *Amat.* 137b–139a.
[89] Pl. *Amat.* 139a.

ἀλλὰ μὴ οὐχ οὕτως, ὦ φίλε, ἔχωσι, μηδ᾽ ᾗ τοῦτο φιλοσοφεῖν, περὶ τὰς
τέχνας ἐσπουδακέναι, οὐδὲ πολυπραγμονοῦντα κυπτάζοντα ζῆν οὐδ
πολυμαθοῦντα, ἀλλ᾽ ἄλλο τι, ἐπεὶ ἐγὼ ᾤμην καὶ ὄνειδος εἶναι τοῦτο καὶ
βαναύσους καλεῖσθαι τοὺς περὶ τὰς τέχνας ἐσπουδακότας.

But I expect that they are not really so, my friend, and that the practice
of philosophy is not zealously to pursue technical accomplishments or
obsessively to live stooping down or seeking learning over a wide
spread of fields, but something else, since I consider this to be an insult
and those who zealously pursue technical accomplishments to be called
mere mechanics.[90]

At the start of his definition of philosophy, Socrates' interlocutor had
suggested that the types of craft in which it was particularly important to demonstrate competence were those requiring intellect and
not the work of the hands.[91] Now Socrates implies that all craft is of
the latter sort and responds to it with the scorn for the banausic
typical of much of Plato's work.[92] Before we discover what philosophy is, we learn that it is *not* to pursue crafts, to live intently and
stooping down, or to demonstrate *polymathie*. Yet the equation of
polymathie on the one hand with craft and of philosophy on the
other with knowledge of temperance and justice leaves a wide range
of activities unplaced in the middle. What, for instance, of the young
men eagerly debating the theorems of Anaxagoras and Oenopides at
the start of the dialogue?[93] If such learning does not itself bring
knowledge of justice and of temperance, is it therefore to be excluded
from the field of philosophy? It seems almost absurd to suggest that
work so abstract could belong to the banausic, but Socrates has
identified no third category to which such activities can be assigned.

The phrasing employed by Socrates at 137b for all the activities
that he rejects is indeed striking. The specific use of the verb *polypragmonein* suggests the intensity of engagement and coheres with
the zealous pursuit of craft in the preceding phrase.[94] The more
substantive issue is the object of that same pursuit. For those who
live stooping over may recall the beasts of the *Republic* denied man's
capacity to look aloft and doomed to live stooping down to the

[90] Pl. *Amat.* 137b.
[91] Pl. *Amat.* 135b.
[92] Pl. *Resp.* 495e, 590c; *Leg.* 644a, 741e, 743d.
[93] Pl. *Amat.* 132b: μάλ᾽ ἐσπουδακότε.
[94] The use of the frequentative κυπτάζω instead of κύπτω further expresses the
idea of zealous or intense engagement.

ground.[95] Yet the initial setting of the dialogue in a school and the introduction of an athlete scornful of any abstract science may also suggest the representation of the *phrontisterion* in Aristophanes' *Clouds*. Here one of the first sights to greet the boorish Strepsiades is that of the stooping pupils of Socrates. His guide assures Strepsiades that they are contemplating the world below, but to the countryman they look like nothing so much as men rooting for bulbs.[96] The capacity of the same stance to suggest at once abstract scientific contemplation and the most banausic of occupations is at the heart of the joke. To any reader of *The Lovers* reminded of this scene and this joke, it may aptly encapsulate what is questionable about the categories with which Socrates addresses the issue of *polymathie*.

(5) CICERO, SENECA, AND POLYBIUS ON USEFUL AND USELESS LEARNING

What makes *The Lovers* so intriguingly incomplete is its reticence with respect even to some of the fields of investigation it itself explores. How exactly does Socrates respond to the questions posed by Ionian science and does he truly regard their silence on the great questions of ethics as enough to exclude them from the realm of philosophy? To any devoting themselves to essentially abstract inquiry, this may indeed be a matter for concern, and it can be a deterrent from discussion of the heavens to believe, as does the athlete, that to do so is just to drivel on to no useful effect. Seneca addresses just such concerns in *Epistle* 65 when he describes how he devoted a day spent ill in bed to contemplation of Platonic, Aristotelian, and Stoic theories of causation. Has the philosopher whose concern with ethics overwhelms even the scientific subject matter of his *Natural Questions* surrendered to the useless subtleties (*subtilitatem inutilem*) of abstraction?[97] As the letter progresses, the specific problem that Seneca himself has examined gives way to the further

---

[95] Pl. *Resp.* 586a: κεκυφότες εἰς γῆν.

[96] Ar. *Nub.* 188–92, esp. 191: ἐγκεκυφότες.

[97] Sen. *Ep.* 65. 16. For the critique of oversubtle logical play, see Scarpat (1965), 157–67 discussing Sen. *Ep.* 45. 13; 48. 4; 88. 43.

question of whether he had any right to address it in the first place.[98] Seneca never finally tells us whether there really are three, four, or five effective causes, but he gives an eloquent account of the propriety of his putting the question in the first place.[99]

The same preoccupation with defining appropriate fields of study is prominent elsewhere in the philosopher's work as well. We have already considered Seneca, *De Otio* 5. 3 and its claim that Nature herself has given man a curious spirit and invited him to study her mysteries.[100] Yet here the discourse of licit and illicit investigation also intersects with that of the useful and the useless. For this section of the *De Otio* opens with the claim that Nature has created man for the dual ends of contemplation and of action.[101] To prove the point Seneca invites his readers to consider how great is their own desire to discover things previously unknown and how greatly they are aroused by every type of tale.[102] This is then illustrated by reference to our tendency to undertake journeys of discovery, to flock to spectacles, to dig into mysteries, to peruse volumes of antiquities, and to listen to accounts of the customs of the barbarians.[103] Self-examination thus tells us that we are indeed driven by that curious spirit that Nature has given us.[104] There is, moreover, no doubt that the catalogue of scientific questions that Seneca now introduces represents a more elevated application of that curiosity than the investigations listed in 5. 2.[105] What is, however, disputed is whether the lower level applications exist in a continuum with the higher or are positively set against them.[106] If we finally conclude that the former interpretation is correct, this is in spite of the fact that some

[98] Note esp. Sen. *Ep.* 65. 15 for the imagined challenge from Lucilius.

[99] Sen. *Ep.* 65. 19–22. Contrast Epict. *Diss.* fr. 1 = Stob. *Flor.* 2. 1. 31 and its final disavowal of grand scientific theories (ταῦτα οὐκέτι ἀναγκαῖον πολυπραγμονεῖν).

[100] See Ch. 4 Sect. 4.

[101] Sen. *Ot.* 5. 1: 'natura nos ad utrumque genuit, et contemplationi rerum et actioni'.

[102] Sen. *Ot.* 5. 1: 'quantam cupidinem habeat ignota noscendi, quam ad omnis fabulas excitetur'.

[103] Sen. *Ot.* 5. 2.

[104] Sen. *Ot.* 5. 3: 'curiosum nobis natura ingenium dedit'.

[105] For this motif, cf. Sen. *Ot.* 4. 2; *Brev.* 19. 1; *Helv.* 20. 1–2; *Ep.* 65. 16–22; *Q Nat.* 1. *praef.* 3; La Penna (1995).

[106] Joly (1961), 36–8 argues for an essentially adversative relationship between the two modes and therefore aligns the passage with other critiques of useless knowledge such as the attack on the *enkuklios paideia* in Sen. *Ep.* 88. The distinctions drawn at Pl. *Resp.* 475c–e are also relevant to this view. Dionigi (1983), 87–90 argues for greater continuity and sees the *De Otio* as drawing closer to an Aristotelian account of man's natural appetite for learning. Dionigi (1983), 233 further compares Sext. Emp.

of the uses of curiosity in 5. 2 recall activities against which Seneca elsewhere rails as futile and superfluous.

Two texts are of particular importance in Seneca's assault on useless and superfluous modes of study. The first is his assault on encyclopaedic learning in *Epistle* 88. Here he rails against a mode of education that can teach him where Ulysses wandered but not how he himself can avoid wandering from the path.[107] He goes on to describe a particularly egregious example of useless Homeric criticism and scathingly closes 'Such things a man should know who wishes to know many things'.[108] Too much of what passes for education is simply superfluous (*superuacuus*) and has no ethical value whatsoever.[109] The mind that is to accommodate true wisdom must first be stripped clear of the useless furniture of learning.[110]

Closely related to *Epistle* 88 is *De Brevitate Vitae* 13 and the assault on those futile literary questions that have now spread from Greece to Rome.[111] Where once grammarians asked how many oarsmen Ulysses had, which of the *Iliad* or the *Odyssey* was written first, and whether the same man composed them both, now they ask who was the first Roman commander to win a naval battle and who the first to lead elephants in a triumph.[112] This then is the same polemic witnessed at the start of this chapter in the attacks of Philip and Antipater on those grammarians who ask whether the Cyclops kept dogs or who was the father of Proteus. Nor was Seneca alone among the Romans in expressing disdain for such preoccupations.[113] Suetonius, for instance, records the learned studies of the emperor Tiberius, who treasured the Hellenistic poets Euphorion, Rhianus, and Parthenius,[114] and

---

Math. 1. 42: φύσει φιλομαθής ἐστιν ἄνθρωπος καὶ πολὺς ... τῆς ἀληθείας ἵμερος ἐντέτηκε. See also Blumenberg (1983), 260–1.

[107] Sen. *Ep.* 88, esp. 88. 7: 'quaeris Ulixes ubi errauerit potius quam efficias ne nos semper erremus'.

[108] Sen. *Ep.* 88. 41: 'talia sciat oportet qui multa uult scire'.

[109] For *superuacuus* as a key term in this letter, see Sen. *Ep.* 88. 35, 36, 37, 42, 45; Scarpat (1965), 171–4.

[110] Sen. *Ep.* 88. 35–6. For this letter, see also Blumenberg (1983), 261–2.

[111] Note esp. Sen. *Brev.* 13. 2–3: 'Graecorum iste morbus ... ecce Romanos quoque inuasit inane studium superuacua discendi'; Scarpat (1965), 172–3.

[112] Sen. *Brev.* 13. 1–3; Joly (1961), 35; Bös (1995), 53–4. Note how Williams (2003) at 13. 2 finds himself qua commentator drawn into answering some of the questions Seneca scorns. The insidious attraction of such issues is also apparent at 13. 4, where Seneca answers the very question he condemns and is drawn into a lengthy display of his own antiquarian erudition.

[113] See also Juv. 7. 230–6; August. *Ord.* 2. 12. 37.

[114] Suet. *Tib.* 70. 2.

gathered together grammarians to ask them who was the mother of Hecuba, what was the name of Achilles when disguised as a girl, what the Sirens were accustomed to sing.[115] The biographer adds that his subject was so concerned to acquire knowledge of mythological history that he became foolish and a mockery.[116]

The issues with which Seneca engages are no less prominent in the work of Cicero. In the *De Officiis*, for instance, the first of four categories of what is honourable (*honestum*) is the discovery of what is true (*in ueri cognitione*).[117] Cicero, no less than Aristotle and Seneca, testifies to man's innate desire for knowledge,[118] but warns against two types of error. The first is to treat things we do not know as if we do and rashly to assent to such claims.[119] The only antidote to this failing is the application of time and meticulous care to our reflections.[120] The second error is to devote time and energy to matters that are obscure, difficult, and unnecessary.[121] Cicero's phrasing overlaps interestingly with Gellius' explanation of Plutarch's concept of *polypragmosyne*.[122] It also anticipates Seneca's tendency to distinguish between necessary and superfluous objects of study.[123] When, however, he does define that which is honourable and worthy of being known, the laudable subjects of our endeavour and our care, his approach is rather more generous than that of Seneca at his most remorselessly ethical: astrology and geometry, dialectic and civil law are all to be allowed.[124] The only proviso is that such study should not be at the expense of action, which is where virtue is manifested and praise acquired.[125]

[115] Suet. *Tib.* 70. 3.
[116] Suet. *Tib.* 70. 3: 'maxime tamen curauit notitiam historiae fabularis usque ad ineptias atque derisum'.
[117] Cic. *Off.* 1. 18.
[118] Cic. *Off.* 1. 18: 'omnes enim trahimur et ducimur ad cognitionis et scientiae cupiditatem'.
[119] Cic. *Off.* 1. 18: 'ne incognita pro cognitis habeamus hisque temere adsentiamur'.
[120] Cic. *Off.* 1. 18: 'tempus et diligentiam'.
[121] Cic. *Off.* 1. 19: 'res obscuras atque difficiles... easdemque non necessarias'; Joly (1961), 38; Walsh (1988), 79.
[122] Gell. *NA* 11. 16. 8: 'uaria promiscaque et non necessaria rerum cuiuscemodi plurimarum cogitatione et petitione'.
[123] For the distinction between *necessaria* and *superuacua*, see Sen. *Ep.* 45. 4, 10; 48. 12; 49. 5; 88. 37. The equivalent contrast in Greek is that between ἀναγκαῖα and περιττά, for which see Dion. Hal. *Dem.* 32; *De imit.* 9. 2. 13; Plut. *Cat. Mai.* 18. 3; *Mor.* 155D.
[124] Cic. *Off.* 1. 19.
[125] Cic. *Off.* 1. 19.

It is, however, in the *De Finibus* that Cicero reflects most profoundly on human curiosity and our natural appetite to learn. The five books of this study engage first with Epicurean, then Stoic and finally Peripatetic accounts of the first principles of morality. In the first two books, therefore, Cicero finds himself in dialogue with the Epicurean L. Torquatus and his young companion C. Triarius;[126] in the third and fourth his interlocutor is the most famous of Roman Stoics, Cato the Younger; and in the fifth he looks back to his time in Athens studying under the philosopher Antiochus and keeping company with M. Piso, T. Pomponius, his brother Q. Cicero, and the youthful L. Cicero.[127] The participation in the first and third dialogues of figures marked out by their lack of years is itself significant because it encourages consideration of the moral value of that education which they are still in the course of receiving. These passages are particularly revealing for the matters at issue in this chapter.

In the first book Cicero challenges Torquatus to explain what pleasure he and Triarius derive from reading, from history, and from the study of the poets.[128] Simply to reply that such study gives Torquatus pleasure, just as it did his ancestors, will not do because neither Epicurus nor Metrodorus would ever offer such a defence.[129] What Cicero here confronts is the noted hostility of Epicurus himself to the same liberal education assaulted by Seneca in *Epistle* 88, and he goes on to express the regret that Epicurus not only lacked such training himself but also sought to deter others from it.[130]

The issue of education is less prominent in the second dialogue with Cato the Younger, but it is by no means entirely overlooked. In

---

[126] Cic. *Fin*. 1. 13. Note also 1. 14 for Torquatus' admission that Triarius shares Cicero's regret that Epicurus omits the literary ornament of a Plato or an Aristotle. A disciple neither of Torquatus nor of Cicero, Triarius becomes a surrogate for the reading audience of books 1–2.

[127] Cic. *Fin*. 5. 6 stresses the 'adulescentia' of L. Cicero. For his later career and its premature end, see Cic. *Verr*. 2. 4. 25, 137, 145; *Att*. 1. 5. 1. The awareness of promise unfulfilled adds pathos to his role in book 5.

[128] Cic. *Fin*. 1. 25: 'quid tibi, Torquate, quid huic Triario litterae, quid historiae cognitioque rerum, quid poetarum euolutio, quid tanta tot uersuum memoria uoluptatis adfert?'

[129] Cic. *Fin*. 1. 25: 'nec mihi illud dixeris: "haec enim ipsa mihi sunt uoluptati, et erant illa Torquatis." numquam hoc ita defendit Epicurus neque Metrodorus aut quisquam eorum qui aut saperet aliquid aut ista didicisset'.

[130] Cic. *Fin*. 1. 26: 'de cetero uellem equidem aut ipse doctrinis fuisset instructior ... aut ne deterruisset alios a studiis. quamquam te quidem uideo minime esse deterritum'. For an account of Epicurus' views on education, see Reid (1925) ad loc. For Torquatus' answer to these points, see Cic. *Fin*. 1. 71–2.

the third book, though Cato rejects the view of the heterodox Stoic, Erillus of Carthage, that the greatest good is to live with knowledge,[131] he does endorse scientific inquiry as part of our embrace of the good, and asks who is so boorish or so hostile to the study of nature as to shun matters worthy of knowledge and which it is indeed a pleasure to study.[132] At the start of book 4, Cicero is therefore able to assert the essential coherence of the Platonic, Aristotelian, and Stoic study of nature and to set it against the more limited aims of the Epicureans.[133]

Yet it is when Cicero turns to those writing in the tradition of Aristotle that he finds himself most firmly engaged with human curiosity and with the proper ends of learning. In book 4 he associates with Aristotle and Xenocrates the view that man's mind has an ingrained love of knowledge,[134] while in book 5 infant curiosity is treated as the first manifestation of our doing that which we are born to do.[135] Curiosity and the love of knowledge are therefore essential to our being, but that does not mean that they should be allowed free rein. Two passages in particular underline this point. The first comes at 5. 6 and forms part of the advice of M. Piso to the young L. Cicero. The setting, it will be recalled, is Athens and the five Romans strolling together in the now empty grounds of the Academy reflect on what it means to them to visit places so haunted by the memory of those great men whom they have studied and adored. L. Cicero, in particular, is a student of oratory and confesses that he has been to the riverbank to see where Demosthenes trained his voice and to the tomb where Pericles lies buried. Piso therefore treats the young man to a lesson on the value of visiting such places of memory:

> tum Piso: 'atqui, Cicero,' inquit 'ista studia, si ad imitandos summos uiros spectant, ingeniosiorum sunt; sin tantum modo ad indicia ueteris memoriae cognoscenda, curiosorum. te autem hortamur omnes, currentem quidem ut spero, ut eos quos nouisse uis imitari etiam uelis.'

---

[131] Cic. *Fin.* 3. 31: 'cum scientia uiuere'.

[132] Cic. *Fin.* 3. 37: 'quis autem tam agrestibus institutis uiuit aut quis contra studia naturae tam uehementer obduruit ut a rebus cognitione dignis abhorreat easque sine uoluptate aut utilitate aliqua non requirat et pro nihilo putet?' Cato also allows for the study of great men of history.

[133] Cic. *Fin.* 4. 11–14; Bös (1995), 42–3.

[134] Cic. *Fin.* 4. 18: 'insitus menti cognitionis amor'.

[135] Cic. *Fin.* 5. 42–3. Note esp. 42 for when infants 'animaduertuntque ea quae domi fiunt *curiosius*, incipiuntque commentari aliquid et discere et eorum quos uident uolunt non ignorare nomina'. See also Bös (1995), 45, 48 and n. 17.

Then Piso said: 'Yet, Cicero, those pursuits are the stuff of men of genius if they look to the imitation of the greatest men; but if they only look to gaining familiarity with markers of ancient memory, then they are the stuff of the curious. And we all urge you, who are, as I hope, indeed under way, also to want to imitate those you wish to learn of.'[136]

To visit the tomb of Pericles simply in order to be able to say that you have been there is nothing to be proud of. To go to the same place in order to further the imitation of his example certainly is. The former is the stuff of the *curiosi*, the latter of the *ingeniosi*, and there can be no doubt to which category L. Cicero is encouraged to aspire to belong.[137]

The same M. Piso is then invited to expound the Peripatetic viewpoint, not least for the benefit of L. Cicero, and this he agrees to do.[138] It is he therefore who gives the account of infant curiosity which we have already considered and who at 5. 49 again distinguishes that mode of learning typical of the *curiosi* from that of the greatest men. For here Piso translates the Homeric song of the Sirens and then explains its attraction to the hero. Ulysses, he argues, could not be ensnared by mere ditties (*cantiunculis*). What the Sirens really offer is knowledge (*scientia*), and it should provoke no surprise that this is prized even more highly than his fatherland by a man desirous of wisdom (*sapientiae cupido*).[139] At this point, however, a clarification is in order. For Piso seems here to reflect that undifferentiated knowledge is a very broad category, and he therefore adds that it is the mark of *curiosi* to want to know everything, whatever it may be,[140] while the highest men are led by contemplation of greater things to the desire of knowledge.[141]

Who then are the *curiosi* to whom Piso here refers? As has already been seen so often in the works of Cicero, the answer is to be sought in Greek writing on *polypragmosyne*. To be more specific, the dis-

---

[136] For this motif, cf. Str. 2. 5. 17.

[137] Bös (1995), 45.

[138] Cic. *Fin.* 5. 8.

[139] For the song of the Sirens and the promise of knowledge, Dionigi (1983), 94 compares Sext. Emp. *Math.* 1. 42.

[140] Cic. *Fin.* 5. 49: 'atque omnia quidem scire, cuiuscumque modi sint, cupere curiosiorum'.

[141] Cic. *Fin.* 5. 49: 'duci uero maiorum rerum contemplatione ad cupiditatem scientiae summorum uirorum est putandum'; Labhardt (1960), 211; Joly (1961), 38; Beagon (2011), 71. For an analysis of this passage that turns more on the balance between study and action, see Buffière (1956), 380–6.

tinction drawn between the intellectual interests of the *curiosi* and those of the greatest men is most closely to be paralleled in a passage of Polybius to which reference has already been made on more than one occasion in this study. For when at 9. 1 Polybius distinguishes the three different audiences for history, the statesman who will be drawn to and learn from his own account of nations and cities and rulers corresponds closely to the *ingeniosi* and the *summi viri* of De Finibus 5. 6 and 5. 49. Such men also have a great deal in common with Ulysses, whom, as was noted in Chapter 3, Polybius elsewhere describes as the man most blessed with the qualities of leadership and as the ideal picture of the man of affairs.[142] In opposition to this ideal audience for his work, Polybius places those who care to listen to a story (*philekoos*) and therefore take pleasure in the genealogical mode, and those of active curiosity and a taste for the recondite (*polypragmon kai perittos*) who seek out the accounts of colonies, foundations, and kinship to be found in the works of an Ephorus.[143]

The distinctions drawn by Polybius may usefully be brought into relation with a famous passage from the *Hippias Maior* of Plato. For here the sophist Hippias of Elis lists as the special favourites of his listeners many of the themes that Polybius places in the two categories that he himself rejects.[144] There is also a common element of oral performance between what Hippias offers and what Polybius refers to when he associates genealogical history with those who like to listen to a story. This rather disparaging phrase in turn reflects Socrates' reply to Hippias and his comparison of the sophist's historical narratives with the pleasant stories old women tell to children.[145] The global term applied to his own themes by Hippias is 'archaeology' (*archaiologia*), but Momigliano sees in it the earliest form of that which he defines as antiquarianism.[146] Though he does not cite the division of history presented by Polybius, he would surely place the rejected modes of investigation under the same heading and

---

[142] Polyb. 9. 16. 1; 12. 27. 10–11. For discussion, see Ch. 3 Sect. 3.

[143] For helpful discussion of this passage, see Beister (1995), 339–49.

[144] Pl. *Hipp. Mai.* 285d: περὶ τῶν γενῶν…τῶν τε ἡρώων καὶ τῶν ἀνθρώπων, καὶ τῶν κατοικίσεων, ὡς τὸ ἀρχαῖον ἐκτίσθησαν αἱ πόλεις, καὶ συλλήβδην πάσης τῆς ἀρχαιολογίας ἥδιστα ἀκροῶνται, ὥστ᾽ ἔγωγε δι᾽ αὐτοὺς ἠνάγκασμαι ἐκμεμαθηκέναι τε καὶ ἐκμεμελετηκέναι πάντα τὰ τοιαῦτα.

[145] Pl. *Hipp. Mai.* 285e–286a: πρὸς τὸ ἡδέως μυθολογῆσαι.

[146] Momigliano (1950), 285–9.

see in this further evidence for the emerging divide between political history and antiquarianism.[147]

What connects *De Finibus* 5. 6 and 49 and Polybius 9. 1 is their critique of the indiscriminate indulgence of the thirst for knowledge: the tourist ticks off one site after another without considering what lessons each may hold for his own career; the man who thirsts after knowledge of each and every sort loses the opportunity to concentrate on that which truly matters; and the student of colonies, foundations, and kinship buries himself in recondite curiosities and fails to learn those lessons that the statesman will garner from the study of kings and cities and peoples. What the majority will surely find less entertaining, the more receptive minority will discover to be eminently more useful.[148] That utility, moreover, is also dependent on one's ability to stay the course with Polybius and allow him to fulfil the promise made in the first book of the *Histories* to bring the events of a full fifty-three years into one synoptic view.[149] To Polybius the whole is necessarily greater than the sum of the parts and it is the job of the historian to perceive and describe the relationships that make for that whole.[150] This manifesto for a higher mode of historiography and with it the scornful critique of the antiquarian is scarcely exhausted today.[151]

(6) VARRO, ARCHELAUS, AND THE CURIOSITY OF THE PARADOXOGRAPHER

Discourses of useful and useless knowledge are apt to be hijacked by the high-minded and austere. What though of those in antiquity who

---

[147] Momigliano (1950), 288: 'History was chiefly political history. What remained outside was the province of learned curiosity—which the antiquarians could easily take over and explore systematically.'

[148] For this approach as less entertaining but more useful, see Polyb. 9. 1. 2; 9. 2. 5.

[149] Polyb. 1. 4. 2: ὑπὸ μίαν σύνοψιν.

[150] Note Polyb. 1. 3. 4 for the *Histories* as a bodily whole.

[151] Finley (1985), 5–6 taking issue with Momigliano (1950), 311: 'It will be apparent that I retain a rather old-fashioned notion of history as a systematic account over a long enough period of time not only to establish relationships, connections, causes and consequences but also to show how change occurs and to suggest why. Unhappily I cannot agree that the old distinction between antiquarianism and historiography has lost its point, that a "new notion" of human development has in actual practice "left little space for mere descriptions of the past".'

had no time for grand narratives and systematic investigations, who were unembarrassedly attracted to the strange, the disparate, and the obscure? Polybius is, for sure, an admirable and hugely impressive writer, but there was many another historian happy to pander to the undiscriminating curiosity of his readers. Pliny the Younger thus confesses the charm of a historiography built out of the trivia of myth and chatter,[152] and the writers of the *Historia Augusta* are quite frank about the sort of material that they and their readers enjoy.[153] In what remains of this chapter I will therefore turn to further representatives of this less elevated mentality. In particular I will consider the paradoxographers, will examine their cheerfully parasitic relationship to more systematic works of scholarship, and will consider the terms in which they celebrate that which they admire.

It is surely fitting that M. Terentius Varro should enjoy a place of honour in any account of ancient curiosity. For just as Strabo acclaims Callimachus as 'a man of great learning if any other were', so St Augustine endorses Varro as the most learned and most curious of the Romans.[154] What earns this compliment first and foremost must be the antiquarian's reconstruction of the origins and customs of his people in works such as *De Vita Populi Romani* and *De Gente Populi Romani*, and Arnobius notes in the latter the meticulous calculations (*curiosis computationibus*) underpinning the great scholar's claim that fewer than 2000 years divided the time of the Flood from

---

[152] Plin. *Ep.* 5. 8. 4: 'sunt enim homines natura curiosi, et quamlibet nuda rerum cognitione capiuntur, ut qui sermunculis etiam fabellisque ducantur'.

[153] SHA *Prob.* 2. 7–8: 'sum enim unus ex curiosis, quod infitias ire non possum, ince<n>dentibus uobis, qui, cum multa sciatis, scire multo plura cupitis'; SHA *Aurel.* 10. 1: 'friuola haec fortassis cuipiam et nimis leuia esse uideantur, sed curiositas nil recusat'. Contrast [Anon.] *Itin. Alex.* 2 on the sources employed and the necessary limits the author has set on his own curiosity in order to produce a work of general utility: 'quosque istic qua potui tibi circumcisa satis curiositate collegi, adhibito sane uerborum cultu restrictius, quoniam uoti communis utilitas non priuatae iactantiae gloria petebatur.' For discussion, see the excellent Tabacco (2000), 77–9.

[154] August. *De Doct. Christ.* 1. 17: 'Varro quo nescio utrum apud eos quisquam talium rerum doctior uel curiosior esse possit'; *De civ. D.* 6. 2: 'quis Marco Varrone curiosius ista quaesiuit? quis inuenit doctius? quis considerauit adtentius? quis distinxit acutius? quis diligentius pleniusque conscripsit? qui tametsi minus est suauis eloquio, doctrina tamen atque sententiis ita refertus est, ut in omni eruditione, quam nos saecularem, illi autem liberalem uocant, studiosum rerum tantum iste doceat, quantum studiosum uerborum Cicero delectat.' For further such tributes to Varro's learning and productivity, see Cic. *Att.* 13. 18. 2; *Brut.* 60; Dion. Hal. *Ant. Rom.* 2. 21; Plut. *Rom.* 12. 3; Quint. *Inst.* 10. 1. 95; Gell. *NA* 4. 9. 1; 4. 16. 1; 19. 14. 1; Apul. *Apol.* 12.

the consulship of Hirtius and Pansa.[155] Yet what characterizes these works is also evident in all that remains of Varro's enormous oeuvre and the questions to be addressed in these pages emerge instead from his three-book dialogue on agriculture, the *De Re Rustica*.

The second book of the *De Re Rustica* is set in Epirus in 67 BC, at which time Varro was serving alongside Pompeius Magnus in the war against the pirates. The subject of the dialogue is the pasturing of animals, and each of the various speakers has gained some expertise in the matter, many of them through landownership in Epirus itself.[156] Different speakers address different species, but each adheres to the formal division of the topic presented by Scrofa at 2. 1. 12–24.[157] This begins with the meticulous classification of beasts into three groups of three: smaller animals consisting of sheep, goats, and swine; larger animals comprising oxen, asses, and horses; and finally those animals which are kept not for the profit derived from them, but for the purpose of the above groups, or as a result of them, that is mules, dogs, and herdsmen.[158] There then follows the catalogue of nine questions to be asked with regard to each of the nine divisions: the proper age at which to buy and keep each species; their proper characteristics; the best breed; the law of purchase; where, when, and how it is best to take the animals to pasture; how to breed from them; how to feed their young; how to maintain their health; how many to have in the herd.[159]

---

[155] Varro, *De Gente Populi Romani* fr. 9 Peter = Arn. *Adv. nat.* 5. 8. 7: 'Varro ille Romanus multiformibus eminens disciplinis et in uetustatis indagatione rimator in librorum quattuor primo quos de gente conscriptos Romani populi dereliquit curiosis computationibus edocet, ab diluuii tempore, cuius supra fecimus mentionem, ad usque Hirti consulatum et Pansae annorum esse milia nondum duo'.

[156] Varro, *Rust.* 2. 2. 20 and 2. 10. 11 for Atticus and Cossinius breeding sheep in Epirus; 2. 5. 12 for Atticus and Vaccius owning cattle; 2. 6. 1 for Murrius raising Reatine donkeys in the province, then selling them to the people of Arcadia; 2. 7. 1 for both Atticus and Lucienus as horse-breeders.

[157] Scrofa's zeal for formal division is also apparent at Varro, *Rust.* 1. 5. 3 and 1. 6. 1. For discussion of this aspect of his contribution, see Skydgaard (1968), 10–25; Martin (1971), 244: 'il se montre soucieux jusqu'à la manie de diviser et de subdiviser la matière qu'il traite'; White (1973), 460–1; Diederich (2007), 36–52, 410–19; Kronenberg (2009), 83–4, 86, 91–2. For a broader attempt to describe Scrofa's agronomy on the basis of what Varro and Columella say about him, see Martin (1971), 237–55. For arguments suggesting that the mania for subdivision owes more to Varro himself, see Heurgon (1978), p. xl comparing Gell. *NA* 3. 10. 17 on the *Hebdomades* and August. *De civ. D.* 19. 1 on Varro's division of all philosophers past, present, and future into 288 schools. For reasons to distinguish the Scrofa created by Varro from one or more Scrofae of history, see Kronenberg (2009), 76–81.

[158] Varro, *Rust.* 2. 1. 12.

[159] Varro, *Rust.* 2. 1. 13–24.

The insistence on formal division and systematic treatment of each topic is indeed striking. Yet this is not just a discipline that Varro imposes on his dialogue. It is also a structure against which he can react and which has the perhaps unexpected effect of highlighting those very observations that resist integration into the more orderly whole. A key example comes at *De Re Rustica* 2. 3. 5, where the resident expert on goats, Cossinius, interjects into his remarks under the fourth heading of purchase a quite irrelevant observation from Archelaus on the respiratory system of certain examples of the breed:

> de quibus admirandum illut, quod etiam Archelaus scribit: non ut reliqua animalia naribus, sed auribus ducere solere pastores curiosiores aliquot dicunt.

> Concerning which creatures there is also that remarkable statement that Archelaus also makes: some more attentive shepherds say that they [sc. goats] are not accustomed to breathe, as other animals do, through their noses, but through their ears.[160]

The claim itself is undoubtedly a strange one, but so is its location. Both issues merit further consideration.

Who could possibly believe that goats breathe through their ears?[161] One answer might be someone who also holds that the female partridge conceives on hearing the voice of the male,[162] or that you can tell a hare's age by counting the number of its orifices.[163] For both these opinions are attributed to the same Archelaus in the course of the *De Re Rustica* and the type of claim that he purveys is indeed a part of the general discourse of the dialogues.[164] Though Varro repudiates the *miracula* of the Sasernae,[165] he himself reports how once he heard the tale of an Arcadian pig too fat to rise and, when he went to inspect

---

[160] Archel. F 1 Giannini.

[161] Arist. *Hist. an.* 492a14–15 attributes the claim to Alcmeon but dismisses it as false. This must be the natural scientist and alleged pupil of Pythagoras, Alcmeon of Croton. See also Diederich (2007), 117 and n. 709.

[162] Archel. F 12 Giannini = Varro, *Rust.* 3. 11. 4.

[163] Archel. F 2 Giannini = Varro, *Rust.* 3. 12. 4; cf. Plin. *HN* 8. 218.

[164] It is significant that Varro, *Log. Gallus Fundanius de admirandis* fr. 54 Semi = Non. p. 218. 16 M also mentions the partridge. The claim that the partridge conceives through hearing derives from Arist. *Hist an.* 541a27–9. See Lehmann (2006), 560.

[165] Varro, *Rust.* 1. 2. 28. The type of *miraculum* here at issue appears to be the use of magical cures and incantation. See also Varro, *Rust.* 1. 2. 25 for the same writers' advice on how to ward off bugs. For this aspect of the work of the Sasernae, see Kolendo (1973), 63–4. For general accounts of the Sasernae, see Martin (1971), 81–5; Kolendo (1973); Heurgon (1978), 115–16.

this wonder (*res admiranda*), found that the pig was indeed so immobile that a shrew had bitten into its flesh and made its nest in the resultant cavity.[166] Scrofa likewise reports a matter incredible but true (*res incredibilis... sed... uera*) regarding the conception of horses in Spain;[167] Vaccius repeats the surprising claim (*admirandum scriptum*) that a castrated bull can still impregnate a cow if put to her immediately after the operation;[168] and Lucienus tells a seemingly incredible story (*tametsi incredibile*) of what happened when a blindfolded stallion was persuaded to cover a mare.[169]

All these then are most curious stories, but the terms which Varro employs in order to describe them are other than *curiosus*. In the specific passage from which we began, object-oriented curiosity is expressed through the initial *admirandum illut*; where *curiosus* is employed is in describing the disposition that permitted the herdsmen to make the discovery in the first place. Archelaus himself, to whom Varro attributes the tale, was an Alexandrian paradoxographer of the third century BC and the author of epigrams on strange creatures addressed to King Ptolemy.[170] He also wrote a similar work in prose entitled the *Idiophue*,[171] and the title of the work suggests the adjective *idion* often used in paradoxographical literature to indicate a claim that is unusual or 'singular'.[172] Further investigation of the same sources also reveals a number of other adjectives focused on the claim and indicating its wondrous or bizarre character.[173] Yet to devote any great energy to cataloguing those adjectives with which

---

[166] Varro, *Rust.* 2. 4. 12.

[167] Varro, *Rust.* 2. 1. 19. For more on horses conceiving from the wind, see Sect. 7. I do not understand on what basis Ross jr (1987), 165 treats this passage of Varro as any more 'serious' than Verg. *G.* 3. 280–3.

[168] Varro, *Rust.* 2. 5. 14.

[169] Varro, *Rust.* 2. 7. 9.

[170] See e.g. the epigrams on scorpions born from crocodiles and wasps from horses and on snakes born from men cited at Antig. *Mir.* 19. 4 and 89 = Archel. F 4, 5, and 10 Giannini.

[171] For the *Idiophue*, see Ath. 409C; Diog. Laert. 2. 17; Schol. Nic. *Ther.* 823. The fullest and most satisfactory discussion of Archelaus I have found is that of Fraser (1972), i. 778–80 and ii. 1086–90.

[172] See Antig. *Mir.* 7; 15. 3; 19. 1; 85; 89; 124b; 142. Note that Antig. *Mir.* 89 refers back to material quoted from Archelaus and Aristotle at 19. 3–5 while 124a overlaps with Archel. F 3 Giannini = Anecd. gr. Boissonade I pp. 417–18.

[173] Antig. *Mir.* 9. 2: τερατωδέστερον; 15a. 2: ξένον; 20. 1: θαυμάσια; 22. 2–3: τερατῶδες; 25a. 1: θαυμαστά; 25c: θαυμαστόν; 105. 1: θαυμασιωτάτην; 128b: τερατωδέστερον. Note that 105. 1 reproduces the expression of wonder already present at Arist. *Hist. an.* 580b10–14.

the literature of the surprising indicates that very quality in the stories it tells would itself be futile. Nor would it come any closer to revealing the more subject-oriented Greek terms that Varro translates as *curiosiores*. It is this more demanding task that I propose to undertake in the ensuing section of this argument. From there I will return to Varro's undermining of his own systematic structure and attempt to reconstruct some of the aesthetic of the paradoxographer.

(7) ANTIGONUS AND THE AESTHETIC OF THE PARADOXOGRAPHER

It was noted above that Tiberius, the constant investigator of literary and mythological arcana, was also a devotee of the profoundly difficult Hellenistic poets Euphorion, Rhianus, and Parthenius. It is therefore worth adding that, when the epigrammatist Theodoridas pays tribute to Euphorion, it is with the statement that he is capable of composing something *perisson*;[174] and that, in dedicating to Gallus his *Sufferings of Love*, Parthenius describes the Roman poet as one in pursuit of the *peritton*.[175] The same adjective that Polybius applies contemptuously to the student of foundations, colonies, and kinship and that Seneca renders in Latin—and no less disapprovingly—as *superuacuum* is one that the devotees of a quite different aesthetic could embrace and make their own.[176]

A further representative of the culture of Hellenistic Greece, and a child of the same century as Euphorion and Rhianus, is the paradoxographer Antigonus of Carystus.[177] This writer's *Mirabilia* col-

---

[174] Euphorion test. 7 van Groningen = Theodoridas at *Anth. Pal.* 7. 406. 1: Εὐφορίων, ὁ περισσὸν ἐπιστάμενός τι ποῆσαι. Lightfoot (2009), 209 aptly renders this as 'who well understood the special turn of phrase'.

[175] Parth. *Amat. narr.* praef. 2. On this point, see Wiseman (1979), 151–3; Lightfoot (1999), 370-1. Lightfoot is surely right to question whether the use of περιττός by Simylus *Suppl. Hell.* 728 has any technical sense.

[176] For *superuacuum* translated as περισσόν, see *CGL* (1888), ii. 405.

[177] See von Wilamowitz-Moellendorff (1881), 16–26. The authenticity of this collection is questioned in Musso (1976); Dorandi (1999), pp. xiv–xvii. Musso bases his arguments on the structure of the completed work and its relationship to the Byzantine culture of excerpting and pseudonymous production. He does not engage with von Wilamowitz-Moellendorff (1881), 23–4 and the demonstration that no author later than 240 BC is cited and that Antig. *Mir.* 18, 78, 84 refers to three wonders localized in Carystus.

lects wonders of the natural world from historians and geographers such as Timaeus,[178] Theopompus,[179] Ctesias,[180] and Herodotus.[181] It is also an important direct and indirect source for Archelaus.[182] Yet the bulk of his work consists of stories drawn from the *Historia Animalium* of Aristotle,[183] or from the prior paradoxographical collection of Callimachus.[184] The *Mirabilia* is scarcely one of the best known works of classical literature, but it is peculiarly rewarding for the issues under examination in this chapter. In particular, close attention must be paid to how Antigonus introduces not only individual wonders but also continuous series of wonders taken from the same author. For if we look closely at what he says here and at the relationship he establishes with his sources both major and minor, it will be possible to describe with more authority the aesthetic of the paradoxographer.

I begin with the introduction Antigonus offers to some of his minor sources. At *Mirabilia* 7, Antigonus praises the poet of the *Homeric Hymn to Hermes* for his reference to the stringing of the lyre with the guts of sheep,[185] and notes that, inasmuch as the poet knows that the guts of sheep are euphonous while those of rams are not, he is to be identified as in all respects a man of intellectual energy with a taste for the abstruse (*polypragmon kai perittos*).[186] At 24 Antigonus claims that the ruse by which Odysseus sits down in order to calm the dogs of Eumaeus proves Homer to be painstaking and *polypragmon*,[187] and at 19 he commends Philetas as thoroughly

[178] Antig. *Mir.* 1. 1; 134; 140. 2; 152 b. 2.
[179] Antig. *Mir.* 14; 15a. 3; 119. 1; 137; 141–3; 164; 170; 173.
[180] Antig. *Mir.* 15b; 145–6; 150; 165–6.
[181] Antig. *Mir.* 21. 3.
[182] Antig. *Mir.* 19. 3–4; 89. 2 cite Archelaus directly. For indirect evidence, see Antig. *Mir.* 19. 1; 81; 124a and b, which reproduce material attested elsewhere as deriving from Archel. F 11, 12, 3, and 8 Giannini respectively but without citation of Archelaus.
[183] Antig. *Mir.* 16a; 19. 5; 20. 1; 22. 2–3; 25c; 27–88; 90–115; 144; 169. 1.
[184] Antig. *Mir.* 45. 2; 129–66; 168–73. Note that Antigonus' citations of Callimachus also reproduce Callimachus' own citations of his sources.
[185] *Hymn. Hom. Merc.* 51. For a defence of θηλυτέρων as cited by Antigonus over συμφώνους as transmitted in the manuscripts of the hymns, see Vergados (2007).
[186] Antig. *Mir.* 7: πολυπράγμονα πανταχοῦ καὶ περιττὸν ὄντα. For such citations, see also Antig. *Mir.* 45, which describes Callimachus as περίτρανος εἶναι βουλόμενος; von Wilamowitz-Moellendorff (1881), 21–2.
[187] Antig. *Mir.* 24: ἐπιμελὴς καὶ πολυπράγμων. For the verse in question, see Hom. *Od.* 14. 31. Note also Plin. *HN* 8. 146: 'impetus eorum et saevitia mitigatur ab homine considente humi.'

periergos for his account of how to regenerate bees through burial of
the corpse of a cow.[188] These terms are striking on more than one
level. On the one hand, they offer a clear parallel to what was earlier
identified as distinctive in the passage of Archelaus on ear-breathing
goats as quoted by Varro: the attribution of the discovery to the
peculiarly attentive disposition of the herdsmen.[189] Here too the poet
of the *Hymn to Hermes* has clearly paid close attention to the musical
qualities of the intestines of sheep as opposed to rams while Homer
himself has looked carefully at how a dog will react to a man sitting
down. On the other, the very phrase with which Polybius disparages
the devotees of ktistic history (*polypragmon kai perittos*) is here
employed by Antigonus in praise of the author of the *Hymn to
Hermes*, and almost a century before the master of pragmatic history
took up his pen. What is striking here is not just the confirmation
that an aesthetic existed that valued things quite unlike those celebrated by the devotees of serious and useful learning. Rather what is
most significant is the revelation that the agenda is being set, the
language of criticism coined, by the frivolous and only then adopted
by the grave. The writer we might expect to oppose and to react is
actually leading the way.[190]

[188] Antig. *Mir.* 19. 2: ἱκανῶς ὢν περίεργος. See also Spanoudakis (2002), 69.
[189] That this is a habitual mode of citation in Archelaus is also indicated by the
indirect evidence of Pliny the Elder. Note in particular the formula employed at Plin.
HN 2. 109 with regard to the claim that the number of lobes on the liver of a mouse or
a shrew rises and falls in harmony with the waxing and waning of the moon: 'quin et
soricum fibras respondere numero lunae *exquisiuere diligentiores*, minimumque
animal, formicam, sentire uires sideris interlunio semper cessantem.' This claim is
also made at Antig. *Mir.* 124a and before him by Archel. F3 Giannini = Anecd. gr.
Boissonade I pp. 417–18, and it seems reasonable to assume that the reference to
more careful observers is also his. For a similar formula regarding the mating habits
of land animals, see Plin. *HN* 10. 181: 'equos et canes et sues initum matutinum
adpetere, feminas autem post meridiem blandiri *diligentiores* tradunt'.
[190] An important parallel for this mode of citation is offered by Schol. Theoc. *Id.*
2. 48c, which records the claim of οἱ ... περιττοὶ καὶ πολυπράγμονες that *hippomanes*
is not, as Theocritus indicates, a plant but rather a glutinous substance somewhat
smaller than a dried fig that mares habitually lick off the forehead of a newborn foal,
and which the practitioners of love-magic particularly prize. The scholion draws
heavily on Arist. *Hist. an.* 577a9–13, cf. 605a2–8 and is paralleled by Antig. *Mir.* 20. 3;
Verg. *Aen.* 4. 515–16; Plin. *HN* 8. 165. Yet Arist. *Hist. an.* 572a8–22 records an
alternative tradition identifying *hippomanes* as a secretion from love-mad mares and
connects it to the claim that they can conceive from the wind. This is then embraced
by Verg. *G.* 3. 280–3; Ov. *Am.* 1. 8. 8; Tib. 2. 4. 57–8. For the claim that *hippomanes* is
a plant, see Hes. fr. 350 M-W = Serv. at Verg. *G.* 3. 280; Dioscor. 2. 173; Ps.-Dioscor.
4. 40; Theophr. *Hist. pl.* 9. 15. 6. What emerges in the ancient treatment of this issue is
a peculiarly learned game in which the authority of Hesiod and Theocritus is set

I turn now to the two major sources of the *Mirabilia*. In the case of Callimachus, Antigonus is a paradoxographer drawing on a paradoxographer and making a selection from a selection. The only criterion offered for those items chosen is that they struck him as worth hearing.[191] Here again one might look to Polybius' scornful description of the devotee of genealogical history as one who loves to listen to a story (*philekoos*) and see in Antigonus' words a preemptive rehabilitation of this attitude. With Aristotle, however, matters are rather different. In the first of three references to what he makes of the philosopher, Antigonus commends the material he has collected as the best source from which to excerpt information on the special abilities of animals in matters such as combat, the treatment of wounds, the acquisition of life's necessities, the love of parents and children, and powers of memory.[192] The third and closing reference notes the considerable production of Aristotle and professes either to have excerpted from it or to have recalled as much as Antigonus was able.[193] Most extensive and most important of all, however, is the second reference that Antigonus interjects into his citations of Aristotle. Here Antigonus refers to the seventy books of natural history composed by Aristotle, praises the care taken over this work,[194] and notes the central role given to explanation of the phenomena described.[195] Yet, for the purposes of Antigonus' selection, it will suffice just to offer a summary treatment of what amongst these works and others is strange and surprising.[196]

Antigonus may wish us to believe that he has worked his way through a full seventy volumes of Aristotle on nature, but every claim reported from *Mirabilia* 27–88 and 90–115 actually derives from the

against two somewhat implausible claims both represented by the peculiarly respectable figure of Aristotle. What the scholion implies is what Archelaus suggests of the ear-breathing goats: those who miss the 'true' explanation do so because they fail to display the instincts of the truly curious and observant. This is all, as Thomas (1988) at Verg. *G.* 3. 280–3 observes, an eminently Alexandrian motif.

[191] Antig. *Mir.* 129: πεποίηται δέ τινα καὶ ὁ Κυρηναῖος Καλλίμαχος ἐκλογὴν τῶν παραδόξων, ἧς ἀναγράφομεν ὅσα ποτὲ ἡμῖν ἐφαίνετο εἶναι ἀκοῆς ἄξια.

[192] Antig. *Mir.* 26.

[193] Antig. *Mir.* 115. The distinction is between direct transcription from the text and citation from memory.

[194] Antig. *Mir.* 60: πάνυ πολλὴν ἐπιμέλειαν πεποιημένος ἐν τοῖς πλείστοις αὐτῶν.

[195] Antig. *Mir.* 60: οἷον ἔργῳ, οὐ παρέργῳ χρώμενος τῇ περὶ τούτων ἐξηγήσει... καὶ πεπείραται ἐξηγητικώτερον ἢ ἱστορικώτερον ἐν ἑκάστοις ἀναστρέφεσθαι.

[196] Antig. *Mir.* 60: τὸ ξένον καὶ παράδοξον ἔκ τε τούτων καὶ τῶν ἄλλων ἐπιδραμεῖν.

first nine books of the *Historia Animalium*.[197] Those from 27–60 are all taken from book 9 while 61–88 and 90–115 largely reproduce the order in which they are presented in the work as a whole.[198] This is significant and bears further consideration. For just as the Scrofa of *De Re Rustica* 2. 1. 12–24 insists on a systematic division of animals into nine classes and then the rigorous examination of each under nine separate headings, the *Historia Animalium* is a work governed from the first by the principle of division, be it the distinction between those parts of the body that divide into parts uniform (flesh into flesh) and those that divide into parts not uniform (hands do not divide into hands) or the ensuing division of all living creatures by genus (*genos*) and by species (*eidos*).[199] This then is a rigorous and systematic approach where the individual example is consistently integrated into the grand scheme of the work as a whole. Antigonus can therefore praise Aristotle for his determination to put explanation above simple description, but his own response to the *Historia Animalium* is to dismantle the explanatory superstructure and to leave behind only the most entertaining individual details. At *Mirabilia* 61–4, for instance, he draws on the opening chapters of the first book of the *Historia* and their account of basic modes of differentiating between animals. Where, however, *Historia Animalium* 487a11–b7 distinguishes animals by manner of life, actions, and customs as well as parts, then introduces the basic division between creatures of sea and land, *Mirabilia* 61 excerpts only the claim that all land animals possessed of lungs breathe, but that wasps and bees

---

[197] Antigonus draws on the preliminary storehouse of data that is the *Historia Animalium* and skips the more analytical *De Partibus Animalium* and *De Generatione Animalium*. For claims regarding the enormity of Aristotle's output in the field of biology, cf. Plin. *HN* 8. 44, who refers to Aristotle writing fifty books of natural science and attributes this energy to Alexander's hunger for knowledge of the animal world (*Alexandro Magno rege inflammato cupidine animalium naturas noscendi*). For documentation of each of Antigonus, sources in this section, see Giannini (1965) ad loc. For sceptical remarks on Alexander and Aristotle, see Romm (1989).

[198] Antig. *Mir.* 61–88 and 90–1 in particular pick out examples from books 1–5 in the order in which they are presented. See also Antig. *Mir.* 92–5 for four passages from book 8 and Antig. *Mir.* 97 and 99–105 for seven items from book 6. Antigonus consistently preserves Aristotle's original ordering.

[199] Arist. *Hist. an.* 486a23–5. Note also Arist. *Hist. an.* 490b6–14 for the division of animals into seven basic classes. In adopting the terms genus and species, I follow the translation of Peck (1965), 5, but it is important to take note of the same author's warning against regarding Aristotle as the forefather of Linnaean taxonomy. For discussion of how Aristotle divides his data and key bibliography on this question, see Hankinson (1995), 123–7 and 335–6.

do not do so. Where *Historia Animalium* 489a30–5 distinguishes blooded from bloodless creatures, *Mirabilia* 63 draws out only the claim that many creatures are bloodless and that this is so for all with more than four feet. In the first instance the sea-creatures are lost and in the second the blooded, and with them both goes any sense of division and differentiation. The central claim is omitted, the intriguing addendum comes to the fore.

What Antigonus makes of Aristotle offers an intriguing parallel for the manner in which the rigidly systematic *De Re Rustica* 2 absorbs the paradoxographical material of Archelaus. There is some debate among scholars as to whether the eighty-one-fold division of the topic is meant to reflect the interests of Scrofa himself or rather the latest instance of a peculiarly Varronian mania.[200] What surely matters, however, is that, if Varro is responsible for the overall structure, he is no less the author of its subversion through reference to Archelaus and the ear-breathing goats. For if this material is absorbed, still it is not integrated. It stands apart and represents a peculiarly irrelevant— if thoroughly entertaining—addition to what has just been said of the correct formula for the purchase of these creatures. This is essential to the literary character of the work as a whole.

What then is the aesthetic of the paradoxographer? It is most obviously one that prizes the wondrous or surprising aspects of places, creatures, and things. Yet it is also one that celebrates those whose curiosity induces them to pause and observe those wonders, herdsmen and Homer alike. Finally, it is an aesthetic of selection and of collection. The paradoxographer delights in drawing from the historian, the geographer, and the scientist all that is most intriguing that they have to tell. This is the process of selection. He then collects all this material in the form of entries that sit alongside but do not follow from or lead into one another. They remain beautiful and fascinating in and of themselves.[201]

Polybius aspires to write a history that is both pragmatic in aim and universal in scope. Contents are therefore chosen for their value to statesmen and insofar as they can be subordinated to the grand structure of the work as a whole. There is room for *polypragmosyne* in such a work, but only for that *polypragmosyne* that can discipline itself and resist haring off after every stray detail to catch its attention. Anyone unable to accept such a regime is apt to be dismissed as

---

[200] See Sect. 6.

[201] Bös (1995), 111–12 quoting Marrou (1938), 148–57, esp. 150–1 makes interestingly similar remarks on the state of scientific writing in the age of Augustine.

polypragmon kai perittos. To the paradoxographer, however, there could be no greater compliment.

(8) CONCLUSION

It may be of value briefly to reflect on a statement quoted just a few pages earlier from the works of Pliny: those more precise (*diligentiores*) have discovered that the number of lobes on the liver of a shrew rises and falls in harmony with the waxing and waning of the moon.[202] Pliny here reports a claim also to be found in Antigonus and in Archelaus before him, and the stress on more precise observation is typical of both.[203] Yet how exactly would one conduct this experiment? First one would require twenty-eight shrews slaughtered on successive days of the lunar cycle. It would then be necessary to extract from each of these rather tiny creatures its even tinier liver, and finally to tot up the infinitely more minute lobes growing on each one. All without a microscope. If anyone actually did undertake such research, he must indeed have been possessed of unusually precise powers of observation. The alternative conclusion is that this is but a reflection of Alexandrian miniaturism, the expression of an aesthetic value disguised as science.

The indictment of wilfully trivial and arcane modes of scholarship is expressed, much like the indictment of a flamboyantly ornamental style of composition, in essentially ethical terms. Where a writer or orator revels unashamedly in his own verbal conceits, he may be held to privilege the medium over the message and thus to forget the primary purpose of communication. Where he pursues one fascinating topic after another with no concern for their practical importance, or ambition to integrate them into a systematic body of thought, he may be deemed to waste his talents and to cheat the reader of truly edifying instruction. Old, learned, respectable bald heads shake in disapproval. Yet it is precisely in the presumption of this disapproval that the aesthetic commitment is to be found: the very language that gives vent to the moral indignation of the censorious is embraced by the frivolous as the encapsulation of an artistic principle. Wholesome literature be damned!

[202] Plin. *HN* 2. 109.
[203] Antig. *Mir.* 124a; Archel. F3 Giannini = Anecd. gr. Boissonade I pp. 417–18.

Conclusion

This study has covered a great deal of material and a wide range of authors. It may be useful briefly to bring together the most important results of the investigation.

This is not the first work of scholarship to engage with the significance of *polypragmosyne* and its synonyms in Greek literature or of *curiositas* in Latin. Ehrenberg's seminal study remains a fundamental point of reference for anyone working on the earliest manifestations of the concept in the Greek writers of the fifth and fourth centuries BC.[1] Labhardt's study of *curiositas* has proved no less important a point of reference for students of Latin literature and the same may well prove true for the more recent study of Bös.[2] Yet even in these works a number of limitations are apparent. Ehrenberg finds no interest in references to *polypragmosyne* in the Greek literature of the Hellenistic age and beyond, and both Labhardt and Bös study the Latin material in substantial isolation from the Greek. More generally, there is a tendency for modern scholarship on the topic to cluster around particular periods and works. Most scholars of Periclean Athens have something to say about *polypragmosyne*, and there is scarcely a study of the *Metamorphoses* of Apuleius that does not reflect on the problem of *curiositas*. Elsewhere, by contrast, comment is superficial if not entirely absent.

My work on this topic began with a particular author whose understanding of *polypragmosyne* was as fascinating as it was neglected: Polybius. Where Ehrenberg could see nothing but the exhaustion of a once vigorous concept, I perceived the beginning of something new and strikingly interesting in its own right. The

---

[1] Ehrenberg (1947).
[2] Labhardt (1960); Bös (1995).

resultant focus on the Greek literature of the Hellenistic and Roman periods has proved fruitful in and of itself. Yet it has also contributed a great deal to my understanding of what the Roman writers mean by *curiosus* and *curiositas*. Where previous studies have often displayed a rather one-dimensional understanding of the Greek terms that these words translate, I have found it consistently illuminating to move between languages and to treat Greek and Latin writers as operating within a single intellectual tradition. As Greek understanding of *polypragmosyne* and *periergia* changes, so the semantic range of *curiosus* and *curiositas* expands. It is this perception that allows Philo of Alexandria to offer the closest parallel for the *curiosi* of Catullus 7 or the distinction between different modes of historical writing at Polybius 9. 1 to identify more clearly the *curiosi* disparaged by Cicero at *De Finibus* 5. 6 and 49.

In the Greek literature of the fifth and fourth centuries, *polypragmosyne* is as apt to describe the behaviour of one state towards another as it is to indicate the conduct of the individual citizen towards his peers. The former concept is never entirely forgotten and it is more than just a sterile rhetorical exercise for Cassius Dio to make Caesar at Vesontio rehearse some of the most famous arguments found in Thucydides in support of the policy of intervention and expansion with which it is associated. Yet this remains an essentially Greek discourse, and where Latin writers imagine what their subjects say of them, there is no equivalent complaint of *curiositas*. Such language is reserved instead for the individual meddler, be he the busybody of the comic stage, the censorious observer of Catullus, or the prying rival of Petronius.

The great change in usage from Polybius onwards is the association of *polypragmosyne* and its synonyms with the world of knowledge. The volunteer prosecutor of the fifth and fourth centuries could be sure that he would be charged with *polypragmosyne* and sykophancy, and must perforce have expended no little energy on researching the misdemeanours of the defendant. Yet from the Hellenistic period onwards there emerges a recurrent association of *polypragmosyne* with more innocent, often entirely commendable forms of investigation. This is apparent in all that has been written here of history, geography, and natural science and it underpins Plutarch's advice that we redirect the passion of curiosity from study of our neighbours' failings to the workings of nature or at least to the flaws and vices of an earlier age. Latin usage of *curiosus* from Cicero onwards reflects this understanding.

As part of this new association of *polypragmosyne* with scholarship and research, there emerge various connected discourses. The first of these relates specifically to geography and to this discipline's relationship with empire. Geographers and ethnographers can produce memoranda for those about to enter lands at the borders of the known world. More often they follow in the footsteps of the conqueror and map the worlds that he has opened up. The crucial model here is that of Alexander, of those scholars who followed him to India, and of the soldiers and sea captains who described the wonders that he revealed. Where he furnishes Nearchus with a fleet and sends him out into the Indian Ocean, Scipio Aemilianus does the same for Polybius in the seas off North Africa. There is no little *imitatio Alexandri* in all this.

The second discourse is that which distinguishes licit and illicit fields of inquiry. Plato identifies *polypragmosyne* as the opposite of doing that which is proper to oneself, and this formulation remains fundamental to accounts of what man does and does not have the right to study. For now the *polypragmon* is determined to transcend limitations imposed by others on his right to know. He intrudes on mysteries open only to the initiate, meddles with the hazardous world of magic, ascends to the heavens, and sinks down to the world below in pursuit of knowledge that the gods have reserved unto themselves. Where Seneca seeks to defend inquiry into the heavens, it is therefore with the assertion that nature wishes man to be curious and that such fields are entirely proper to us.

The last discourse regards useful and useless inquiry. The Greek critics associate *periergia* with a wantonly ornate style, that is to say with a language that is all curlicues and filigree. This is also reflected in how Quintilian, and perhaps Varro before him, use *curiosus* within their vocabulary of criticism. Where *periergia* in language places peripheral ornament over simple communication, in terms of content it manifests itself in a preference for the strange and the trivial over the serious and the systematic. In Polybius a scholar must be *polypragmon*, but one who is not only *polypragmon* but also *perittos* will fritter away his energies on those fields of inquiry against which he defines the political utility and systematic structure of his own pragmatic history. Cicero likewise associates the *curiosi* with an indiscriminate pursuit of knowledge and contrasts this with the

higher topics that will attract men of true distinction. Yet the high-
minded and censorious do not have it all their own way. There is a
consistent strand in Hellenistic literature that positively relishes that
which is out of the way and bizarre, and this carries over to Rome.
This is reflected in the mythological problems addressed by the
grammarians and in the strange data culled by the paradoxographers
from writers eminently more serious than themselves. They are
honoured to be called *polypragmones kai perittoi* and employ such
language in order to compliment those who devote particularly
careful attention to matters that others might dismiss as trivial and
absurd. In Varro those shepherds who notice that goats breathe
through their ears are *curiosiores*; in Pliny those scientists who
observe that the number of lobes on the liver of a shrew increases
and decreases in harmony with the waxing and the waning of the
moon are *diligentiores*. The derivation of both claims from the paradoxographer Archelaus can be no accident.

The ancient understanding of *polypragmosyne* undergoes many a
shift and a change across the centuries and its study has led me in
many unexpected and entirely entertaining directions. Yet even at its
most diverting the topic is also one of considerable importance. Close
examination of which associations survive the heyday of Athenian
power and which do not prompts reflection on what was so remarkable about the city and its institutions. Reflection on what it means to
Polybius and others to look to Roman expansion in order to acquire
new worlds to map concentrates the mind on the compromises
required of a Greek intellectual operating in a world of Roman
power. The cheerfully parasitic relationship of the paradoxographer
to the great works of systematic scientific investigation may amuse
us; but when what he has excerpted is all that remains, and great
advances in learning are a thing of the distant past, it becomes more
important to ask what were the conditions that permitted truly
original thought to flourish and why they did not endure. All this
and much more besides is at stake when we ask ourselves what the
ancients meant when they spoke of *polypragmosyne*.

Bibliography

Adkins, A. W. H. (1976) '*Polupragmosune* and "Minding One's Own Business"', *CPh* 71: 301–27.

Allan, W. (2001) *Euripides, The Children of Heracles with an Introduction, Translation and Commentary*, Warminster.

Allison, J. W. (1979) 'Thucydides and Πολυπραγμοσύνη', *AJAH* 4: 10–22.

Alpers, K. (1980) 'Innere Beziehungen und Kontraste als "Hermeneutische Zeichen" in den Metamorphosen des Apuleius von Madaura', *WJA* 6: 197–207.

Andersson, T. J. (1971) *Polis and Psyche: A Motif in Plato's Republic*, Göteborg.

André, J.-M., and Baslez, M.-F. (1993) *Voyager dans l'antiquité*, Paris.

Arrowsmith, W. (1973): 'Aristophanes' Birds: The Fantasy Politics of Eros', *Arion* 1: 119–67.

Ash, R. (2007) 'The Wonderful World of Mucianus', in E. Bispham, G. Rowe, and E. Matthews (eds.), *Vita Vigilia Est: Essays in Honour of Barbara Levick*, London, 1–17.

—— (2011) 'Pliny the Elder's Attitude to Warfare', in Gibson and Morello (2011), 1–19.

Asheri, D. (2007) *A Commentary on Herodotus, Books I–IV*, Oxford.

Barrett, W. S. (1964) *Euripides, Hippolytus: Edited with Introduction and Commentary*, Oxford.

Barton, C. (1992) *The Sorrows of the Ancient Romans*, Princeton.

Barton, T. (1994) *Ancient Astrology*, London.

Bassett, E. L. (1963) 'Scipio and the Ghost of Appius', *CPh* 58: 73–92.

Beagon, M. (2011) 'The Curious Eye of the Elder Pliny' in Gibson and Morello (2011), 71–88.

Bearzot, C. (2007) 'Ἀπραγμοσύνη, Identità del meteco e valori democratici in Lisia', in Bearzot, *Vivere da democratici: Studi su Lisia e la democrazia ateniese*, Rome, 121–40.

Beister, H. (1995) 'Pragmatische Geschichtsschreibung und Zeitliche Dimension', in C. Schubert and K. Brodersen (eds.), *Rom und der Griechische Osten: Festschrift für Hatto H. Schmitt zum 65. Geburtstag*, Stuttgart, 329–49.

Bellincioni, M. (1979) *Lucio Anneo Seneca, Lettere a Lucilio, Libro XV: Le lettere 94 e 95: Testo, introduzione, versione e commento*, Brescia.

Benedict, B. (2001) *Curiosity: A Cultural History of Early Modern Inquiry*, Chicago.

Bengtson, H. (1954–5) 'Q. Caecilius Metellus Celer (cos. 60) und die Inder', *Historia* 3: 229–36.

Berger, E. H. (1903) *Geschichte der wissenschaftlichen Erdkunde der Griechen*, 2nd edn., Leipzig.

Berno, F. R. (2003) *Lo specchio, il vizio e la virtù: Studio sulle Naturales Quaestiones di Seneca*, Bologna.

Berti, E. (2000) *M. Annaei Lucani Bellum Civile Liber X*, Florence.

Bessone, L. (2008) *Senectus imperii: Biologismo e storia romana*, Padua.

Blössner, N. (1997) *Dialogform und Argument: Studien zu Platons Politeia*, Stuttgart.

Blumenberg, H. (1983) *The Legitimacy of the Modern Age*, tr. R. Wallace, Cambridge, Mass.

Bond, G. W. (1981) *Euripides, Heracles: With Introduction and Commentary*, Oxford.

Bös, G. (1995) *Curiositas: Die Rezeption eines antiken Begriffes durch Christliche Autoren bis Thomas von Aquin*, Paderborn.

Bramble, J. C. (1974) *Persius and the Programmatic Satire*, Cambridge.

Bréhier, E. (1925) *Les Idées philosophiques et religieuses de Philon d'Alexandrie*, 2nd edn., Paris.

Bringmann, K. (1965) *Studien zu den politischen Ideen des Isokrates*, Göttingen.

Briscoe, J. (1981) *A Commentary on Livy Books XXXIV–XXXVII*, Oxford.

Brock, R. (1998) 'Mythical Polypragmosyne in Athenian Drama and Rhetoric', in M. Austin, J. Harries, and C. Smith (eds.), *Modus Operandi: Essays in Honour of Geoffrey Rickman*, BICS suppl. 71: 227–38.

Buffière, R. (1956) *Les Mythes d'Homère et la pensée grecque*, Paris.

Burkert, W. (1985) *Greek Religion*, tr. J. Raffan, Oxford.

Callari, L. A. (1989) 'Curiositas: Simbologia religiosa nelle "Metamorphosi" di Apuleio', *Orpheus* 10: 162–6.

Capelle, W. (1932) 'Griechische Ethik und römischer Imperialismus', *Klio* 25: 86–113.

Carter, D. M. (2011) (ed.) *Why Athens?*, Oxford.

Carter, L. B. (1986) *The Quiet Athenian*, Oxford.

Christ, M. R. (1998) *The Litigious Athenian*, Baltimore and London.

Citroni Marchetti, S. (1982) 'Iuvare mortalem: L'ideale programmatico della *Naturalis Historia* di Plinio nei rapporti con il moralismo stoico-diatribico', *Atene a Rome* 27: 124–48.

Clarke, K. C. (1999) *Between Geography and History: Hellenistic Constructions of the Roman World* (Oxford).

—— (2001) 'An Island Nation: Re-reading Tacitus' Agricola', *JRS* 91: 94–112.

Collard, C. (1975) *Euripides, Supplices: Edited with an Introduction and Text*, 2 vols., Groningen.

Comfort, H. (1933) 'Aulularia 561 ff.', *AJPh* 54: 373–6.

Conte, G. B. (1994) *Genres and Readers*, tr. G. W. Most, Baltimore and London.

Cotta Ramosino, L. (2001) 'La guerra e lo sviluppo delle conoscenze geografiche in Plinio: Tra condanna e valorizzazione', in M. Sorti (ed.), *Il pensiero sulla guerra nel mondo antico*, Milan, 209–23.

Daston, L., and Park, K. (1998) *Wonders and the Order of Nature 1150–1750*, New York.

Davidson, J. (1990) 'Isocrates against Imperialism: An Analysis of the De Pace', *Historia* 39: 20–36.

DeFilippo, J. G. (1990) '*Curiositas* and the Platonism of Apuleius' "Golden Ass"', *AJPh* 111: 471–92.

Demont, P. (1990) *La Cité archaïque et classique et l'idéal de la tranquillité*, Paris.

De Romilly, J. (1963) *Thucydides and Athenian Imperialism*, tr. P. Thody, Oxford.

Di Benedetto, V. (1971) *Euripide: Teatro e società*, Turin.

Diederich, S. (2007) *Römische Agrarhandbücher zwischen Fachwissenschaft, Literatur und Ideologie*, Berlin.

Dienelt, K. (1953) 'Ἀπραγμοσύνη', *WS* 66: 94–104.

Diggle, J. (2004) *Theophrastus, Characters: Edited with Introduction, Translation and Commentary*, Cambridge.

Dihle, A. (1980) 'Plinius und die geographische Wissenschaft in der römischer Kaiserzeit', in *Tecnologia, economia e società nel mondo romano: Atti del convegno di Como 27/28/29 settembre 1979*, Como, 121–37.

Dilts, M. R. (2002) *Demosthenis Orationes I*, Oxford.

Dion, R. (1977) *Aspects politiques de la géographie antique*, Paris.

Dionigi, I. (1983) *L. Anneo Seneca De Otio (dial. VIII): Testo e apparato critico con introduzione, versione e commento*, Brescia.

Dorandi, T. (1999) *Antigone de Caryste, Fragments: Texte établi et traduit*, Paris.

Dougan, T. W. (1905) *M. Tulli Ciceronis Tusculanarum Disputationum Libri Quinque*, 2 vols., Cambridge.

Dover, K. J. (1974) *Greek Popular Morality in the Time of Plato and Aristotle*, Oxford.

—— (1993) *Aristophanes, Frogs: Edited with an Introduction and Commentary*, Oxford.

Dunbar, N. (1995) *Aristophanes, Birds: Edited with Introduction and Commentary*, Oxford.

Dyck, A. (1996) *A Commentary on Cicero, De Officiis*, Ann Arbor.

Edelstein, L., and Kidd, I. G. (1972–88) *Posidonius, The Fragments*, 4 vols., Cambridge.

Ehrenberg, V. (1947) 'Polypragmosyne: A Study in Greek Politics', *JHS* 67: 46–67.

Engels, J. (1999) *Augusteische Oikumenegeographie und Universalhistorie im Werk Strabons von Amaseia*, Stuttgart.

—— (2010) 'Strabo and the Development of Ancient Greek Universal Historiography', in A. Fear and P. Liddel (eds.), *Historiae Mundi: Studies in Universal History*, London, 71–86.

Ernout, A. (1949) *Les Adjectifs latins en -osus et en -ulentus*, Paris.

Festugière, A. J., and Nock, A. D. (1954) *Corpus Hermeticum*, 4 vols., Paris.

Finley, M. I. (1985) *Ancient History: Evidence and Models*, London.

Fontaine, M. (2004) 'Agnus κουρίων (Plautus, *Aulularia* 561–564)', *CPh* 99: 147–53.

Fordyce, C. J. (1961) *Catullus: A Commentary*, Oxford.

Fraser, P. M. (1972) *Ptolemaic Alexandria*, 3 vols., Oxford.

Frick, C. (1880) *Pomponii Melae De Chorographia Libri Tres*, Leipzig.

Fuhrmann, M. (2000) *Anaximenes, Ars Rhetorica*, Munich.

Gabba, E. (1955) 'Sulla "Storia romana" di Cassio Dione', *RSI* 67: 289–333.

—— (1984) 'Scienza e potere nel mondo ellenistico', in G. Giannantoni and M. Vegetti (eds.), *La scienza ellenistica: Atti delle tre giornate di studio tenutesi a Pavia dal 14 al 16 aprile 1982*, Naples, 11–37.

Gallazzi, C., Kramer, B., and Settis, S. (2008) *Il papiro di Artemidoro*, Milan.

Garland, R. (1995) *The Eye of the Beholder: Deformity and Disability in the Graeco-Roman World*, London.

Giannini, A. (1965) *Paradoxographorum Graecorum Reliquiae*, Milan.

Gibson, R. K., and Morello, R. (2011) (eds.) *Pliny the Elder: Themes and Contexts*, Leiden.

Giua, M. A. (1985) 'Storiografia e regimi politici in Tacito, Annales IV, 32–33', *Athenaeum* 63: 5–27.

Goetz, G., and Gundermann, G. (1888) *Corpus Glossariorum Latinorum*, 7 vols., Leipzig.

Gomme, A. W. (1956) *A Historical Commentary on Thucydides: The Ten Years' War*, vol. ii. *Books II–III*, Oxford.

Gow, A. S. F., and Page, D. L. (1965) *The Greek Anthology: Hellenistic Epigrams*, 2 vols., Cambridge.

—— —— (1968) *The Greek Anthology: The Garland of Philip and Some Contemporary Epigrams*, 2 vols., Cambridge.

Gowers, E. (1993) *The Loaded Table: Representations of Food in Latin Literature*, Oxford.

Grethlein, J. (2003) *Asyl und Athen: Die Konstruktion kollektiver Identität in der griechischen Tragödie*, Stuttgart.

Griffiths, J. G. (1975) *Apuleius of Madaura, The Isis-Book* (Leiden).

Grossmann, G. (1950) *Politische Schlagwörter aus der Zeit des Peloponnesischen Krieges*, Diss. Basel.

Gruen, E. (1984) *The Hellenistic World and the Coming of Rome*, 2 vols., Berkeley and Los Angeles.

—— (1998) *Heritage and Hellenism: The Representation of Jewish Tradition*, Berkeley and Los Angeles.

Habermehl, P. (2006) *Petronius, Satyrica 79–141: Ein philologisch-literarischer Kommentar*, vol. i, Berlin and New York.

Hajdu, I. (2002) *Kommentar zur 4. Philippischen Rede des Demosthenes*, Berlin.

Hankinson, R. J. (1995) 'Philosophy of Science', in J. Barnes (ed.), *The Cambridge Companion to Aristotle*, Cambridge, 109–39.

Harding, P. (1973) 'The Purpose of Isokrates' *Archidamos* and *On the Peace*', *CSCA* 6: 137–49.

—— (1981) 'In Search of a Polypragmatist', in G. S. Shrimpton and D. J. McCargar (eds.), *Classical Contributions: Studies in Honour of Malcolm Francis McGregor*, New York, 41–50.

Harrison, A. R. W. (1968–71) *The Law of Athens*, 2 vols., Oxford.

Harrison, S. J. (2000) *Apuleius: A Latin Sophist*, Oxford.

Harvey, D. (1990) 'The Sykophant and Sykophancy: Vexatious Redefinition?', in P. Cartledge, P. Millett, and S. Todd (eds.), *Nomos: Essays in Athenian Law, Politics and Society*, Cambridge, 103–21.

Hauser, M. (1954) *Der römische Begriff Cura*, Diss. Basel.

Hazebroucq, M.-F. (1997) *La Folie humaine et ses remèdes: Platon, Charmide ou De la modération*, Paris.

Healy, J. F. (1999) *Pliny the Elder on Science and Technology*, Oxford.

Heath, T. (1921) *A History of Greek Mathematics*, 2 vols., Cambridge.

Hense, O. (1890) 'Ariston bei Plutarch', *RhM* 45: 541–54.

Heurgon, J. (1978) *Varron, Économie rurale: Livre premier*, Paris.

Hijmans jr., B. L. (1995) 'Appendix III. Curiositas', in Hijmans et al. *Apuleius Madaurensis, Metamorphoses Book IX: Text, Introduction and Commentary*, Groningen, 362–79.

Holford-Strevens, L. (2003) *Aulus Gellius: An Antonine Scholar and His Achievement*, rev. edn., Oxford.

Hornblower, S. (1991) *A Commentary on Thucydides*, vol. i. *Books I–III*, Oxford.

Huart, P. (1968) *Le Vocabulaire de l'analyse psychologique dans l'œuvre de Thucydide*, Paris.

Huff, T. E. (2011) *Intellectual Curiosity and the Scientific Revolution: A Global Perspective*, Cambridge.

Hunink, V. (1997) *Apuleius of Madauros, Pro Se De Magia (Apologia): Edited with a Commentary*, 2 vols., Amsterdam.

Hunter, R. (2009) 'The Curious Incident... *Polypragmosyne* and the Ancient Novel', in M. Paschalis, S. Panayotakis, and G. Schmeling (eds.), *Readers and Writers in the Ancient Novel*, Groningen, 51–63.

204 *Bibliography*

Inwood, B. (2005) *Reading Seneca*, Oxford.

Jebb, R. (1906) *Sophocles, The Plays and Fragments: Part III, The Antigone*, Cambridge.

—— (1908) *Sophocles, The Plays and Fragments: Part V, The Trachiniae*, Cambridge.

Jocelyn, H. D. (1973) 'Homo sum: Humani nil a me alienum puto', *Antichthon* 7: 14–46.

Johnson, P. J. (1996) 'Constructions of Venus in Ovid's *Metamorphoses* V', *Arethusa* 29: 125–49.

Joly, R. (1961) 'Curiositas', *L'Antiquité classique* 30: 33–44.

Kenney, E. J. (1990) *Apuleius: Cupid and Psyche*, Cambridge.

Kenny, N. (1998) *Curiosity in Early Modern Europe: Word Histories*, Wiesbaden.

—— (2004) *The Uses of Curiosity in Early Modern France and Germany*, Oxford.

Kent, R. G. (1938) *Varro, On the Latin Language*, Cambridge, Mass. and London.

Keulen, W. H. (2007) *Apuleius Madaurensis, Metamorphoses Book I: Text, Introduction and Commentary*, Groningen.

Kirichenko, A. (2008) 'Satire, Propaganda, and the Pleasure of Reading: Apuleius' Stories of Curiosity in Context', *HSCP* 104: 339–71.

Kleve, K. (1964) 'ΑΠΡΑΓΜΟΣΎΝΗ and ΠΟΛΥΠΡΑΓΜΟΣΎΝΗ: Two Slogans in Athenian Politics', *SO* 39: 83–8.

Kolendo, J. (1973) *Le Traité d'agronomie des Saserna*, Wroclaw.

Kramer, J. (2001) *Glossaria Bilinguia Altera (C. Gloss. Biling. II)*, Munich and Leipzig.

Kroll, W. (1980) *C. Valerius Catullus: Herausgegeben und Erklärt*, 6th edn., Stuttgart.

Kronenberg, L. (2009) *Allegories of Farming from Greece and Rome: Philosophical Satire in Xenophon, Varro, and Virgil*, Cambridge.

Kyhnitzsch, E. (1894) *De Contionibus quas Cassius Dio Historiae Suae Intexuit cum Thucydideis Comparatis*, Diss. Leipzig.

Labhardt, A. (1960) 'Curiositas: Notes sur l'histoire d'un mot et d'une notion', *MH* 17: 206–24.

Laederich, P. (2001) *Les Limites de l'empire: Les Stratégies de l'imperialisme romain dans l'œuvre de Tacite*, Paris.

Lana, I. (1980) 'Scienza e politica in età imperiale romana (da Augusto ai Flavi)', in *Tecnologia, economia e società nel mondo romano: Atti del convegno di Como 27/28/29 settembre 1979*, Como, 21–43.

Lancel, S. (1961) '"Curiositas" et préoccupations spirituelles chez Apulée', *Revue de l'histoire des religions* 160: 25–46.

La Penna, A. (1995) 'Towards a History of the Poetic Catalogue of Philosophical Themes', in S. J. Harrison (ed.), *Homage to Horace: A Bimillenary Celebration*, Oxford, 314–28.

Lateiner, D. (1982–3) '"The Man Who Does Not Meddle in Politics": A Topos in Lysias', *CW* 76: 1–12.

Lefèvre, E. (1994) *Terenz' und Menanders Heautontimorumenos*, Munich.

Lehmann, Y. (2006) 'Le Merveilleux scientifique dans le *Logistoricus Gallus Fundanius De Admirandis* de Varron', in J. Champeaux and M. Chassignet (eds.), *Aere Perennius: Hommage à Hubert Zehnacker*, Paris, 553–62.

Lenchantin de Gubernatis, M. (1937) *Livii Andronici Fragmenta*, Turin.

Lenfant, D. (2004) *Ctésias de Cnide, La Perse; L'Inde; Autres Fragments*, Paris.

Lightfoot, J. L. (1999) *Parthenius of Nicaea*, Oxford.

—— (2009) *Hellenistic Collection*, Cambridge, Mass. and London.

Linforth, I. M. (1919) *Solon the Athenian*, Berkeley.

Litsch, E. (1893) *De Cassio Dione Imitatore Thucydidis*, Diss. Freiburg.

Loraux, N. (1986) *The Invention of Athens: The Funeral Oration in the Classical City*, tr. A. Sheridan, Cambridge, Mass.

McCartney, E. (1960) 'Vivid Ways of Indicating Uncountable Numbers', *CPh* 55: 79–89.

Madvig, J. N. (1876) *M. Tulli Ciceronis De Finibus Bonorum et Malorum Libri Quinque*, 3rd edn., Copenhagen.

Magnien, V. (1950) *Les Mystères d'Éleusis*, Paris.

Malitz, J. (1983) *Die Historien des Poseidonios*, Munich.

Manuwald, G. (2001) *Fabulae Praetextae: Spuren einer literarischen Gattung der Römer*, Munich.

Marincola, J. (2007) 'Odysseus and the Historians', *Syllecta Classica* 18: 1–79.

Marrou, H.-I. (1938) *Saint Augustin et la fin de la culture antique*, Paris.

Martin, R. (1971) *Recherches sur les agronomes latins et leurs conceptions économiques et sociales*, Paris.

Mason, H. J. (1994) 'Greek and Latin Versions of the Ass-Story', *ANRW* II. 34. 2: 1665–1707.

Mathieu, G. (1925) *Les Idées politiques d'Isocrate*, Paris.

Mazzucchi, C. M. (1992) *Dionisio Longino Del Sublime*, Milan.

Merkelbach, R. (1962) *Roman und Mysterium in der Antike*, Munich.

Mette, H. J. (1956) 'Curiositas', in *Festschrift Bruno Schnell zum 60. Geburtstag am 18. Juni 1956 von Freunden und Schülern Überreicht*, 227–35.

—— (1962) 'Die περιεργία bei Menander', *Gymnasium* 69: 398–406.

Mewaldt, J. (1929) 'Fundament des Staates', in F. Focke et al. (eds.), *Genethliakon Wilhelm Schmidt zum siebzigsten Geburtstag*, Stuttgart, 69–93.

Millar, F. (1964) *A Study of Cassius Dio*, Oxford.

Moles, J. L. (1993) 'Truth and Untruth in Herodotus and Thucydides', in C. Gill and T. P. Wiseman (eds.), *Lies and Fiction in the Ancient World*, Exeter, 88–121.

Momigliano, A. (1950) 'Ancient History and the Antiquarian', *Journal of the Warburg and Courtauld Institutes* 13: 285–315.

—— (1979) *Alien Wisdom*, Cambridge.

—— (1980) 'Polybius between the English and the Turks', in Momigliano, *Sesto contributo alla storia degli studi classici e del mondo antico*, Rome, 125–41.

Montiglio, S. (2005) *Wandering in Ancient Greek Culture*, Chicago.

Moreschini, C. (1972) 'Ancora sulla Curiositas in Apuleio', in *Studi classici in onore di Quintino Cataudella*, Catania, iii. 517–24.

—— (1978) *Apuleio e il platonismo*, Florence.

Muecke, F. (1993) *Horace, Satires II with an Introduction, Translation and Commentary*, Warminster.

Müller, C. W. (2000) *Euripides Philoktet: Herausgegeben, übersetzt und kommentiert*, Berlin and New York.

Murphy, T. (2004) *Pliny the Elder's Natural History: The Empire in the Encyclopedia*, Oxford.

Murray, O. (1972) 'Herodotus and Hellenistic Culture', *CQ* 22: 200–13.

Musso, O. (1976) 'Sulla struttura del Cod. Pal. Gr. 398 e deduzioni storico-letterarie', *Prometheus* 2: 1–10.

Naas, V. (2002) *Le Projet encyclopédique de Pline l'Ancien*, Rome.

—— (2011) 'Imperialism, *Mirabilia* and Knowledge: Some Paradoxes in the *Naturalis Historia*', in Gibson and Morello (2011), 57–70.

Nestle W. (1926) *'ΑΠΡΑΓΜΟΣΥΝΗ* (zu Thukydides II 63)', *Philologus* 81: 129–40.

Netz, R. (2009) *Ludic Proof: Greek Mathematics and the Alexandrian Aesthetic*, Cambridge.

Nicolet, C. (1991) *Space, Geography and Politics in the Early Roman Empire*, Ann Arbor.

North, H. (1966) *Sophrosyne: Self-Knowledge and Self-Restraint in Greek Literature*, Ithaca, NY.

Obbink, D. (1996) *Philodemus On Piety, Part 1: Critical Text with Commentary*, Oxford.

O'Donnell, J. J. (1992) *Augustine Confessions*, 3 vols., Oxford.

Ogilvie, R. M., and Richmond, I. (1967) *Cornelii Taciti De Vita Agricolae*, Oxford.

Osborne, R. (1990) 'Vexatious Litigation in Classical Athens: Sykophancy and the Sykophant', in P. Cartledge, P. Millett, and S. Todd (eds.), *Nomos: Essays in Athenian Law, Politics and Society*, Cambridge, 83–102.

Parroni, P. (1984) *Pomponii Melae De Chorographia Libri Tres: Introduzione, edizione critica e commento*, Rome.

Peck, A. L. (1965) *Aristotle, History of Animals I–III*, Cambridge, Mass. and London.

Penwill, J. L. (1975) 'Slavish Pleasures and Profitless Curiosity: Fall and Redemption in Apuleius' *Metamorphoses*', *Ramus* 4: 49–82.

Petersmann, H. (1973) *T. Maccius Plautus, Stichus*, Heidelberg.

Prescott, H. W. (1907) '*Agnus Curio* in Plautus *Aulularia* 562, 563', *CPh* 2: 335–6.

Rademaker, A. (2005) *Sophrosyne and the Rhetoric of Self-Restraint: Polysemy and Persuasive Use of an Ancient Greek Value Term*, Leiden.

Raubitschek, A. E. (1958) 'Ein neues Pittakeion', *WS* 71: 170–2.

Redfield, J. (1985) 'Herodotus the Tourist', *CPh* 80: 97–118.

Reid, J. S. (1925) *M. Tulli Ciceronis De Finibus Bonorum et Malorum Libri I, II*, Cambridge.

Reitz, C. (1982) *Die Nekyia in den Punica des Silius Italicus*, Frankfurt am Main.

Reitzenstein, R. (1927) *Die hellenistischen Mysterienreligionen*, 3rd edn., Leipzig.

Ritchie, W. (1964) *The Authenticity of the Rhesus of Euripides*, Cambridge.

Roller, D. W. (2003) *The World of Juba II and Kleopatra Selene: Royal Scholarship on Rome's African Frontier*, London.

Romm, J. S. (1989) 'Aristotle's Elephant and the Myth of Alexander's Scientific Patronage', *AJPh* 110: 566–75.

Ross jr, D. O. (1987) *Virgil's Elements: Physics and Poetry in the Georgics*, Princeton.

Rostovtzeff, M. (1941) *The Social and Economic History of the Hellenistic World*, 3 vols., Oxford.

Rüdiger, H. (1963) 'Curiositas und Magie: Apuleius und Lucius als literarische Archetypen der Faust-Gestalt', in H. Meier and H. Sckommodau (eds.), *Wort und Text. Festschrift für Fritz Schalk*, Frankfurt am Main, 57–82.

Sandy, G. (1972) 'Knowledge and Curiosity in Apuleius' *Metamorphoses*', *Latomus* 31: 179–83.

Scarpat, G. (1965) *La lettera 65 di Seneca*, Brescia.

Schlam, C. C. (1968) 'The Curiosity of the Golden Ass', *CJ* 64: 120–5.

—— (1992) *The Metamorphoses of Apuleius: On Making an Ass of Oneself*, Chapel Hill, NC and London.

Schmidt, G. (1985) *Platons Vernunftkritik oder die Doppelrolle des Sokrates im Dialog Charmides*, Würzburg.

Schmidt, V. (1982) 'Apuleius *Met*. III. 15 F. Die Einweihung in die Falschen Mysterien (Apuleiana Groningana VII)', *Mnemosyne* 35: 269–82.

Scobie, A. (1975) *Apuleius Metamorphoses (Asinus Aureus), I. A Commentary*, Meisenheim am Glan.

Scott, W. (1924), *Hermetica*, 4 vols. (Oxford).

Shattuck, R. (1996) *Forbidden Knowledge*, New York.

Skydgaard, J. (1968) *Varro the Scholar: Studies in the First Book of Varro's De Re Rustica*, Copenhagen.

Souilhé, J. (1962) *Platon, Œuvres complètes*, vol. xiii. 2, Paris.

Spaltenstein, F. (1990) *Commentaire des Punica de Silius Italicus (livres 9 à 17)*, Geneva.

Spanoudakis, K. (2002) *Philitas of Cos*, Leiden.

Stein, M. (1992) *Definition und Schilderung in Theophrasts Charakteren*, Stuttgart.

Stockert, W. (1983) *T. Maccius Plautus Aulularia*, Stuttgart.

Syndikus, H. P. (1984) *Catull. Eine Interpretation, Erster Teil: Einleitung; Die kleinen Gedichte*, Darmstadt.

Tabacco, R. (2000) *Itinerarium Alexandri: Testo, apparato critico, introduzione, traduzione e commento*, Florence.

Tandoi, V. (1964) 'Albinovano Pedone e la retorica giulio-claudia delle conquiste I', *SIFC* 36: 129–68.

—— (1967) 'Albinovano Pedone e la retorica giulio-claudia delle conquiste II', *SIFC* 39: 5–66.

Tasinato, M. (1994) *Sulla curiosità*, Parma.

Theiler, W. (1982) *Poseidonios, Die Fragmente*, 2 vols., Berlin and New York.

Thomas, R. F. (1988) *Virgil, Georgics*, 2 vols., Cambridge.

Thomson, J. O. (1948) *History of Ancient Geography*, Cambridge.

Too, Yun Lee (2008) *A Commentary on Isocrates' Antidosis*, Oxford.

Tosi, R. (1991) *Dizionario delle sentenze latine e greche*, Milan.

Tränkle, H. (1977) *Livius und Polybios*, Basel.

Tuckey, T. G. (1951) *Plato's Charmides*, Cambridge.

Tzanetou, A. (2011) 'Supplication and Empire in Athenian Tragedy', in D. M. Carter (2011), 305–24.

Usener, H. (1887) *Epicurea*, Leipzig.

Ussher, R. G. (1960) *The Characters of Theophrastus: Edited with Introduction, Commentary and Index*, London.

Ussing, J. L. (1878) *T. Macci Plauti Comoediae II*, Copenhagen.

van Mal-Maeder, D. (1997) '*Lector, intende: laetaberis*: The Enigma of the Last Book of Apuleius' *Metamorphoses*', *GCN* 8: 87–118.

van Paassen, C. (1957) *The Classical Tradition of Geography*, Groningen.

van Wyk Cronjé, J. (1986) *Dionysius of Halicarnassus, De Demosthene: A Critical Appraisal of the Status Quaestionis*, Hildesheim.

Vergados, A. (2007) 'The *Homeric Hymn to Hermes* 51 and Antigonus of Carystus', *CQ* 57: 737–42.

Vermaseren, M. J. (1963) *Mithras: The Secret God*, London.

Vinh, G. (2011) 'Athens in Euripides' *Suppliants*: Ritual, Politics, and Theatre', in D. M. Carter (2011), 325–44.

Visentin, C. (1999) 'La *ΝΕΩΤΕΡΟΠΟΙΙΑ* di Atene in Tucidide: Tra impulso costruttivo e trasgressione', *Aevum* 73: 43–52.

Vlahogiannis, N. (1998) 'Disabling Bodies', in D. Montserrat (ed.), *Changing Bodies, Changing Meanings: Studies on the Human Body in Antiquity*, London and New York, 13–36.

Volk, K. (2001) 'Pious and Impious Approaches to Cosmology in Manilius', *MD* 47: 85–117.

von Möllendorff, P. (2000) *Auf der Suche nach der verlogenen Wahrheit: Lukians Wahre Geschichten*, Tübingen.

von Scala, R. (1890) *Die Studien des Polybios*, Stuttgart.

von Wilamowitz-Moellendorff, U. (1881) *Antigonos von Karystos*, Berlin.

—— (1895) *Euripides Herakles*, 2nd edn., Berlin.

Walbank, F. W. (1948) 'The Geography of Polybius', *C&M* 9: 155–82.

—— (1957–79) *A Historical Commentary on Thucydides*, 3 vols., Oxford.

—— (1962) 'Polemic in Polybius', *JRS* 52: 1–12.

—— (1972) *Polybius*, Berkeley, Los Angeles, and London.

—— (2002) *Polybius, Rome and the Hellenistic World: Essays and Reflections*, Cambridge.

Walsh, P. G. (1988) 'The Rights and Wrongs of Curiosity (Plutarch to Augustine)', *Greece and Rome* 35: 73–85.

Watson, L. C. (2003) *A Commentary on Horace's Epodes*, Oxford.

White, K. D. (1973) 'Roman Agricultural Writers I: Varro and His Predecessors', *ANRW* I. 4: 439–97.

Whitmarsh, T. (2011) *Narrative and Identity in the Ancient Greek Novel*, Cambridge.

Wick, C. (2004) *M. Annaeus Lucanus Bellum Civile Liber IX: Einleitung, Text und Übersetzung, Kommentar*, 2 vols., Leipzig.

Wilgaux, J. (2009) ''Υγιὴς καὶ ὁλόκλαρος: Le Corps du prêtre en Grèce ancienne', in P. Brulé (ed.), *La Norme en matière religieuse en Grèce ancienne*, Liège, 231–42.

Wilkins, J. (1993) *Euripides, Heraclidae with Introduction and Commentary*, Oxford.

Williams, G. D. (2003) *Seneca, De Otio De Brevitate Vitae*, Cambridge.

Wilson, C. H. (1966) 'Thucydides, Isocrates, and the Athenian Empire', *Greece and Rome* 13: 54–63.

Winkler, H. (1933) *Rom und Aegypten im 2. Jahrhundert v. Chr.*, Leipzig.

Winkler, J. J. (1985) *Auctor & Actor: A Narratological Reading of Apuleius' Golden Ass*, Berkeley, Los Angeles, and London.

Wiseman, T. P. (1979) *Clio's Cosmetics: Three Studies in Greco-Roman Literature*, Leicester.

Wisse, J., Winterbottom, M., and Fantham, E. (2008) *M. Tullius Cicero, De Oratore Libri III: A Commentary on Book III. 96–230*, Heidelberg.

Wlosok, A. (1969) 'Zur Einheit der Metamorphosen des Apuleius', *Philologus* 113: 68–84 = (1999) 'On the Unity of Apuleius' *Metamorphoses*', tr. M. Revermann, in S. J. Harrison (ed.), *Oxford Readings in the Roman Novel*, Oxford, 142–56.

Woodman, A. J. (1998) *Tacitus Reviewed*, Oxford.
Woolf, G. (2011) *Tales of the Barbarians: Ethnography and Empire in the Roman West*, Oxford.
Zecchini, G. (1978) *Cassio Dione e la guerra gallica di Cesare*, Milan.
Zuntz, G. (1955) *The Political Plays of Euripides*, Manchester.

Index Locorum

Achilles Tatius:
1. 2. 1: 87 n. 174
2. 3. 3: 87 n. 174
2. 20. 1: 88 n. 175
2. 38. 1–2: 87 n. 174
2. 38. 2: 164 n. 23
2. 38. 5: 87 n. 174
5. 10. 7: 87 n. 171
5. 12. 2: 59 n. 28
5. 27. 3–4: 87 n. 174

Acts of the Apostles:
4. 19. 19: 8 nn. 32–34

Aelian

Ep. Rust.

14: 81 n. 129
fr. ed. Domingo-Ferasté
46: 15 n. 68
46a: 133 n. 21
46b: 133 n. 22
55b: 133 n. 22

NA

9. 35: 134 n. 33
11. 17: 133 n. 20
16. 16: 134 n. 33

VH

3. 17: 10 n. 40
3. 19: 163 n. 14
12. 1: 8 n. 29; 163 n. 14;
    164 n. 22
13. 1: 164 n. 22

Aeschines

3. 172: 26 n. 53
3. 229: 165 n. 30

Aeschylus
PV

887–893: 17 n. 4

Afranius ed. Ribbeck[3]

189–91: 61 n. 42
250: 61 n. 42

Alexander of Aphrodisias
in Arist. *Top.*
156 l. 20–157 l. 17: 6 n. 12

Alexis ed. Kassel-Austin

145. 1: 60 n. 36

Anaxandrides ed. Kassel-Austin:

40: 136 n. 38

Anaxarchus ed. Diels-Kranz:

B1: 171 n. 71

Anaximenes
Ars rhet.

29. 7: 52 n. 221
29. 18: 23 n. 36
35. 8: 52 n. 221

Andocides

1. 33: 26 n. 51
3. 33: 52 n. 221

Anthologia Palatina:

7. 11–13: 162 n. 3
7. 89: 17 n. 4; 96 n. 26
7. 190: 162 n. 3
7. 406. 1: 188 n. 174
9. 190: 162 n. 3
11. 20. 1: 162 n. 11
11. 20. 5–6: 162 n. 12
11. 321. 2–3: 162 n. 6
11. 321. 5: 162 n. 9
11. 321. 5–6: 162 n. 10
11. 322: 161–2
11. 322. 3: 162 n. 3
11. 347. 2: 162 n. 7
11. 347. 3–4: 162 n. 10
11. 347. 5–6: 162 n. 12
11. 347. 6: 162 n. 8

Antigonus of Carystus
Mir.

1. 1: 189 n. 178
7: 187 n. 172; 189 n. 186

4: 82 n. 136
5: 82 n. 136

Plato

Amat.

132a–b: 172 n. 76
132b: 172 n. 77; 174 n. 93
132c–133b: 172 n. 78
133c: 172 n. 80
133c–e: 173 n. 81
134a–c: 173 n. 82
134c–d: 173 n. 83
135b: 174 n. 91
135b–c: 173 n. 84
135c–d: 173 n. 85
135e–136b: 173 n. 86
136b–d: 173 n. 87
137b: 174
137b–139a: 173 n. 88
139a: 173 n. 89

Ap.

18b–c: 131 n. 10
18c: 132 n. 12
19b: 6–7 and n. 20; 33; 132 n. 11; 151;
   152 n. 156
31c: 33 and n. 102

Chrm.

153a: 18 n. 14
153c: 18 n. 14
157d: 18 n. 12
161b: 17 n. 6
161b–c: 17 n. 6
161c: 18 n. 8
161e: 18 n. 7
162b: 18 n. 8
162b–c: 17 n. 6
171d–e: 18 n. 13

Cri.

52b: 96 n. 28

Grg.

462d–465e: 164 n. 28
521d: 20 n. 21
525d: 20 n. 21
526a: 20 n. 21
526c: 20 n. 21; 93 n. 9

Hipp. Mai.

285d: 182 n. 144
285e–286a: 182 n. 145

Leg.

644a: 174 n. 92
741e: 174 n. 92
743d: 174 n. 92
759c: 136 n. 38
820e–822d: 132 n. 14
821a: 6–7 and n. 21; 132
   n. 15; 151
952d1: 76 n. 108

Menex.

239b: 41 n. 157
249a–b: 20 n. 23

Resp.

368c–369a: 21 n. 28
370b: 19 n. 15
374a: 19 n. 15
394e: 19 n. 15
397e: 19 n. 15
400e: 19 n. 15
406 d–e: 19 n. 15
421b: 19 n. 15; 21 n. 26
423c–d: 19 n. 18
431b–c: 21 n. 30
431c–432b: 21 n. 31
431d–e: 20 n. 25
433a: 19 n. 15 and n. 17
433a–b: 16–17
433d: 19 n. 15
434a–b: 19 n. 20
434a–c: 19 n. 19
441d: 19 n. 15
442b: 19 n. 15
443b: 19 n. 15
443c: 21 n. 29
443d–e: 21 n. 31
444a: 21 n. 29
444a–b: 20 n. 24; 21 n. 32
475c–e: 172 n. 75; 176 n. 106
495e: 174 n. 92
519e: 21 n. 26
549c: 6 n. 15; 59 n. 28
549c–550c: 21 n. 29
565a: 20 n. 22; 22 n. 34
586a: 175 n. 95
590c: 174 n. 92
620c–d: 25 n. 49

Plautus

Amph.

894–895: 59 n. 29

Index

Abraham 151–2

Accius, L. and diction 168–9

accuratus 142

Achilles, his name when disguised as a girl 178

Achilles Tatius 87–8

Acoreus, in Lucan 123–4

Acropolis 133``

Actaeon, in Ovid and Apuleius 136–8, 150

admirandum 187

Adrastus, king of Argos 41–45

Adriatic 110

Aelian 7–8, 10 n. 40, 15; on curiosity and the divine 132–4

Aelius Gallus, friend of Strabo 109; expedition of 109

Aeolus 128

Aeschines, on the diction of Demosthenes 165

Aeschylus 132 n. 17

Aesop: and the *aperiergos* 11; and the lark 47, 69–70

Aetolia 100 and n. 50

Afranius, L. and *curiosus* 61 and n. 42

Africa: circumnavigation of 105; Atlantic coast of 117; northern coast of 111, 128; southern shore of 117

Aglauros 132–3, 143

Agricola, Cn. Iulius 121–2

Agrippa, M. Vipsanius 110–11

Ajax Oileus 71–2

alazon: in Theophrastus, New Comedy, and Aristotle 51

Alcibiades: in Plutarch 46; in Thucydides 37, 91, 124–7, 129

Alcmena, in Euripides' *Heracleidae* 44

Alcmeon of Croton: on ear-breathing goats 186 n. 161

Alexander, false-prophet in Lucian 71

Alexander the Great: and expansion of geography 102, 108–10, 128; and the gymnosophists 104–6; in Pliny the Elder 111–12; fleets of 112; in *Histories* of Strabo 114; absent from Mela's *Chorographia* 117; and Trajan 123; and Nearchus, 106, 197

Alexandria 14; and visit of Scipio Aemilianus 107–8; science and aesthetics 83, 194

Alexis, and *periergos* 60 n. 36

alienus 62, 65, 157 n. 190

alioquin 140–1

allotriopragmosyne 20

allotrios 62, 123 n. 196

Ammon, oracle of Jupiter 82 and n. 135

Ampelusia 117

Anacharsis: in Herodotus 95; in Lucian and Diogenes Laertius 95 n. 21

Anaxagoras 172, 174

Anaxarchus, and critique of *polymatheia* 171

Ancus Marcius, in Cassius Dio 124–5, 127

Annius Plocamus 111

Antigonus of Carystus: paradoxographer 188–94; modes of citation 189–90; and Aristotle 189, 191–3; and Callimachus 191; on the shrew and its liver 190 n. 189, 194

Antigonus Gonatas, in Polybius 100

Antiochus III, in Polybius and Livy 77–9, 100

Antipater, epigrams of 162, 177

Antiphanes, epigrams of 161–2

Antipho, in the *Eunuchus* 62–4

antonyms 10–11, 56

anxius 140, 148 n. 128

aperiergos 10–11, 165–6

aperittos 166

Aphrodite: anger of 87; in astrology 149 n. 137; girdle of 164

Apion, grammarian 115

apodemia 93–7, 129

apragmon/apragmosyne: and quietism 10, 22, 24–5, 26–30, 37, 45, 50; as antonym 56; and gods as

Callimachus: and Catullus 7 82;
favourite of the grammarians 161–2;
acclaimed for his learning 162 and
n. 4, 184; coupled with Euphorion
and Parthenius 162 n. 5; quoted
by Antigonus of Carystus 189, 191
Callirhoe, in Chariton 85–7
Camarina 36
Cambyses, in Herodotus 35, 96
Candaules, and wife in Herodotus 17,
95–6
Canidia, in *Epodes* 5 and 17 80–1
Capaneus: in Euripides' *Supplices*
42 n. 159; statue of in Ardea 71–2
Capri 120
Carmania 106
Carneades 126
Carthage: and Athenian war-aims 37;
and 3rd Punic War 101, 104; and
resistance to navigation 102
Caspian Sea 117
Cassius Dio 7, 91; and Thucydides
123, 124–7, 196; on Vespasian 123;
on Trajan 123; on Septimius
Severus 123
Castor and Pollux, temple of in
Ardea 72
catachresis 66–8
Cato, M. Porcius: the Elder 97; the
Younger 179–80
Catullus: on *curiosi* 79–84, 196; style of
poems 7 and 64 170
Celer, Q. Metellus 117–118
Celts 103, 120, 128
Ceylon 111
Chaerea, in the *Eunuchus* 62–4
Chaireas, in Chariton 85–7
Chaldaea, and astrology 151–3, 157
Charisios, in the *Epitrepontes* 61
Chariton: and curiosity 85–7; and
jealousy 86–7
Charmides, in Plato's *Charmides* 17–22
Charondas, as lawmaker 25 n. 50
Chauci, German tribe 113
Chilon 17, 53
Chios 38
Chloe, in *Daphnis and Chloe* 87
Chremes, in *Self-Tormentor* 13, 64–5,
73–4, 76
Chrysippus, as researcher and writer 69
Cicero, L. Tullius 179–81

Cicero, M. Tullius: ravenous for gossip 13,
14–15, 72–3; coins *curiositas* 57;
coins *formositas* 57 n. 22; on the gods
of Epicurus 59, 88; on Chrysippus as
researcher and writer 69; as reader of
the *Self-Tormentor* 73–4; usage of
curiosus 72–6; on the slave
Nicostratus 88 n. 175; on curiosity
and the divine 132, 135–6; on
indiscriminate curiosity 139, 178–83,
197–8; and the *De Officiis* 178; and
the *De Finibus* 179–83, 196
Cicero, Q. Tullius 179
Cilicia 108
Cineas, in Plutarch 58 and n. 27
city, and country 10, 11, 26, 30, 45
Claudius, emperor: as meddler 59 n. 28;
and conquest of Britain 111,
117 n. 164; and Annius Plocamus
111; and Mauretania 116
Claudius Ptolemaeus 148–50, 160
Cleisthenes, praised by Isocrates in the
Antidosis 28
Cleon 13, 125–6
Cleopatra, in Lucan 123–4
Cleophon, attacked by Isocrates in *On
the Peace* 38
Clinia, in the *Self-Tormentor* 65
Clitipho, in the *Self-Tormentor* 65
Clitiphon, in Achilles Tatius 87–8
Clodius Pulcher, P. and Bona
Dea 135–6
comets 156–8
Conops, in Achilles Tatius 88
Corbulo, Cn. Domitius: and Nero 111;
in Germany 113; as source for Pliny
the Elder 111, 113, 117
Corinth 36–37, 39–40, 46, 92, 101–2
Cornelius Lentulus, L. at Lysimachia 77
Corpus Hermeticum 130–1
Corycum, Ionian 114–15
Cos 38
Cossinius, in *De Re Rustica* 186
Creon, in the *Supplices* 76
Critias, in Plato's *Charmides* 18
Ctesias of Cnidus, on Persia and
India 93–4, 107; quoted by Antigonus
of Carystus 189
Croesus, in Herodotus 92, 95
Cupid, in the *Metamorphoses* 138, 143,
150